SIX
MEASURES
OF
JSL
PRAGMATICS

TECHNICAL REPORT #14

# SIX
# MEASURES
# OF
# JSL
# PRAGMATICS

by SAYOKO OKADA YAMASHITA

SECOND LANGUAGE TEACHING & CURRICULUM CENTER
University of Hawai'i at Mānoa

Funds for the publication of this technical report were provided in part by a grant to the University of Hawai'i under the Language Resource Centers Program of the US Department of Education.

ISBN 0–8248–1914–4

*Book design by Deborah Masterson*

Distributed by
University of Hawai'i Press
Order Department
2840 Kolowalu Street
Honolulu, HI 96822

# ABOUT THE
# NATIONAL FOREIGN LANGUAGE RESOURCE CENTER

The Second Language Teaching and Curriculum Center of the University of Hawai'i is a unit of the College of Languages, Linguistics, and Literature. Under a grant from the US Department of Education, the Center has since 1990 served as a National Foreign Language Resource Center (NFLRC). The general direction of the Resource Center is set by a national advisory board. The Center conducts research, develops materials, and trains language professionals with the goal of improving foreign language instruction in the United States. The Center publishes research reports and teaching materials; it also sponsors a summer intensive teacher training institute. For additional information about Center programs, write:

Dr. Richard Schmidt, Director
National Foreign Language Resource Center
East-West Road, Bldg. 1, Rm. 6A
University of Hawai'i
Honolulu, HI 96822

or visit our Web site: http://www.lll.hawaii.edu/nflrc

# NFLRC ADVISORY BOARD

Kathleen Bardovi-Harlig
*Center for English Language Teaching*
*Indiana University*

John Clark
*Defense Language Institute*
*Monterey, California*

James Pusack
*Project for International Communication Studies (PICS)*
*University of Iowa*

Ronald Walton
*National Foreign Language Center*
*Washington, DC*

Representatives of other funded NFLRCs

*I dedicate this book to my father,*
*Jinichiro Okada (1912–1996),*
*with love and respect.*

# CONTENTS

## CHAPTER 6: DISCUSSION

## CHAPTER 7: CONCLUSION

## APPENDICES

# ABSTRACT

This study investigated differences among test formats for measuring the cross-cultural pragmatic competence of English speaking learners of Japanese. A total of six direct and indirect, and open-response and selected-response, type tests were used to gather data from forty-seven North American English speaking learners of Japanese as a second or foreign language. Various statistical procedures (including descriptive statistics, internal consistency reliability estimates, inter-rater reliability and intra-class correlation coefficients, Pearson product-moment correlation coefficients, a factor analysis, a two-way MANOVA, and univariate follow-up statistics) were applied to investigate the reliability and validity of each test. The multiple-choice discourse completion test had many problems, but the other five tests (i.e., the self-assessment, the language lab oral production test, the open discourse completion test, the roleplay test, the roleplay-self-assessment test) were found to be highly reliable and reasonably valid. In addition, the results indicate that, with a few minor adjustments, the translated versions of measures of cross-cultural pragmatics, developed originally in English by Hudson, Detmer, and Brown (1992, 1995) for testing cross-cultural pragmatics of learners of ESL, can also be used with English speaking populations who are studying Japanese language.

Moreover, the participants' length of exposure to the target culture was found to be related to performance on the two oral production pragmatics tests. The levels of proficiency of the participants also appear to be associated with the three pragmatics productive language tests. Practicality is also discussed from various perspectives.

# ACKNOWLEDGMENTS

I wish to extend my gratitude to the many people whose expertise, time, and support made the completion of this project possible. I would especially like to thank Dr. James Dean Brown. His interest in the work I was doing, the time he spent working with me and his perceptive comments were invaluable to me. Without his knowledge of the fields of statistics and second language learning and teaching, and without his guidance, encouragement, support, and patience, the completion of this project would never have been possible.

I am also very grateful to Dr. Thom D. Hudson for his willingness to let me use his research tools (referred to as Hudson et al. 1992, 1995) in my study. He also gave me enormous amounts of information about how I should prepare for data collection for this study and how to use it. I am grateful to him for his support and encouragement.

Special thanks go to Dr. Gabriel Kasper, one of the world's leading scholars in the field of cross-cultural pragmatics. Her knowledge and expertise inspired me a great deal. She was willing to help and advise me whenever I asked her for help. Her own work on cross-cultural pragmatics served as a model and inspiration.

I would also like to thank Dr. Noel R. Houck for assisting me with her knowledge of cross-cultural pragmatics, and for the time she spent reading and commenting on this report with numerous suggestions and sound advice. Her professional knowledge in the field and her suggestions were invaluable.

I am also very grateful to Dr. Ken G. Schaefer for his support and encouragement through my course work at the Temple University Japan. He was always there when I really needed help. Without his support and encouragement, I would never have finished my course work at Temple University Japan nor this project.

In addition, I would like to extend my gratitude to the Temple University Japan Graduate Program. I would like to thank Dr. Rod Ellis for inspiring me in the field of second language acquisition and classroom teaching for the first two years of the program. I was lucky to have him as an adviser in the beginning stages of my study. Also, I would like to thank Prof. Paul Nation for helping me work on the initial planning of this research. Special thanks also go to all the Temple University Japan 3rd Doctoral Cohort members, whose friendship and support as well as criticism and suggestions made this project possible.

I would also thank my interlocutor, Mr. S. Saito, who did the same 30 minute roleplays again and again with more than fifty participants for four months, and also the four raters, Mr. H. Tokiyama, Ms. C. Ushioda, Ms. M. Taguchi, and Ms. M. Nigo, who spent so much time viewing six 120 minute videotapes, listening to five

120 minute audiotapes, and reading the OPDCT responses of 47 participants for rating. I also wish to thank Atsuko Ushimaru very much for working with me on the translation of the OPDCT. I would also like to thank Brian and Mary Ann Platt for proofreading earlier versions of this report.

Finally, I would like to extend my deepest appreciation to the 47 participants who were willing to participate in my study and who completed all of these six time-consuming and complicated tests without fail, as well as my colleagues of International Christian University, Professors K. Tatematsu of Inter-University Center, H. Hoshino and M. Tsujimura of Waseda University, and M. Kitazawa of Temple University Japan who suggested that their students volunteer for my study.

SIX
MEASURES
OF
JSL
PRAGMATICS

# CHAPTER 1: INTRODUCTION

## BACKGROUND

In the past few decades, a number of cross-cultural, interlanguage pragmatics or speech act studies have been conducted. Many such studies investigated the use of speech acts such as making a request or an apology, expressing a sentiment of gratitude, and so forth and compared the performance of native speakers and non-native speakers in the use of the target language. Besides observing authentic, natural occurrences, various methods of study have been used to elicit the particular speech acts involved including different kinds of questionnaires and discourse completion tests (with or without a rejoinder), as well as closed-response or open-response roleplays.

Hudson, Detmer, and Brown (1992) were interested in developing prototype measures for assessing cross-cultural pragmatic competence. Aware of the variability of speech act realizations created by (a) the social properties of the speech events, and the speaker's strategic, actional, and linguistic choices for achieving communicative goals (pp. 1–2), and by (b) particular types of data collection procedures and associated instruments, they focused their studies on cataloging and testing cross-cultural contrasts. Their aim was to provide a framework for cross-cultural pragmatics tests using English and Japanese, which could serve as a model for the development of proficiency tests of pragmatics in other languages (p. 2).

Many pioneer works have tried to determine how native and non-native speakers realize speech acts (i.e., to what extent these realizations are different), what the characteristics of non-native speakers' speech act realizations are, and whether there is interference from the first language of the learners. However, a main concern expressed in Hudson, Detmer, and Brown (1995) was that most of the languages which had been studied were non-Asian languages such as English, Hebrew, German, and Dutch. Adding more information about an Asian language to the database on studies of cross-cultural pragmatics was viewed as essential. Thus, for their study's prototype group, they chose Japanese learners in Hawai'i who were studying English as a second language (ESL).

Some studies on native Japanese pragmatics and Japanese ESL learners' interlanguage pragmatics have been reported (see Yoshinaga, Maeshiba, and Takahashi, 1992 for an exhaustive bibliography). Also, interest is increasing in studying JSL (Japanese as a second language) or JFL (Japanese as a foreign language) learners' cross-cultural pragmatics competence or speech act realizations in communication for requests (Ikoma, 1993; Kashiwazaki, 1993), and refusals (Ikoma and Shimura, 1993; Shimura, 1993; Yokoyama, 1993). Some studies, such as Ikoma (1993), used an eliciting method called DCT, or *discourse completion test*, as a measuring tool, while others, like Kashiwazaki's (1993) study, relied on authentic

Yamashita, Sayoko Okada (1996). *Six measures of JSL pragmatics*. (Technical Report #14). Honolulu: University of Hawai'i, Second Language Teaching and Curriculum Center.

(naturalistic) data. Unfortunately, to date, no studies have investigated or compared data elicitation methods in the cross-cultural pragmatics studies of JSL learners. While the learner's acquisition of communicative competence in a target language is of great interest in the field of foreign and second language pedagogy, testing cross-cultural pragmatics should also be considered a very crucial step for researchers and language teachers alike. Finding reliable, effective, and valid methods of testing cross-cultural pragmatics will contribute not only to research in pragmatics but also to the more general areas of language teaching and learning.

## GOALS OF THIS STUDY

The primary goal of this project is to find effective methods for testing the cross-cultural pragmatics of English speaking learners of Japanese (both JSL and JFL) — tests that can serve as pragmatics proficiency tests. Three pragmatics measures were translated into Japanese from the English language prototype tests developed by Hudson et al. (1992, 1995). This project followed the framework used by Hudson et al. to investigate the pragmatics of Japanese learners of English as a second language in Hawai'i. Their purpose was to explore how reliable, valid, and effective their six English language cross-cultural pragmatic measures were. The findings of the present study should contribute to our ability to develop reliable, valid, and effective pragmatics testing measures for learners of the Japanese language. The findings will ultimately contribute a great deal to JSL and JFL pedagogy where such methods of testing cross-cultural pragmatics have not yet been fully developed. Since this study used the framework proposed by Hudson, Detmer, and Brown (1992, 1995), their works will be briefly reviewed here.

## MODEL OF THIS STUDY

### HUDSON, DETMER, AND BROWN (1992)

In their first book, Hudson, Detmer, and Brown (1992) reviewed the literature on pragmatics and cross-cultural pragmatics. They first discussed generic concerns of defining and assessing interlanguage pragmatics citing theories of Hymes (1972), Canale (1988), Canale and Swain (1980), Bachman and Palmer (1989), and so forth. In summarizing, Hudson et al. (1992) said that "contemporary concerns with the role of pragmatics in communicative competence have added the dimension of language context to investigations into language proficiency" (p. 5). Then they discussed a number of problems with defining the causes of pragmatic failure and difficulties in generalizing specification of traits which reflect pragmatic failure, citing the works of Blum-Kulka (1982), Olshtain and Blum-Kulka (1985), Thomas (1983) and others. Hudson et al. (1992), after examining different parameters, decided to use the concepts of relative power, social distance, and absolute ranking of impositions which Brown and Levinson (1987) proposed for the variables in their speech act realization testing project. They proposed a framework for assessing pragmatic competence in various target languages (though they were aiming at developing a framework for Japanese and American English) after examining the relevant literature in Japanese and American English cross-cultural pragmatics such as Beebe and Takahashi (1989), Beebe, Takahashi, and Uliss-Weltz (1990), Clancy (1986), Ide (1989), and others.

Hudson et al. (1992) employed multiple modalities in their instruments in order to examine variability due to data collection procedures (also known as the *method effect*). Three different classifications of test methods (indirect measures of pragmatic knowledge, direct measures of pragmatic ability, and self-assessment of pragmatic skill) were proposed. Further, each of these three classifications was subdivided into two test sub-methods (cued-response and free-response methods). The basis for a multitrait-multimethod matrix for test validation (after Campbell and Fiske, 1959) was provided. A variable distribution table (Hudson et al. 1992, p. 16) presented in Table 1 in this section indicated the distribution and interactions of the three variables (power, distance, and imposition) and three speech acts (requests, refusals, and apologies) that would be tested. Preliminary results were presented at the end of Hudson et al. (1992).

Table 1: Variable distribution table from
Hudson, Detmer, and Brown (1995, p. 6)

| | | Cell Number and Attributes | | | | | | | |
|---|---|---|---|---|---|---|---|---|---|
| **Speech Act** | | | | | | | | | |
| Request | | 1 | 2 | 3 | 4 | 5 | 6 | 7 | 8 |
| Refusal | | 9 | 10 | 11 | 12 | 13 | 14 | 15 | 16 |
| Apology | | 17 | 18 | 19 | 20 | 21 | 22 | 23 | 24 |
| **Variables** | | | | | | | | | |
| Power | P | + | + | + | + | − | − | − | − |
| Distance | D | + | + | − | − | + | + | − | − |
| absolute Ranking of imposition | R | + | − | + | − | + | − | + | − |

## HUDSON, DETMER, AND BROWN (1995)

Hudson, Detmer, and Brown (1995) described how they developed and piloted the open-ended discourse completion test (DCT), oral-aural instruments (listening lab test, structured interview or roleplay, and oral assessment), and self-assessment. They also presented revised frameworks for power and distance relationships, and for degree of imposition of the three speech acts. Their Tables 3 and 4 (pp. 10 and 11) listed the relationships of people such as a manager (+Power/+Distance) versus a job applicant (−Power/+Distance), and degree of imposition such as destroying property (Apology/+Imposition) versus knocking over but not destroying property (Apology/−Imposition).

Then they reported the percent of agreement among native speakers from a pilot study. Native American-English speakers and non-native (Japanese studying English as a second language) speakers' DCT data were analyzed using a coding scheme based on a combination of the Cross Cultural Speech Act Realization Project (CCSARP) in Blum-Kulka, House, and Kasper (1989b) and Beebe, Takahashi, and Wliss-Weltz (1990). Hudson et al. (1995) list the strategies used in their Table 7 (pp. 14–15). These strategies include alerters (such as attention getters), head acts (such as grounders), illocutionary force indicating devices (such as "I'm sorry"), supportive moves (such as imposition minimizers), and modifications (such as downgraders like politeness markers and upgraders like intensifiers). Two coding systems were employed and revised on the basis of observed L1 interference in the non-native speaker data. Hudson et al. (1995) also provided native speaker and non-native speaker samples of coded responses (using codes for each strategy presented above) and uncoded responses (listing actual full-sentence responses for DCT), and analyzed the similarities and differences for specific speech acts as produced by both native and non-native speakers. They reported some changes in item specifications based on the native and non-native speaker DCT results. They also presented information about other on-going testing measures such as their multiple-choice DCT, their oral-aural instruments, and their self-assessment formats. Appendixes included all six types of testing measures, rating sheets, interviewer guidelines, and a training manual for native speaker raters. The self-assessment and roleplay self-assessment tests in English which Hudson et al. (1995) developed were used directly in this study without modifications. The OPDCT, multiple-choice DCT, Listening Lab test, and roleplay scenarios presented in Hudson et al. (1995) were modified considerably including translation into Japanese and some modification of situations to better fit the Japanese cultural context. The resulting measures were all used to test American English learners of Japanese in order to assess their proficiency in Japanese pragmatics.

## ORGANIZATION

This report consists of seven chapters. The following is a brief description of each chapter. The beginning part of chapter 1 (the current chapter) presents a brief introduction to the background studies that are directly related to the current study. The chapter then briefly describes and reviews the study of Hudson, Detmer, and Brown (1992, 1995) as their study is the theoretical base of the current study. Then this section describes the organization of this report giving a short summary of each chapter. Definitions and abbreviations are given at the end of chapter 1 so as to supply a baseline understanding of the important terms used in this report.

Chapter 2 reviews the literature of related fields of study. It first overviews the current studies on cross-cultural pragmatics. Then it surveys the literature on the different methods used in this study for the measurement of cross-cultural pragmatics such as discourse completion tests, roleplay tests, language lab oral production tests, as well as self-assessments and ratings.

Chapter 3 presents the results and findings of a pilot study that was conducted with both native speakers of Japanese and American learners of Japanese. At the end of chapter 3, the research questions are posited.

Chapter 4 focuses on the research design and methodology including the following subsections: (a) methods, (b) participants, (c) materials, (d) procedures (test administration and scoring), (e) analysis, and (f) additional comments on data collection.

Chapter 5 presents the results. Chapter 6 is the discussion section. Chapter 7 provides the conclusions, pedagogical implications, and suggestions for further study.

# DEFINITIONS AND ABBREVIATIONS

The most important definitions and abbreviations which are used in this report are listed next in alphabetical order. The definitions are taken directly from the literature. Some of the definitions (e.g., pragmatic competence, illocutionary acts, etc.) are still controversial in the literature. Instead of trying to define them in my own words (and thereby adding to the confusion), I have defined the terms as they appear in the literature, in some cases citing two or more people. Special abbreviations used only in this study are marked with an asterisk.

*Cloze test*: A procedure commonly used for estimating overall English language proficiency by deleting every nth word from a reading passage and replacing each word with a blank (Brown, 1983). Students are then required to fill in the blanks. Cloze has been found to be a stable, reliable, and sensitive measure of the sentential and inter-sentential components of the language (Bachman, 1982; Brown, 1983; Chavez-Oller, Chihara, Weaver, and Oller, 1985; Jonz, 1987, 1990).

*Competence*: The knowledge and ability that underlie language use (Hymes, 1972).

*Context*: A set of propositions, beliefs, knowledge, commitments, and so forth on the part of the participants in a discourse situation (Olshtain, 1996).

*Cross-cultural pragmatics*: "Culturally colored interactional styles create culturally determined expectation and interpretative strategies, and can lead to breakdowns in intercultural and interethnic communication" (Gumperz, 1978).

*Degree of Imposition*: "A potential expenditure of goods and/or services by the hearer" (Hudson, Detmer, and Brown, 1992, p. 7).

*DCT (Discourse completion task or test)*: "Written questionnaires which include a number of brief situational descriptions, followed by a short dialogue with an empty slot for the speech act under study" (Kasper and Dahl, 1991).

*Distance*: "A social parameter referring to the degree of familiarity between the interlocutors" (Olshtain and Blum-Kulka, 1985, p. 18).

*EFL*: English as a foreign language

*ESL*: English as a second language

*Hiragana*: the basic Japanese syllabic character system used for Japanese words

*Illocution*: "Illocutionary function is used to convey *force* and *how* language is to be taken" (Austin, 1962) [emphasis in the original]; some of the English verbs and verb phrases associated with illocutionary acts are — state, assert, describe, warn, remark, comment, command, order, request, apologize, promise, and so forth (Searle, 1965); it is concerned with the creation of some sort of effect on the addressee (Flowerdew, 1990). *Perlocution* or perlocutionary acts, on the other hand, "have to do with those effects which our utterances have on hearers which go beyond the hearer's understanding of the utterance (e.g., convincing, persuading, annoying, amusing, and frightening)" (Searle, Kiefer, and Bierwisch, 1980, p. vii).

*Interlanguage*: a type of 'Learner language' which is viewed as an independent social or psychological phenomenon (Phillipson, Kellerman, Selinker, Sharwood Smith, and Swain, 1991).

*Interlanguage pragmatics*: "the study of nonnative speakers' use and acquisition of pragmatic and discourse knowledge in a second language" (Kasper, 1989).

*JFL*: Japanese as a foreign language

*JSL*: Japanese as a second language

*Kanji*: Chinese characters borrowed in Japanese

*Katakana*: the basic Japanese syllabic character system used for foreign words

*LL\**: Language lab oral production test. Situations are given aurally from a tape, and the participant is asked to respond orally. Each response is recorded on another tape. (This procedure was called "Listening Lab DCT" in Hudson et al. 1995)

*MCDCT\**: Multiple-choice discourse completion test

*NS*: Native speaker

*NNS*: Non-native speaker

*OPDCT\**: Open-response discourse completion test

*Perlocution*: see *Illocution*

*Power*: "A social parameter referring to the degree to which the speaker, participating in the interaction can impose his plans at the expense of his interlocutor's plans" (Olshtain and Blum-Kulka, 1985, p. 18).

*Pragmatics*: "the study of language usage" (Leech, 1983, p. 5); "the cognitive, social, and cultural study of language and communication" (Verschueren, Ostman, and Blommaert, 1995, p. 1).

*Pragmatic competence*: "Entails a variety of abilities concerned with the use and interpretation of language in contexts, or most prominently the ability to use and interpret nonliteral forms, such as metaphorical uses of language and indirect requests…" (Bialystok, 1993, p. 43)

*Pragmatic failure*: "A hearer perceives the force of a speaker's utterance as other than the speaker intended s/he should perceive it." (Thomas, 1983, p. 94)

*Pragmatic transfer*: "The influence exerted by learners' pragmatic knowledge of languages and cultures other than L2 on their comprehension, production, and acquisition of L2 pragmatic information" (Kasper, 1992).

*Roleplay (or RP\*)*: "A type of skit in which learners assume the identity of individual characters in a given situation and engage in a conversation that reflects the personalities, needs, and desires of the characters they are asked to portray" (Eckard and Kearney, 1981, p. 20). The term *roleplay* is sometimes written *role-play*, or *role play*. *Roleplay* is used throughout this report.

*RPSA\**: Roleplay self-assessment. A procedure wherein students assess their performance in a previously videotaped roleplay.

*SA\**: Self-assessment, or self-report, is "the learner's own perspective which is an internal or self-directed activity" (Oscarson, 1989, p. 1).

*Speech acts*: "The unit of linguistic communication in which production of words or of sentences is regarded as the performance of speech acts. An act is something that we 'do' or a piece of active behavior by an agent" (Vershueren, Ostman, and Blommaert, 1995, p. 497); "The minimal unit of speech that has rules in terms both of where and when they may occur and of what their specific features are — many of these are culturally named acts, such as complaining, apologizing, commenting, advising, and so on" (Hymes, 1972).

# CHAPTER 2: REVIEW OF THE LITERATURE

## THEORETICAL OVERVIEW

Within second or foreign language pedagogy and research, communicative competence has been the focus and subject of discussion for a number of years (Bachman, 1990; Canale, 1983; Canale and Swain, 1980; Faerch and Kasper, 1986; Gumperz, 1972; Hymes, 1972). When Chomsky (1965) introduced the notions of *competence* and *performance* to describe language ability, he claimed that *competence* only referred to the linguistic system or the speaker-hearer's knowledge of his language (i.e., grammar), and *performance* referred to the actual use of language in concrete situations. In contrast, scholars like Hymes (1972) and Campbell and Wales (1970) opposed Chomsky's competence-performance dichotomy and proposed, in its place, a notion of communicative competence that should be included as a part of language ability. They claimed that communicative competence covers not only grammatical competence but also contextual or sociolinguistic competence (i.e., knowledge of the rules of language use). Bachman (1990) further modified and refined a framework of principles, and presented theoretical models of language ability (see "Components of communicative language ability in communicative language use" and "Components of language competence" in Bachman, 1990, pp. 85 and 87). In his model of "components of language competence," Bachman proposed that two features characterize communicative language use: organizational competence (which comprises grammatical and textual competencies) and pragmatic competence (which comprises illocutionary and sociolinguistic competencies). According to Bachman, all of these components interact with each other and with features of the situation in which language is to be used (Bachman, 1990, p. 86). In terms of testing language ability, Bachman (1990) proposed that, "if we develop and use language tests appropriately, we must base them on clear definitions of both the abilities we wish to measure and the means by which we observe and measure these abilities" (p. 81).

Recently, the study of cross-cultural pragmatics has become particularly important in second language acquisition pedagogy and testing. People are now aware of the fact that even if a second language learner uses grammatical forms correctly in the target language, misunderstandings may still arise between second language learners and native speakers due to pragmatic (either sociopragmatic or pragmalinguistic) failure (Thomas, 1983; also see chapter 7 in Wolfson, 1989 for an overview of miscommunication). Questioning the cause of such failures reveals that they may possibly be due to the fact that (a) there is not always a direct correspondence between literal meanings and actual speech act performances, and/or (b) speech act realizations might be interpreted differently cross-culturally, as numerous studies in cross-cultural or interlanguage pragmatics have reported (for instance, see collections of studies in Blum-Kulka, House, and Kasper, 1989b; Kasper and Blum-Kulka, 1993). Among those studies, variability is perceived as a serious issue. Kasper and Dahl (1991) have cited a problem which they call "a double layer of variability." They listed two types of variability: "(1) that which reflects the social properties of the speech event, and the strategic, actional, and linguistic choices by which interlocutors attempt to reach their communicative goals; and (2) the variability induced by different instruments of data collection" (p. 215).

Hudson, Detmer, and Brown (1992) became interested in the variability of type (2) and proposed prototype measures of cross-cultural pragmatics (Hudson, Detmer, and Brown, 1995). They studied cross-cultural pragmatics of Japanese learners of English as a second language (ESL) using six prototype measures that they developed — namely, a self-assessment, a language lab production test, an open-ended discourse completion test, a multiple-choice discourse completion test, a roleplay, and a roleplay self-assessment. This study was designed to test the cross-cultural pragmatics of American learners of Japanese as a second and foreign language (JSL/JFL) by using translated and somewhat modified Japanese versions of the same six tests which Hudson et al. (1992, 1995) developed.

The remaining sections of this chapter will continue by reviewing the literature on: (a) issues of elicitation and self-assessment in measures used in cross-cultural pragmatics study and (b) issues of comparing test methods.

## CROSS-CULTURAL PRAGMATICS TESTING MEASURES

### DATA COLLECTION MEASURES

The data collection measures employed in cross-cultural pragmatics studies can be described on a relative continuum as shown in Kasper and Dahl (1991, p. 217). In Figure 1, they illustrate the relationships among such methods as rating tasks, multiple-choice questionnaires, and interviews, all of which provide information about learners' perceptions/comprehension of alternative speech act realizations. Discourse completion tasks, as well as closed-response and open-response roleplays are categorized as tasks which provide production data. Studies of pragmatics using such measures were well reviewed by Kasper and Dahl (1991). In the current section, measures which are relevant to this study will be up-dated and reviewed.

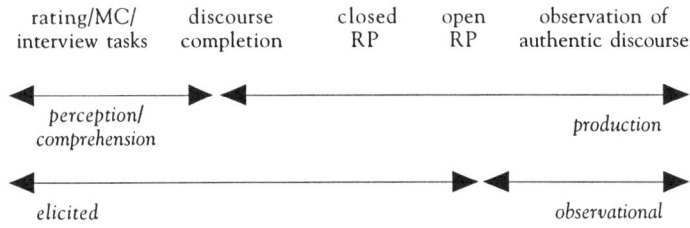

**Figure 1. Eliciting measures for cross-cultural pragmatics
(Kasper and Dahl, 1991, p. 217)**

## SPEECH ACTS AND VARIABLES IN THE TESTS

Among various kinds of speech acts, requests, refusals, and apologies have been most often investigated in cross-cultural pragmatics studies (Beebe, Takahashi, and Uliss-Weltz; 1990; Blum-Kulka, 1989; Blum-Kulka and House, 1989; Blum-Kulka, House, and Kasper, 1989b; Hartford and Bardovi-Harlig, 1996; Olshtain, 1989; Cohen and Olshtain, 1981, 1983; Niki and Tajika, 1994). These speech acts are appropriate for contrasting English and Japanese speech act realization (Hudson, Detmer, and Brown, 1995, p.6); hence, they are included in the six cross-cultural pragmatics tests in this project.

Also, three variables, degree of imposition, power, and social distance were selected for the tests because they are identified as the three independent and culturally sensitive variables that subsume all other variables and play a principled role in speech act behavior (Hudson et al. 1995; also Brown and Levinson; 1987, Fraser, 1990). The definitions and descriptions of the variables used in this study are summarized next (adapted by Hudson et al. 1995, pp. 4–5):

*Imposition* represents the expenditure of goods and/or services by the hearer, or the obligation of the speaker to perform the act. When the speech act is "requests," +Imposition (+I) is a great expenditure of goods, services, or energy required by hearer to carry out the request, whereas –Imposition (–I) is a small expenditure of goods, services, or energy required by hearer to carry out the request. When the speech act is "refusals," +I is a great expenditure of goods, services, or energy requested of the speaker, whereas –I is a small expenditure of goods, and so forth When the speech act is "apologies," +I is a great severity of offense or speaker's obligation to apologize is great, whereas –I is a small severity of offense or speaker's obligation to apologize is small.

*Power* represents the power of the speaker with respect to the hearer. When the speaker has a higher rank, title, or social position, or is in control of the assets in the situation, the power is indicated as +P, whereas when the speaker has a lower or lesser rank, title, or social position, or is not in control of the assets in the situation, the power is indicated as –P.

*Distance* represents the distance between the speaker and the hearer, or the degree of familiarity and solidarity. +D indicates that the speaker and the hearer do not know or identify with each other, whereas –D indicates that the speaker and the hearer know and or identify with each other.

## SIX CROSS-CULTURAL PRAGMATICS MEASURES

SA (Self-assessment), LL (language lab oral production test), OPDCT (open discourse completion test), RP (roleplay), RPSA (roleplay self-assessment), MCDCT (Multiple-choice discourse completion test) are the six test measures used in this study (in the order they were administered). The rationale for choosing these six particular pragmatics measures has been described in Hudson, Detmer, and

Brown (1992, 1995). The rest of this chapter will review each test in turn. Because of their interrelationships, the measures will be discussed in a different order.

## Open discourse completion tests

The OPDCTs are the most popular measures of cross-cultural or interlanguage pragmatics. Numerous cross-cultural pragmatics studies have used data elicited using OPDCTs to study speech acts such as requests, suggestions, complaints, and so forth (Beebe, Takahashi, and Uliss-Weltz, 1990; Blum-Kulka, 1982, 1983; Blum-Kulka and Olshtain, 1986; Cohen, Olshtain, and Rosenstein 1986; House, 1989; House and Kasper, 1987; Ikoma, 1993; Kasper, 1989; Olshtain and Weinbach, 1987; Takahashi and Beebe, 1987, 1993).

Among those studies, the most ambitious is the Cross Cultural Speech Act Realization Project (CCSARP) (Blum-Kulka, House, and Kasper, 1989b), which greatly inspired and influenced later studies in the field of cross-cultural and interlanguage pragmatics. The CCSARP was organized to investigate cross-cultural and intralingual variations in two speech acts (requests and apologies) which were directly relevant to "face-threatening acts" (Brown and Levinson, 1987). The primary goals of the project were to investigate (a) cross-cultural variation, (b) sociopragmatic variation, and (c) interlanguage variations of the realization patterns of the two speech acts. The researchers studied more than 1000 native speaker students in America, Australia, Great Britain, Canada, Denmark, Germany, and Israel. They also studied over 800 non-native speaker students who were learning three target languages (English, German, and Hebrew) in four different countries (Denmark, US, Germany, and Israel). This project provides a framework for speech act studies. Some major findings are: (a) a universality of conventional indirectness in requestive discourse (Blum-Kulka, 1989), (b) variations of speech act realization for apologies and requests, which were attributed to situational factors (Wolfson, Marmor, and Jones, 1989), (c) verbosity in interlanguage (Blum-Kulka and Olshtain, 1986; House and Kasper, 1987; Faerch and Kasper, 1989), and (d) different operations of transfer from learners of various native languages.

When the "waffling" effect, or verbosity, was reported as a negative characteristic of the DCT (Edmondson and House, 1991), Bergman and Kasper (1993) suggested that the DCT, on the contrary, "provides learners with an opportunity for knowledge display that is precluded for many NNSs by the cognitive demands of face-to-face interaction" (p. 101).

The DCT elicitation method serves as a very effective tool for cross-cultural and interlanguage pragmatics studies in that it can be used to gather a large amount of data easily and in that it is compatible with natural speech occurrences. However, questions have also been raised about its usefulness. One of the issues is the types of DCT forms — whether or not a DCT with a rejoinder makes the response different from that without a rejoinder.

Here are some examples of DCTs with (a) preferred or (b) dispreferred rejoinders and a DCT with (c) no rejoinder reported by Johnston, Kasper, and Ross (1993b). (Rejoinders are shown here in italics).

(a)  You are giving a dinner party for twelve people, but you don't have a bowl big enough for the salad. You go around to your neighbor to see if she has one.

You: _____

*Your neighbor: Yes, I'll just get it for you.*

(b)  At an office party, you had a bit too much to drink and were rude to one of your colleagues. The next day you call her up to check that she was not offended.

You: _____

*Your colleague: Well, it's been a long time since I was insulted like that. You should be ashamed of yourself.*

(c)  You were in a hurry to leave on a trip, and you asked your roommate to mail an express letter for you. When you get back a few days later, the letter is still lying on the table.

You: _____

Johnston, Kasper, and Ross (1993a, 1993b) reported that (a) the presence and type of rejoinder affect responses differentially, (b) the three speech acts that they studied (requests, apologies, and complaints) are affected differentially by rejoinders, (c) speech act realization strategies are affected differentially by rejoinders, and (d) rejoinder type affects responses in a DCT (i.e., studies using different rejoinder types may not be comparable). In contrast, Rose (1992b) found no significant effect for differences between a DCT with rejoinders as compared to one without rejoinders. Clearly, the findings on this issue are contradictory. In authentic conversation, the speaker can sometimes predict or guess the hearer's response, and speak accordingly. On some other occasions, however, the speaker cannot tell what the hearer might respond. Either possibility could happen in real situations. In this study, however, rejoinders were not presented because all the tests including self-assessment had essentially the same format as Hudson et al. (1995), which did not have rejoinders.

Another issue is the use of a written form in order to elicit oral interaction. The realization of intended speech acts in written form might be different from the actual oral performance (Wolfson, Marmor, and Jones, 1989). Cohen and Olshtain (1994) claimed that "since the DCT is a projective measure of speaking, the cognitive process involved in producing utterances in response to this elicitation device may not truly reflect" actual natural speech performance (p. 148). Rintell and Mitchell (1989) found that the lengths of non-native oral responses were longer than the written DCT responses; unfortunately, they did not distinguish between oral and written responses of native speakers. Further study of the possible effects of methodology would be useful. Also, most of the studies of interlanguage pragmatics using DCTs dealt primarily with English or Hebrew as target languages. There is a definite need for studies examining speech act realizations in a wider spectrum of target languages (Blum-Kulka, House, and Kasper, 1989a).

## Listening lab oral production test

Eisenstein and Bodman (1993) used a questionnaire which they wrote. They administered it orally in order to study the influence of intonation and prosodic features. They read each situation to ten native speakers, tape-recorded their responses, and later transcribed those responses. Post hoc interviews revealed that native speakers were uneasy about their responses, which Eisenstein and Bodman (1993) speculated to be due to the lack of interaction. Although transcripts were almost identical to the language of the written questionnaires, the speakers' range of emotion (including prosodic features) and the frequent uneasy pauses in their oral responses were evident in the audiotapes but not in the written questionnaires.

Hudson, Detmer, and Brown (1995) suggested a framework for a listening lab version, in which they let the participants read silently about situations that were taken from an OPDCT and respond to them orally. Later they developed a listening lab version and piloted it with both native English speakers and non-native EFL and ESL learners. To this researcher's knowledge, no other studies have been conducted to date involving an audio-recorded oral DCT.

## Multiple-choice discourse completion tests

Tanaka and Kawade (1982) studied the politeness strategies of native and non-native speakers of English (all graduate students: 53 native speakers of American English and 32 non-native speakers of English from various language backgrounds) using a multiple-choice test. Ten situations were devised to investigate native and non-native speakers' degrees of politeness depending on the delicacy of the situations. They used a questionnaire containing: (a) a picture of each situation, (b) a description of each situation, and (c) six polite responses for each situation (i.e., each situation had six choices). The participants were asked to select the one that they would be most likely to use in each situation. A sample from Tanaka and Kawade (1982, p. 26) follows:

> It's raining heavily. You want to borrow an umbrella from Mr. Brown. He is the owner of a grocery store and an old acquaintance of yours.
>
> 1. I want you to lend me an umbrella.
> 2. Would you lend me an umbrella?
> 3. Lend me an umbrella.
> 4. I would appreciate it if you could lend me an umbrella.

5. Can you lend me an umbrella?
6. Lend me an umbrella, will you?

*[a picture accompanies the sample on p. 26 of Tanaka and Kawade, 1982]*

Their multiple-choice design was unique and worked well for their own research purposes. Since it was designed for studying politeness levels of requests, it does not reflect differences in pragmatic-based strategies such as whether or not the speaker uses hints or uncompleted sentence endings (as reported in Lebra, 1976; Clancy, 1986).

Rose (1992a, 1994) used a MCDCT (he called it a multiple-choice questionnaire or an MCQ) and compared it with an OPDCT. He conducted his study in order to (a) initiate a contrastive study of requests in Japanese and American English using the OPDCT, and (b) explore the validity of the OPDCT in non-Western contexts (i.e., Japanese) by using the MCDCT. A total of 46 Americans (23 females and 23 males) took the OPDCT in English, and 89 Japanese students in the US (47 females and 42 males) took the OPDCT which had been translated into Japanese. Since he knew that Japanese communication is characteristically face-to-face interaction, Rose had strong doubts about using the OPDCT for Japanese participants because of their reluctance to use (i.e., write in an OPDCT) some of the expressions elicited by his OPDCT (e.g., "hinting" for a request). In support of his ideas, he found that the responses of Japanese native-speakers (38 female Japanese women's college students living in Japan) on a Japanese version of the MCDCT, which included hints in appropriate situations, were accurate. From these findings, he raised questions about the validity of the OPDCT, especially in non-Western contexts.

There are almost no cross-cultural or interlanguage pragmatics studies which use the MCDCT or any kind of multiple-choice type measures besides the studies reviewed above. Language pragmatics is the study of human communication style and oral interaction. Although methods such as roleplay and the observation of authentic speech are indispensable for analysis of speech acts, we sometimes need measures such as multiple-choice instruments which can be used to collect data easily in a short period of time and make the analysis, either for research or pedagogical purposes, an easier process.

## Roleplays

In a roleplay, it is possible to simulate conversational turns and to have the interlocutor apply conversational pressures that are not present in a DCT (Cohen and Olshtain, 1994, p. 148). Thus, studies which investigated a variety of speech acts such as making requests, apologies, or invitations; initiating and responding; and so on used the roleplay method (Cohen and Olshtain, 1981, 1993, 1994; Edmondson, House, Kasper, and Stemmer, 1984; Eisenstein and Bodman, 1993; Fiksdal, 1989; Fraser, Rintell, and Walters, 1980; Kasper, 1984; Olshtain, 1983; Rintell and Mitchel, 1989; Scarcella and Brunak, 1981; Tanaka, 1988; Trosborg, 1987). As video equipment has been widely used and become common in SLA research, more and more cross-cultural and interlanguage pragmatics studies have been conducted using video-taped roleplays. Although most of the studies have examined speech acts in the same target language, English, the non-native speakers' L1 background was varied, including languages such as Arabic, Japanese, German, and Danish. The advantage of roleplay tests is that they allow examination of speech act performance in its full discourse context and sequential organization in terms of negotiation of meaning, the strategy choice, and politeness investment, all of which are strong characteristics of authentic conversation (Kasper and Dahl, 1991). Eisenstein and Bodman (1993) concluded that, while written and oral questionnaire data mirror words and expressions, roleplays reveal the interactive aspects of the function more fully (p.75). Kasper and Dahl (1991) further concluded that roleplays could even have an advantage over authentic conversation because they are replicable and allow for the comparative study of non-native speakers with L1 and L2 speaker control groups (p. 229). One disadvantage is that roleplays require the time-consuming task of transcribing the data (Kasper and Dahl, 1991).

## Self-assessment and roleplay self-assessment

Various types of self-assessment tools have come into style since the development of new language teaching approaches, such as student-centered, needs-oriented, and individual based instruction. If assessment by the learners themselves were wholly accurate, it would help a great deal they would not have to rely solely on their teacher's appraisal of their language learning and in that they would be able to make their teachers aware of their individual learning needs (Blanche, 1988). Self-assessment could also be used to diagnose students' proficiency levels. The researchers are often concerned with how autonomous the language learner's self-assessment is. Blanche (1988) extensively reviewed literature on self-assessment in the testing of foreign language proficiency. His review came to the following conclusions: (a) "the accuracy of most students' self-estimates often varies depending on the linguistic skills and materials involved in the evaluations" (p. 81), (b) "self-assessed scores may often be affected by subjective errors due to past academic records, career aspirations, peer-group or parental expectations, lack of training in self study, and so forth," (c) descriptions of concrete linguistic situations which the learner can size up in behavioral terms can help to yield the accurate answers for self-test items, (d) self-assessment appeared to have increased the learners' motivation, (e) more proficient participants tended to underrate their linguistic abilities, and (f) most learners would find it comparatively easier to assess their purely communicative skills (p. 82). Other researchers have also reported that self-assessment estimates are generally accurate (Bachman and Palmer, 1981; Davidson and Henning, 1985; Oskarsson, 1978).

Oskarsson (1978) outlined possible forms of self-assessment for adult language learners and suggested steps for developing methods for self-assessment. His book included a review of relevant literature and research, suggestions for material development, and sample forms of various types of self-assessment. He proposed that authentic language situations provide the most valid opportunities for self-assessment, which may ultimately test one's communicative ability (p. 25).

Although the above comment may have meaningful implications for the current study of pragmatics testing, the self-assessment form that was offered in his book (on p. 47) was still fairly primitive, using the *Yes-No* question type (e.g., I can apologize — [ ]Yes/[ ]No).

LeBlanc and Painchaud (1985) conducted a study of the use of self-assessment as a placement test for a second language program. They reported some advantages of self-assessment questionnaires, such as that they take much less time than regular proficiency tests, data gathering is easier, and students are themselves involved with the important responsibility of their own placement.

In the area of pragmatics testing, Bergman and Kasper (1993) asked (a) "How are contextual factors in a variety of offense contexts perceived by Thai and American informants?" (b) "How is the selection of apology strategies determined by contextual factors?" and (c) "What patterns of intracultural and intercultural variability are observable in the selection of apology strategies by Thai NNS of English as compared to NS of Thai and American English?" (p.87). Thai students (n=423) were asked to rate themselves on a self-assessment questionnaire of 20 items, each of which specified a different offense context, on a five-point rating scale for four context-internal factors (plus and minus Distance and plus and minus Power, after Brown and Levinson, 1987) and two context-external factors (plus and minus Degree of Imposition, after Brown and Levinson, 1987). Their self-assessment questionnaire basically asked the participants how they interpreted or comprehended the given situation and context, but did not ask how they would react or what they would say themselves in the real situation.

Many types of self-assessment questionnaire, similar to that reviewed above, have been proposed. Two major types are (a) assessment to show how the learner grasps or comprehends the given situation (an example of such assessment is presented by Bergman and Kasper, 1993; Shimamura, 1993), and (b) assessment of the performance of the learner him/herself in a given situation. In this second type, a situation is described, and the learners are asked how well they would respond in that particular situation (on a five-point Likert scale), but no actual production is required (Hudson, Detmer, and Brown, 1995).

## EFFECTIVENESS OF DIFFERENT MEASURES (COMPARING TEST MEASURES)

A number of studies of cross-cultural pragmatics using multiple methods and studies which compared the strengths and weaknesses of different pragmatic research methods have appeared in the last decade (Beebe and Takahashi, 1989; Bergman and Kasper, 1993; Blum-Kulka, House, and Kasper, 1989b; Cohen and Olshtain, 1994; Hartford and Bardovi-Harlig, 1992; Hudson, Detmer, and Brown, 1992, 1995; Kasper and Dahl, 1991; Olshtain and Blum-Kulka, 1985; Rose, 1992a; Sasaki, 1995a, 1995b; Wolfson, Marmor, and Jones, 1989).

Bergman and Kasper (1993) studied NS and NNS apology perception and performance using two test methods. One of the methods was the use of an assessment questionnaire in which participants were asked to rate different offense contexts on a five-point rating scale for four context-internal factors and two context-external factors. Another of Bergman and Kasper's methods involved the use of a Dialogue Construction (DC) questionnaire which included the same offense contexts as the assessment questionnaire. With the DC questionnaire, participants were asked to create a dialogue between the offender and the offended person after they read the offense context. Bergman and Kasper (1993) summarized the findings of apology strategies elicited by each method. The findings regarding the characteristics of measure types are (a) both methods demonstrated participants' sociopragmatic knowledge of apology, (b) the "waffling" effect was evident in the DC questionnaire, and (c) a DCT type of questionnaire provides learners with an opportunity to display knowledge which does not always appear in face-to-face interaction. The authors claimed that this type of test shows evidence of the extent to which the learner's available pragmatic knowledge is readily accessible in a real conversation (p. 101).

Rintell and Mitchell (1989) asked whether or not using a roleplay technique to elicit speech act data (oral) would reveal different responses from those elicited employing a DCT (written). In their DCT, they gave a statement explaining the context and asked participants to write what they would say in the given context. For the oral roleplay, the researchers described orally the exact same question (situation) given in DCT and asked the participants to say what the person they are roleplaying would say in the situation. The oral roleplays were tape recorded and transcribed. This roleplay did not have an interlocutor to interact with and was only tape recorded (not video-taped). The researchers claimed that the written and oral production elicited by their two methods were basically very similar except that the oral responses were considerably longer. Two of their salient findings, which appear to have been affected by elicitation methods, were (a) non-native oral data was far longer than the data elicited in the DCT, and (b) there were differences in the frequency of use of direct request strategy forms between oral and written data for both native speakers and nonnative speakers. One concern about the design of their study is that they used the same descriptions in order to elicit oral and written responses, so there may have been a *learning effect* for the test that was administered last.

Sasaki (1995a, 1995b) compared the responses of two speech act realizations (requests and refusals) elicited by open DCTs and roleplays (with a native interlocutor) obtained from 12 Japanese EFL learners (two males and two females each from three levels from low to high intermediate). She had the learners take both tests instead of having different participants for different tests, which was the case with most of the previous studies. She investigated to what extent the responses differed due to different test measures. She found that the two methods elicited different speech samples in terms of the length of the response, their content, and the native speakers' rating of the responses. She concluded that roleplays provide a more authentic measure of pragmatic competence over DCTs.

Eisenstein and Bodman (1993) conducted four experiments using different measures: natural observation, an OPDCT, an oral questionnaire, and roleplays. The oral questionnaire was the same type of measure as introduced and used by Rintell and Mitchell (1989). The authors studied the realization of expressing gratitude performed by native speakers and non-native speakers using the above four methods. They found that the words and expressions used in conveying gratitude both in written and oral questionnaire data, mirrored one another, while the roleplays more fully revealed the interactive aspects of the function (p. 75). Moreover, they point out that roleplays had the advantage of providing the type of data that the researchers expected to study, and it was even more useful than natural data in a way, even though natural data may be more indicative of the whole process. Their study was innovative because they compared the data elicited by four different measures. However, they used different groups of native speakers and non-native speakers for each experiment, so there might have been some inconsistency in the study.

Hudson, Detmer, and Brown's (1992, 1995) studies were the most ambitious ones so far to compare Japanese EFL learners' cross-cultural pragmatics with native English speakers' as baseline data. Their study employed six different measures including the most popular methods, (i.e., written and oral open DCT and roleplays) as well as two kinds of self-assessments, and a multiple-choice DCT. The same group of participants took all six tests. Hudson et al. (1995) analyzed the data qualitatively and quantitatively with various statistical methods. They suggest that the methods in their study should be applied to language learners from different nationalities to see if their various elicitation measures have the same characteristics in other languages (including strengths and weaknesses) as those they reported for English (for more information on their study, see previous chapter).

Since a multiple method approach will allow the tester to achieve cross-validation, it is strongly recommended (Olshtain and Blum-Kulka, 1985, p. 28). For a more extensive overview of multiple method approaches, see Kasper and Dahl (1991), and Olshtain and Blum-Kulka (1985).

# CHAPTER 3: PILOT STUDY

Prior to actually collecting data from learners, informal pilot tests were conducted on non-native speakers as well as native speakers. Since the main question of this study was asking how prototype cross-cultural pragmatic measures which were developed by Hudson et al. (1992, 1995) would work if they were applied to learners of a different language, the current study was designed to use their framework with as few changes from their original design as possible. Even though minimal changes were to be made, it was felt that it would be worthwhile to investigate how well their tests work to the native speakers of Japanese and learners of Japanese. Although the pilot studies for both native speakers and non-native speakers were informal, the results still helped inform the current study. In fact, some changes in test questions as well as a decision about which Japanese writing system to use for the translated version were decided on the basis of the pilot study results. A brief summary of each pilot test will be presented in the following section.

## PILOT STUDY USING NATIVE JAPANESE SPEAKERS

### THE LL TEST BY NATIVE JAPANESE SPEAKERS

The purposes of piloting the LL test on native Japanese speakers were to see how they felt about the testing method and how different or similar their responses were compared to each other and to the non-native speakers. Three native Japanese were asked to tape-record their responses. One female Japanese teacher in her mid-30s responded to LL test-Form A, a female university professor in her mid-40s responded to LL test-Form B, and a male computer company worker in his mid-40s responded to LL test-Form C. One of the participants reported that she felt slightly odd about having to speak to the tape recorder without an interlocutor. She said that she had to use her imagination about what the interlocutor might say. It was felt that the same thing might happen to the non-native JSL/JFL participants. The average length of the responses of the native participants seemed to be similar to those of the advanced non-native participants, that is, such situations as those with a strong degree of imposition and/or minus power tend to be longer, and simple situations such as requesting a napkin in an airplane tended to be very short. These observations about length are not based on anything as formal as analysis of mean length of utterances. However, it would be interesting to investigate the mean length of utterances in a future study.

Another finding in the native pilot LL test is that gender differences (especially femininity) are often observed in the case of minus imposition, plus power, or minus distance. For example, in situation 1 (both in Form A and B), both female native participants used a sentence ending usually used by female. Examples are "A, gomen-nasai. Demo warenakute yokatta-_wa_" (Form A) and "A, gomen-nasai. Daijoubu-_kashira_." However, gender differences are not a focus of study in this study.

## THE OPDCT BY NATIVE JAPANESE SPEAKERS

A total of 36 native speakers were used to pilot the OPDCT (12 for Form A, 10 for Form B, and 14 for Form C; 12 males and 24 females; eleven 20's, nine 30's, seven 40's, five 50's, and three 60's or more of age). The purposes of collecting pilot data from native speakers was to examine: (a) any variation in their responses, (b) the length of their responses, and (c) the amount of time needed for them to fill in the OPDCT.

In analyzing these pilot data, it was possible to categorize most of the responses according to the CCSARP coding manual (Blum-Kulka, House, and Kasper, 1989b). However, there were some Japanese-specific strategies discovered in the apologies (e.g., a dismay strategy; see chapter 6 for further discussion). Most of the responses were written in one sentence, and the length of responses was within the space available (i.e., three solid lines of space were provided for the responses) as shown in the following (taken from Hudson et al. 1995, p. 87; the actual situations in the Japanese version were translated and written in Japanese):

```
Situation: You live in a large apartment building. You are
leaving to go to work. On your way out, you meet your next door
neighbor, whom you haven't seen for a long time.

You: _____

      _____

      _____
```

The time spent for native speakers to fill in the OPDCT was generally between 25 and 90 minutes according to their self-reports. The average time was around 40 minutes for all three Forms. Other findings included the fact that older participants, both males and females, tended to speak more bluntly when they were in roles with high power in such positions as manager of a company or president of a club, and in a much more polite and humble manner in situations where they had less power) and older males (over 50) tended to use a more blunt manner of speaking in many situations.

## ROLEPLAYS BY NATIVE JAPANESE SPEAKERS

The purposes for piloting the roleplays on native Japanese speakers were (a) to familiarize the researcher, a rater, and an interlocutor with the roleplays as one of the eliciting devises for pragmatic tests suggested by Hudson et al. (1995), and (b) to explore what was involved in roleplays in terms of interactions (both verbal and non-verbal) between the speaker and interlocutor, as well as in terms of props and the positions and distances of the two people involved when the Japanese version was used. One of the roleplay videos taped for Hudson et al.'s study about Japanese learners of ESL was available to this researcher. The video captured the facial expressions of the learners clearly but the wider view was lacking (e.g., it was not possible to tell where the participants were situated in the room, how far from the door the participants were standing, or how far the participants were from the props). Since physical distance and/or non-verbal behaviors are often important factors in roleplay performances, a variety of camera angles were explored in the pilot roleplay in order to better capture those aspects.

Three native Japanese speakers were asked to do all eight roleplay situations in the pilot study. One, Mr. T, who was in his 60's, was a member of a drama club when he was a young university student and had recently retired from an insurance company (where he was a *bucho*, or manager) after 35 years' employment. He later became one of the raters in the main study reported here. The second, Mr. S, was in his late 20's and was doing graduate studies in psychology. He later served as the interlocutor for all the non-native participants in this study. The third, Ms. M, was in her early 20's and was a kindergarten teacher at the time.

It was particularly interesting and helpful that Mr. T had rich experience in industry and Ms. M was working at a kindergarten, where differential speech styles are used between her senior teachers, young pupils, and their parents. Their roleplays certainly yielded rich examples of speech styles as well as non-verbal elements. Many of the roles were based on their own experiences. When Mr. T acted out the role of Bucho (manager), he really created a strong impression of being a Bucho.

Mr. S (who was later to be the interlocutor in all of the non-native roleplays) learned the roles from participating himself and observing or roleplaying with Mr. T and Ms. M. He also practiced through his own participation standing the appropriate distances from the participants (the JSL learners) and handling props. Essentially, these piloting sessions served as rehearsal for him as an interlocutor. We learned that even for the native speakers it was very hard to read each scenario (in Japanese) in a short period of time and then perform the roleplays. We also found that it was difficult for the native speakers to do the roleplay situations one after the other consecutively because that required switching roles often, which was confusing. As a result, the Japanese version of the scenarios was rewritten so that the roles, situations, and steps were clearly stated with numbers, 1, 2, 3, and so on in order to help the participants play their roles more easily. Individual variations were also recognized. For instance, the roleplays for the same situation turned out somewhat differently for Mr. T and Mr. S.

## THE MCDCT BY NATIVE JAPANESE SPEAKERS

The purposes for piloting the MCDCT were: (a) to see if correct answers for the Japanese version corresponded to the answer keys of the original English version, and (b) to get feedback from the participants about the appropriateness of the options on the MCDCT. Fourteen native Japanese university students answered the MCDCT (five for Form A, three for Form B, and six for Form C). Some of the forms for situations 2, 7, 11, 13, 18, 21 to 23 did not match the answer keys of the original version. In other words, the participants did not pick the same strategies as the English native speakers did in these eight situations. The answer keys for some forms were adjusted accordingly. Many participants claimed that they had difficulty in selecting only one appropriate answer from the options. Some of the participants wrote down the ways they wanted to respond without selecting an answer from the three possible sentences. Some of the answers they wrote were longer than the answer keys (i.e., all answer keys were within two lines). The answer keys were adjusted on the basis of this pilot information for use in the main study reported here.

## PILOT STUDY USING NON-NATIVE SPEAKERS

### DECIDING WHICH WRITING SYSTEM TO USE
### FOR THE JAPANESE VERSIONS

For non-native speakers, the biggest concern was whether or not the tests should be given in Japanese only or with Roman characters also provided (both for the explanations of the situations and the responses by the participants). In the pilot study, four participants volunteered. Three choices were offered to the participants: (a) English (using the same form used by ESL participants), (b) Japanese only (i.e., *hiragana* and *kanji* with *hiragana* reading), and (c) Roman characters. The Roman version was written as follows (Hebon Roman system is used after Oshima-Takane and MacWhinney, 1995):

```
Bamen 1: Anata wa ookina ie o karite sundeite, aiteiru heya o
hoka no hito ni matagashishiteimasu. Ima anata wa sono hitori no
heya ni, heyadai o moraini kita tokoro desu…
```

One problem with the Roman version is that there are several styles for using Roman characters. For example, the writing of particles in Roman characters as a grammatical unit is not set as a single system.

Other issues included questions of how to give the participants directions, how they should respond, and how to evaluate the responses . One participant who answered the Roman version wrote his answers in *hiragana* and *katakana*, but not with *kanji*. Another participant picked the Japanese version and answered in Roman characters. Two participants picked the English version and answered in Roman characters. All four of them had lived in Japan for more than eight years (i.e., they had lived in a JSL environment) at the time of the pilot test. Some of the participants did not have formal Japanese education. Some of the answers which were written in Roman characters seemed to be limited in expression and usage, while others seemed to be very appropriate even though they were in Roman characters.

As a result, this researcher decided to select only subjects for the main study who had studied formal Japanese, or at least were able to write *hiragana* so that they could take a proficiency test in *hiragana* and use easy *kanji*. This decision was made for three reasons: (a) an existing proficiency test written in *hiragana* and *kanji* could be used as a proficiency test battery (the national Japanese proficiency test also requires *hiragana* proficiency for beginning level), (b) variables could be limited and controlled for a better statistical analysis (i.e., all participants could read situations in Japanese writing, or *hiragana* and easy *kanji*), and (c) raters would be less likely to be biased (i.e., we do not know the effects on raters of rating some language samples based on Roman characters while others are in *hiragana* and *kanji*). In addition, this study was designed and conducted with formal JSL language pedagogy in mind, so including participants who have acquired pragmatic ability only in a natural setting is beyond the current framework.

# PURPOSE OF THIS STUDY

This study applies the framework suggested by Hudson, Detmer, and Brown (1995) in order to investigate the relative effectiveness of six different language measures of cross-cultural pragmatics in Japanese when they are given to learners of Japanese in a JSL setting. The tests include two indirect measures (OPDCT and MCDCT), two direct measures (LL and RP), and two self-assessments (SA and RPSA). The study investigates (a) the relative effectiveness, reliability, and validity of the six measures, (b) theoretical differences between the six measurement approaches, and (c) practical differences in their usefulness for gathering data in future pragmatics research. To those ends, the following research questions were formulated:

1. Are there differences in *reliability* between test formats for measuring the pragmatic competence of English learners of Japanese?
   a. What are the Cronbach alpha reliability estimates for all of the tests?
   b. What are the rater reliabilities for the LL, OPDCT, and RP tests?
      What are the inter-rater reliabilities?
      What are the intra-class reliabilities?
   c. What is the SEM (standard error of measurement) for each test?
   d. To what degree are the +/– variables related? Different?
2. Are forms A, B, C of the SA, LL, OPDCT, and MCDCT tests parallel?
3. Are there differences in *validity* between test formats for measuring the pragmatic competence of English learners of Japanese?
   a. What are the content validity arguments?
   b. What are the criterion validity arguments?
   c. What are the construct validity arguments?
      What does the factor analysis tell us?
      Are there differences in the differential groups' construct validity of the six tests when comparing the pragmatic competence of:
      – different levels of English learners of Japanese?
      – different lengths of exposure to Japanese culture?
4. Are there differences in *practicality* between test formats for measuring the pragmatic competence of English learners of Japanese?

# CHAPTER 4: RESEARCH DESIGN AND METHODOLOGY

## METHODS

Six types of Japanese pragmatic measures, which were designed for assessing JSL learners' pragmatic competence, were compared to explore whether there were differences in task types in terms of reliability, validity, effectiveness, or theoretical or practical differences. The study was conducted in a JSL context, that is, the data were collected in Japan from a variety of American English speaking participants ranging from university students to workers in companies (who were attracted by a flier, see Appendix A). Based on their answers to a background questionnaire (see Appendix B), the participants ranged in age from 19 to 49, had different levels of Japanese proficiency (beginning to advanced levels), and had lived in Japan from 0 (right after the first arrival in Japan) to 22 years. Four native Japanese speakers were involved in rating the participants' pragmatic competence on the open-response tasks (namely, the LL, OPDCT, and RP). Various statistical techniques were used to answer the four main research questions and all of the subordinate questions.

## PARTICIPANTS

A total of forty-seven North American English-speaking learners of Japanese (46 Americans and one English-speaking Canadian) from all language levels (i.e., beginning to advanced levels) were the participants in this study. (Fifty-four American English-speaking learners of Japanese participated in the study originally. However, after deleting the cases who failed to complete all six tasks, only 47 participants remained for the final analysis.)

Proficiency levels for most of the participants were determined on the basis of their scores on a cloze test (the test described in detail in Yamashita, 1994). However, because three of the university students were unable to take the cloze test, their proficiency levels were determined by examining their levels at the institutions they were attending (each level was carefully determined on the basis of the score distributions of the groups in the JSL courses they took).

There were 25 males and 22 females in the group studied. The professions of the participants varied from undergraduate students ($n=23$) and graduate students ($n=10$) to non-students ($n=14$, including office workers, university professors, a lawyer, a judge, language teachers, and housewives). The students were enrolled at three private universities in Tokyo and one graduate institution in Yokohama. Their majors covered a variety of fields including social science, language, mathematics, computer science, economics, international relations, and others. The ages of the participants ranged from 19 to 49, with an average of 26.21. The participants who had just arrived in Japan for the first time were categorized together as the *non-experienced group*. By definition, participants classified in this group had lived in Japan for less than two months. The other group, categorized as the *experienced group*, consisted of participants who had lived in Japan for two months or more.

### Table 2: Overview of participant variables (total *n*=47)

| Gender | n |
|---|---|
| Male | 25 |
| Female | 22 |

| Group | n |
|---|---|
| Undergraduate | 23 |
| Graduate | 10 |
| Non-students | 14 |

| Levels | n |
|---|---|
| Advanced | 15 |
| Intermediate | 20 |
| Beginning | 12 |

| Total length of stay in Japan | n |
|---|---|
| Less than 2 months | 13 |
| 3 months to 1 year | 15 |
| 1 year to 2 years | 5 |
| 2 years to 3 years | 5 |
| 3 years to 4 years | 3 |
| 4 years to 9 years | 3 |
| 9 years or more[1] | 3 |

| Age | n |
|---|---|
| 18–19 | 6 |
| 20–22 | 13 |
| 23–25 | 6 |
| 26–29 | 11 |
| 30–39 | 8 |
| 40–49 | 3 |

| Total months of formal Japanese instruction | n |
|---|---|
| 0 month | 2 |
| less than 12 months | 9 |
| 12 months to 23 months | 16 |
| 24 months to 35 months | 8 |
| 36 months to 47 months | 7 |
| 48 months to 59 months | 3 |
| more than 5 years | 2 |

| Major field or specialty[2] | n |
|---|---|
| Japanese language | 9 |
| Science[3] | 7 |
| Economics[4] | 5 |
| International studies | 4 |
| Asian history | 4 |
| Literature/Communication | 4 |
| Political science/ Law | 3 |
| TESOL | 2 |
| Other | 9 |

[1] The longest length of stay is 22 years.
[2] Participants who left this blank are under "Other". Only first major was used for double majors.
[3] Computers, Psycho-biology, Electrical engineering, Mathematics, Bio-chemistry, Cybernetics, and Psychology are included.
[4] Business and MBA are included.

The purposes of the study were not explained to the participants until after they had completed all six tests. Also, the tests were described as "tasks" (e.g., task 1, task 2, task 3, etc.) or "questionnaires" in order to avoid test anxiety and apprehension. All participants were offered an opportunity to meet with the researcher for a private feedback session after they had completed all six tests. Participants were paid for their time and participation (about US$20.00, or a telephone card, plus a Japanese dictionary worth about US$10.00). Since these tests were very time-consuming, some of the participants were unable to finish all six. A two month period was given for the participants to complete all six tests, and most of the participants took an average of three to five weeks to return the tests to the researcher. However, seven participants did not finish some of the tests and left the country. The tests of the seven participants who did not complete all six tasks were eliminated from the study.

## MATERIALS

Four pragmatics testing instruments (LL, OPDCT, RP, and MCDCT), which were originally created in English by Hudson, Detmer, and Brown, 1995, were translated into Japanese. All four tests were administered with an English supplement. The participants were allowed to see the complete English supplement if they wished. As with the Hudson et al. tests, the two self-assessment sections were given in English. In addition to the six pragmatics tests, a cloze test, developed by this researcher (Yamashita, 1994), was used. The cloze test was written only in *hiragana* and basic *kanji*, and, since it was used as a Japanese proficiency test, no English supplement was provided.

The rating sheets used in Hudson et al. (1995) were also used by this study's native Japanese raters. The directions for rating (from the rater's manual) were given in Japanese (translated by the researcher). Tests SA, LL, OPDCT, and MCDCT had forms A, B, and C. The tests were counterbalanced in such a way that a participant who started test SA with form A would use form B for LL, and form C for OPDCT, so that the *learning effect* could be minimized. See the *Forms* section later in this chapter for more details. Descriptions of each test will be given next (in the order that they were administered).

### Self-assessment of performance on situation description

The self-assessment of performance on situation description, or the SA, (see Appendix C) consisted of twenty-four situations which elicited either a request, refusal, or apology, in which such factors as Power, Degree of Imposition, and Distance were controlled (See Hudson et al. 1995 for details). The description of each situation was given in English. In this test, the participant was not asked to produce any sort of response. Instead, participants were asked to think about what they would say in Japanese in each situation and rate themselves on a five-point Likert scale (according to their ability to respond appropriately in Japanese in the given situation). The sum of the ratings recorded by the participants themselves were their SA score. This test was administered first in the series. The following is an example of the SA test:

```
Situation 8 [Form A]: You are shopping for your friend's
birthday and see something in a display case. You want to look
at it more closely. A salesclerk comes over to you.

Rating: I think what I would say in this situation would be
```

```
           very                            completely
       unsatisfactory   1 - - 2 - - 3 - - 4 - - 5   appropriate
```

## Listening lab production test

The listening lab production test, or the LL test, also consisted of twenty-four short descriptions of situations which elicited either a request, refusal, or apology, in which factors such as Power, Degree of Imposition, and Distance were controlled as in the SA test. Unlike the SA test, the LL test asked participants to listen to each description which was recorded on *Tape* A, and tape-record their responses orally on *Tape* B. The only written material given to the participants was the written English supplement (see Appendix F). Each situation was read twice in Japanese on Tape A. After the second reading, the participants were asked to record their responses in Japanese on Tape B. Participants were asked not to stop the recording of Tape B once they had started the LL test. Participants were allowed to stop, but not to rewind, Tape A if it was necessary. There was no time limit for the LL test, but the average time spent for this test was from 20 to 30 minutes. No tape went beyond 30 minutes. Here is an example of tape-recorded LL test:

```
Situation 8 [Form B]: Anata wa hikooki ni notteimasu. Yuushoku
no jikan ni nari, joomuin ga obon ni shokuji no yooi o
shitekuremashita. Ato wa napkin ga hitsuyoo desu. (Read twice)
```

*[Written English supplement: You are on an airplane. It is dinner time. The flight attendant sets your food on your tray. You need a napkin.]*

```
Sono toki anata wa nan to iimasu ka? [What would you say in the
situation?]
```

*[English translation is not given in this part]*

Each tape-recorded response was rated by three native speakers based on six categories on a five-point Likert scale (see Appendix D). A transcription was made for later use (for qualitative analysis), but not given to raters. The raters were asked to listen to the tapes directly and rate them based on what they heard.

## Open discourse completion test

The open discourse completion test, or the OPDCT (see Appendix E for the OPDCT, Forms A–C), like the SA and LL tests, also consisted of twenty-four short descriptions of situations which elicited either a request, refusal, or apology, in which factors such as Power, Degree of Imposition, and Distance were controlled. Each description was written in Japanese, which is comprised of Chinese characters, *kanji*, and Japanese syllabic components, *hiragana*. In each Japanese description, the *hiragana* were written over each corresponding *kanji* character. This strategy was used for the benefit of participants who can read *hiragana* syllable by syllable, although they might not know the meaning of the *kanji* characters. The participants then wrote in Japanese what they thought they would say in a given situation. Participants were given an English supplement and allowed to see it if they wished, but they were asked to answer everything in Japanese, using the Japanese writing system. No one was allowed to respond in *Roman* characters for reasons explained above.

There was no time limit for the OPDCT, but the average time spent for this test was anywhere from one to two hours according to the participants' self-reported times. One beginner reported that she spent 6.5 hours. Each response was rated by three native speakers based on six categories on a five-point Likert scale. The rating sheet was exactly the same as that used for the LL test.

## Video-taped roleplays

The RP test consisted of eight situations, each of which had three speech acts (i.e., a request, a refusal, and an apology) in which factors such as Power, Degree of Imposition, and Distance were controlled. The participants were given scenarios for the eight situations in Japanese with an English supplement (see Appendixes G and H). Pilot studies of the RP test found that both native and non-native speakers encountered difficulty in quickly understanding the context of the scenarios. In order to help the participants to understand each situation in a short period of time, specific descriptions about *who, when, where,* and *with whom,* were listed under the subtitles. Also, the sequence of the contents of the scenario was listed under numbers, 1, 2, 3, and so on so that the participants would know what they were to say next. Some key words were listed in Japanese to help the participants perform. The participants were asked to prepare one situation at a time to avoid confusion with other situations.

The participants spent an average of two to three minutes preparing for each roleplay with the native speaker of Japanese. The RP of each situation was video-taped, with a tape-recording back-up in case of video-recording failure. One such failure did occur. It will be discussed later. On average, it took a total of about 30 minutes for each participant to complete their eight-situation RP test.

A native Japanese male, age 26, who was a post graduate with a master's degree in psychology, was the interlocuter for the RP test for all 47 participants. The researcher was also in attendance for each video-taping session. When the participant failed to perform a speech act that was suggested in a RP scenario, at the end of each situation, the researcher asked the participants whether they intentionally omitted the speech act, or simply forgot about it. In the case of participants' forgetting a speech act, they were asked to repeat it so that there would not be any missing data from the roleplay tests.

Each situation was rated by degree of appropriateness on a five-point Likert scale by three native-speaker raters (see Appendix I). The rating sheet appeared as follows:

## ROLEPLAY RATING SHEET

Name:_____

Rater:_____

<u>Scene Two — Shopping at a Gift Shop</u>
1. Request

| very unsatisfactory | 1 - - 2 - - 3 - - 4 - - 5 | completely appropriate |

2. Apology

| very unsatisfactory | 1 - - 2 - - 3 - - 4 - - 5 | completely appropriate |

3. Refusal

| very unsatisfactory | 1 - - 2 - - 3 - - 4 - - 5 | completely appropriate |

The participants also rated their own RP video performance. The self-assessment portion of the RP test is another test in and of itself, and is described below.

## Self-assessment of the video-taped roleplay

The participants were asked to watch their own roleplay videotape immediately upon finishing the roleplays and to rate the appropriateness of each situation on a five-point Likert scale. The rating sheet used was the same one used by the native-speaker raters in scoring the participants' RP performances, as described above.

## Multiple-choice discourse completion test

The MCDCT (see Appendix J) consisted of twenty-four situations just like the OPDCT and LL tests. However, instead of writing a response, the participants selected their answer from three possible responses for each situation. The total number of correct responses became the score for the MCDCT. The MCDCT was administered after all of the other tests in order to avoid giving participants ideas for potential response types or patterns for the other tests.

## Forms

As mentioned above, four of the tests (OPDCT, MCDCT, LL, and SA) had three forms (A, B, and C) each, in which the three speech acts (i.e., requests, refusals, and apologies) and levels of Power, Degree of Imposition, and Distance were all counterbalanced. These three forms contained the same balance of Power, Degree of Imposition, and Distance variables but involved different situations. The forms were counterbalanced across the various tests. For example, a participant who had form A on SA, might have form B for the LL test, and form C on the OPDCT. The three forms were used so that the learning effect in repeatedly using exactly the same situations would be minimized. The form used by each participant for the MCDCT, the last test, was the same as the first one they had. It was hoped that this counterbalancing of the order of the forms would produce the least chance of distorting scores due to the learning effect because neither the SA (administered first) nor the MCDCT required any language production.

The translations into Japanese from the original English forms contained minor adjustments to reflect differences in the Japanese language and culture. Examples of such changes include changing "a picture frame on a desk" to "a mini-calendar on a desk" (it is not a Japanese custom to put a family picture on the office desk), or "a store's anniversary party" to "a store's grand sale" (an invitation for a customer to attend a store party is not common in Japanese culture), or "a repair man at a car-garage offering a customer a bite of his lunch" to "offering a customer a cup of coffee," and so forth.

### The English supplements

Each form of all the tests had an English supplement as did the RP scenarios. The supplement was borrowed from English texts developed by Hudson et al. (1995). A written English supplement was attached to each test (LL, OPDCT, MCDCT, and the RP scenario) in reduced font in order to minimize its effect. The participants were told that along with the actual test in Japanese, they could look at the English supplement if they wished. It was necessary for the participants to understand each speech act situation correctly in order to demonstrate their pragmatic competence. Participants were asked to give all of their production responses for the LL, OPDCT, and RP in Japanese. With the SA and RPSA tests, however, the original English versions of the rating sheets were used.

### Cloze test

The cloze test (see Appendix K) was not one of the pragmatics tests. It was given to the participants to determine their proficiency in the Japanese language. Participants were asked to fill in the missing syllable (part of a word) for a folk tale. A seventy-two blank, fixed-ratio cloze test with every ninth character deleted (including KANJI) was used. The cloze test was based on an old folk tale, taken from Yamashita and Ogawa (1994). The acceptable-answer scoring method was based on native-speaker university student data. The average score for the advanced JSL group was 59.31 and that for the intermediate JSL group was 43.65 (Yamashita, 1994, based on a different population from the current study). The descriptive statistics reported in Yamashita (1994) were considered in determining the cut-off points for the present study. (See Yamashita, 1994 for more details about this test.)

## PROCEDURES

### The order of test administration

In the original study (Hudson et al. 1995), it was suggested that the tests be administered in the following order: SA, LL, OPDCT, MCDCT, RP, RPSA. In the present study, the MCDCT was moved to the end because of concern that it would function as a list of potential responses that might give participants hints for the roleplay performances which were to follow immediately after the MCDCT.

With the first group of participants, the cloze test (which is not one of the pragmatics tests) was given on another day after the six pragmatics tests had been completed. But this arrangement produced a problem of missing cloze test data because some of the participants did not return on the second day. So for later groups, the cloze test was given along with the SA test, the first test, so that the researcher could get all of the test results without fail. Figure 2 summarizes these procedures.

### The schedule

Most of the participants took the tests in spring (May to June) of 1995 in the following order: SA, LL, OPDCT, RP, RPSA and MCDCT. Some tests, such as the SA and OPDCT were taken at home (with a written pledge that they would not ask native speakers for help nor consult books). For some tests, such as LL and RP, it was necessary to arrange times to meet with the researcher and the interlocuter for videotaping. All the recordings were done individually. The interlocuter for the RP was always the same person and he used the same props (such as a mug, a dirty free ticket, a camera, vases, a stapler, etc.) in each RP, to insure that the conditions were kept consistent for each participant, and to insure that raters would consistency view the same situation when rating the participants.

|  | Free-response | Selected-response |
|---|---|---|
| Indirect test (Paper and pencil) | OPDCT | MCDCT |
| Semi-direct test (Aural-oral) | LL | SA |
| Direct test (roleplay with a native speaker) | RP | RPSA |
| Scoring system | Rated by native raters | Selected-response by the participant |

Figure 2. Classification of test methods (adapted from Hudson et al. 1995, p. 4)

Places used for video-taping the RP test included: (a) a simulation room at the International Christian University (ICU) campus where a camera, microphones, and lighting were set up regularly for video-taping use; (b) regular classrooms at several campuses (ICU, Waseda University, Temple University, and Inter-University Center) with a portable video-camera; and (c) an individual participant's home in one case, also with a portable video-camera.

The ICU summer group (students in the ICU Summer Course in Japanese from July to August, 1995) and some individual participants who had recently arrived in Japan for the first time took all tests within two weeks of their arrival and were thus treated as JFL (Japanese as a foreign language) speakers and classified into the *non-experienced* group. By definition, the JFL group had lived in Japan less than two months at the time when their tests were administered.

## Ratings by native raters

The participants all wrote their answers to the OPDCT by hand. These hand-written versions were carefully typed by an assistant so that all writing and grammatical errors (including errors in *kanji*) made by the participants were typed as written. This transcription was done in order to avoid any affect on ratings due to poor hand-writing by some of the participants. The transcript was double checked before its completion. The OPDCT responses of all 47 participants and several extra responses (one incomplete test of a participant who was deleted from the final analysis, and two native-speaker OPDCT responses from the pilot study) were randomly reordered and printed. The extra responses were included to check rater consistency. The participants' names were not printed anywhere (so that Asian names would not negatively affect the raters' ratings).

### RATING SHEET

Name: _____

Instrument: DCT / Lang. Lab

Form: _____        Rater: __

| very unsatisfactory | 1 − − − 2 − − − 3 − − − 4 − − − 5 | completely appropriate |

| SITUATION | | | | | |
|---|---|---|---|---|---|
| **Response #** _____ | | | **Response #** _____ | | |
| speech act | 1-2-3-4-5 | | speech act | 1-2-3-4-5 | |
| expressions | 1-2-3-4-5 | | expressions | 1-2-3-4-5 | |
| amount/info | 1-2-3-4-5 | − + | amount/info | 1-2-3-4-5 | − + |
| formality | 1-2-3-4-5 | − + | formality | 1-2-3-4-5 | − + |
| directness | 1-2-3-4-5 | − + | directness | 1-2-3-4-5 | − + |
| politeness | 1-2-3-4-5 | − + | politeness | 1-2-3-4-5 | − + |

In November 1995, the OPDCT responses were sent to three native Japanese Raters (1, 2, and 3) for them to rate based on the rating scale (translated from Hudson et al. 1995). The above is an example of the English language version of the rating scale for the OPDCT and the LL test (see also Appendix D).

It took about two to three weeks for each Rater to do all of the ratings completely. The raters had to rate six categories for each of the twenty-four situations for all 50 participants. The number of data entries for each of the 47 participants who took the OPDCT per rater was 144 (= 6 x 24), which meant a grand total of 6,768 (= 6 x 24 x 47) data points for the final analysis.

The LL taped responses first required editing before the ratings could be done. In order to avoid missing data, participants were asked not to stop tape B (the tape for recording) between each situation until they completely finished responding to all twenty-four of the situations. They were allowed time to think after each situation had been given orally on tape A. As a result, the B Tapes contained many long pauses between situations. The pauses in tape B were deleted for all subjects so that the raters could score them without having to wait between each situation. The tapes of the forty-seven participants were randomly ordered and transferred onto five 120-minute cassette tapes. The tapes were sent to three raters and were rated based on the same scale used for the OPDCT (see Appendixes L and M for the rater's manual). It took about two to three weeks for Raters 1 and 2 to finish them. Rater 3 never finished and gave up. So Rater 4 replaced Rater 3 and finished Rater 3's ratings. The data entries per rater, as with the OPDCT, was 6,768 for the LL analysis.

The RP videos were also edited since they contained long pauses between each scene. The researcher's decision to continue taping from beginning to end was done purposely in order to avoid missing scenes due to stop-and-play switch use. The order of participants was randomized, and their roleplays were dubbed onto new tapes with the pauses having been omitted. Six 120-minute video tapes of the 47 participants (the average length of the RP for each participant was 20 minutes) were sent to Raters 1, 2, and 3. Each speech act within each RP (24 speech acts, three each in eight scenes) was rated based on its degree of appropriateness, and a rating was recorded on a five-point Likert scale. It took each rater three to four weeks to complete the RP ratings.

The RP ratings were completed first, the OPDCT results were second followed by the two other self-assessment tests and the multiple-choice one. The period in which the four raters completed rating these three tests covered a three-month period from mid-September to mid-December, 1995.

## Self-assessment scores

The three self-assessment type tests were completed by the participants. The first test was the SA which contained 24 situations described in English. The participants were asked to think about the situations and to record on a 1 to 5 Likert scale how well they would be able to respond in Japanese for each situation. The second test was the RPSA, in which participants were asked to rate how appropriate their responses were for the RP on a 1 to 5 Likert scale. The same rating sheet was used by the participants in their self-ratings as those used by the native Japanese raters to score the roleplay performances. The third test was a multiple-choice DCT (MCDCT). The participants selected the most appropriate expression from three possible answers for 24 situations. Two expressions were distracters. The best possible score for the MCDCT was 120 (24 items worth 5 points each).

ANALYSIS

The scores for the three tests graded by the raters (OPDCT, LL, and RP) and the scores for the selected-response tests (SA, RPSA, and MCDCT) were entered into a Quattro Pro Spreadsheet program (version 3). All statistical analyses were performed on an IBM PS/55 note N23 computer using SPSS/PC+ Version 4.0.1 (SPSS Incorporated, 1988).

Cronbach's alpha ($\alpha$) coefficient was calculated for each rater's scores for the OPDCT, LL, and RP tests, as well as for the SA, RPSA, and MCDCT in order to estimate the internal consistency of each test. Interrater reliability estimates were calculated using Pearson product-moment correlation coefficients intraclass correlations among the raters' scores. Also, correlation coefficients were calculated for the relationships between plus and minus variables (Degree of Imposition, Power, and Distance) in order to investigate the extent to which the I, P, and D variables were actually taping some common feature. Reliability for each test form (A, B, and C) was also estimated by analyzing the intercorrelations of those forms.

Correlations among all seven tests (the six pragmatics subtests and the cloze test) and a factor analysis procedure were used to examine the convergent and divergent indicators of the construct validity of the tests.

A two-way multivariate analysis of variance and univariate follow-up statistics were used to examine the statistical significance of differences in Japanese cross-pragmatic competence according to the participants' length of exposure to Japanese culture and their levels of Japanese proficiency. This analysis was also related to validity, in this case, differential-groups construct validity.

# ADDITIONAL COMMENTS ON DATA COLLECTION

PARTICIPANTS

In recent years, many Asian-Americans, desiring to learn more about their Asian heritage, have begun to study Japanese. Learners who had strong influences from their ethnic cultural background were carefully omitted from this study. This study was designed to examine only those participants who had had K–12 grades of formal education in North America in order to study strictly "English speaking North Americans." This step was necessary because there were many Asian-Americans in

Japanese courses who had lived in their home country until adolescence and who had had strong linguistic, social, and cultural influences which might affect their cross-cultural pragmatics competence. Since this was a study of cross-cultural pragmatics testing, it was sensible to eliminate such participants.

Also, the participants were limited to those who had at least basic Japanese ability in writing and reading *hiragana*, a basic Japanese writing system (see reasons for this decision under "Open discourse completion" test in the Materials section). Additionally, the participants all volunteered for this study. The researcher did not select the participants randomly, nor did she allow any classroom periods to be used for data collection. An announcement was distributed asking for volunteers to participate in the study (see Appendix A).

## MORTALITY

Since it was a great burden for each participant to complete all six pragmatics tests and the cloze test, some participants gave up after finishing only the SA and LL, or three or four tests. Some students went back to their home country without finishing some of the tests. For the summer course group, the researcher planned carefully and scheduled them from the beginning on a calendar so that every participant could finish the tests in a short period of time before they left. The data for participants who did not complete all the pragmatics tests were omitted from the study ($n=7$ as reported in the beginning of the participant section).

# CHAPTER 5: RESULTS

The purpose of this study was to investigate whether or not there were differences between test formats (direct/indirect and free-response/selected-response; or more specifically, the SA, LL, OPDCT, RP, RPSA, and MCDCT tests) for measuring pragmatic competence of English learners of Japanese. This chapter will provide a technical report of the results as they are related to the research questions that were listed in chapter 3.

## DESCRIPTIVE STATISTICS

Table 3 shows the descriptive statistics for each of the measures in this study. In each case, the number of participants ($N$), number of items tested ($k$), total possible scores, maximum scores, minimum scores, range, mean, standard deviation ($SD$), and Cronbach alpha reliability estimates are given. Forty-seven participants are represented on every measure except for the cloze test (see the explanation about participants in chapter 3).

### Table 3: Descriptive statistics

| Test | $N$ | $k$ | Score* | Max | Min | Range | Mean | $SD$ | Reliability |
|------|-----|-----|--------|--------|-------|-------|-------|-------|-------------|
| SA | 47 | 24 | 120 | 119.00 | 42.00 | 77.00 | 79.43 | 16.45 | .9359 |
| LL | 47 | 24 | 120 | 116.78 | 56.67 | 60.11 | 93.38 | 16.32 | .9920 |
| OPDCT | 47 | 24 | 120 | 113.67 | 67.56 | 46.11 | 92.32 | 12.52 | .9851 |
| RP | 47 | 24 | 120 | 113.67 | 36.67 | 77.00 | 72.78 | 19.76 | .9901 |
| RPSA | 47 | 24 | 120 | 120.00 | 38.00 | 82.00 | 73.66 | 17.92 | .9459 |
| MCDCT | 47 | 24 | 120 | 105.00 | 20.00 | 85.00 | 69.35 | 16.10 | .4652 |
| cloze | 44 | 72 | 72 | 72.00 | 30.00 | 42.00 | 53.55 | 9.36 | .9079 |

*Score = total possible scores

The SA and RPSA were self-assessed by the participants; the LL, OPDCT and RP were rated by raters; the MCDCT was composed of multiple-choice questions; and, the cloze was given as a proficiency test. The actual scores of the LL and OPDCT tests were both 720 (5 x 6 x 24), but both were divided by 6 so that the total scores were more or less parallel to the other pragmatics tests. For the MCDCT, five points were assigned to each correct answer to make the total score 120.

# RELIABILITY

Research question 1 asked if there are differences in *reliability* between test formats for measuring the pragmatic competence of English learners of Japanese. To that end, (a) the internal consistency (Cronbach's alpha) of each test was estimated, (b) the rater reliabilities of the LL, OPDCT, and RP tests were studied, and (c) the standard error of measurements (SEM) was calculated for each test.

## CRONBACH ALPHA

Cronbach alpha reliability estimates for each of the measures are presented in Table 4. These internal consistency reliability estimates for all six pragmatics tests and the cloze test were high except for the MCDCT. Each form of the MCDCT, without exception, showed low reliability (among them, the reliability estimate for Form A was particularly low).

**Table 4: Cronbach alpha reliability estimates for each form and total of each test\*\***

| Test | Form A | Form B | Form C | Total |
|------|--------|--------|--------|-------|
| SA | .9494 [16] | .9430 [15] | .8845 [16] | .9359 [47] |
| LL | .9903 [14] | .9932 [15] | .9928 [18] | .9920 [47] |
| OPDCT | .9832 [16] | .9849 [17] | .9865 [14] | .9851 [47] |
| MCDCT | .1671 [18] | .5017 [15] | .6510 [14] | .4652 [47] |
| RP | * | * | * | .9901 [47] |
| RPSA | * | * | * | .9459 [47] |
| Cloze | * | * | * | .9079 [44] |

\*  Only one form exists for the RP, RPSA, and cloze tests.
\*\* Numbers in [ ] are the total numbers who took each form.

## THE RATER RELIABILITY ISSUE

Table 5 shows four raters' Cronbach alpha internal consistency reliability estimates for the LL, OPDCT, and RP tests, the tests which the native raters scored. The internal consistency reliability estimates for all the raters were high (ranging from .95 to .99). These internal consistency reliability estimates indicate "how consistent the test is in terms of the percent of variance in the scores that is reliable and the percent that is attributable to measurement error" (Brown, 1996, p. 206), and the reliability estimates reported in Table 5 indicate a relatively high level of reliability. The intraclass correlations (Guilford and Fruchter, 1973) shown in Table 5 further indicate the extent of reliability or consistency with all three raters taken together, while taking into account any mean differences as well.

## Table 5: The internal consistency reliability estimates for raters' ratings and the intraclass correlations of the raters

|  | Rater 1 | Rater 2 | Rater 3 | Rater 4 | Intraclass Correlation |
|---|---|---|---|---|---|
| LL | .9825 | .9896 | * | .9903 | .8208 |
| OPDCT | .9472 | .9718 | .9809 | * | .7449 |
| RP | .9678 | .9842 | .9837 | * | .8789 |

* Rater 3 rated the OPDCT and RP tests and the Rater 4 only rated the LL test (see the explanation in chapter 2).

The interrater reliability can also be estimated by examining how much the rater's scores correlate with each other. Tables 6 through 8 report these correlations for the LL, OPDCT, and RP tests, respectively.

### Table 6: Interrater correlations on the LL test

|  | LLR1 | LLR2 | LLR4 |
|---|---|---|---|
| LLR1 | 1.0000 |  |  |
| LLR2 | .8262* | 1.0000 |  |
| LLR4 | .8059* | .8523* | 1.0000 |

*$p<.001$

### Table 7: Interrater correlations on the OPDCT

|  | OPR1 | OPR2 | OPR3 |
|---|---|---|---|
| OPR1 | 1.0000 |  |  |
| OPR2 | .7317* | 1.0000 |  |
| OPR3 | .7813* | .7660* | 1.0000 |

*$p<.001$

### Table 8: Interrater correlations on the RP test

|  | RPR1 | RPR2 | RPR3 |
|---|---|---|---|
| RPR1 | 1.0000 |  |  |
| RPR2 | .8217* | 1.0000 |  |
| OPR3 | .8662* | .7618* | 1.0000 |

*$p<.001$

The full-test reliabilities shown in Table 9 for the LL, OPDCT, and RP tests were based on the Spearman-Brown Prophecy formula as described in Brown, (1996, p. 205). These estimates, of .9257, .8911, and .9056, respectively, indicate how reliable and consistent the test is across raters when all three scores are taken together.

**Table 9: Full-test reliabilities (interrater reliabilities) of the LL, OPDCT, and RP tests**

|  | LL | OPDCT | RP |
|---|---|---|---|
| Interrater reliability | .9257 | .8911 | .9056 |

## THE STANDARD ERROR OF MEASUREMENT

The standard error of measurement (SEM) indicates "the consistency of a set of test scores…this statistic is used to determine a band around a student's score within which that the student's score would probably fall if the test were administered to him or her repeatedly" (Brown, 1996, p. 206). The formula used in Brown (1996, p. 207) was applied to calculate the SEM for the six tests based on the Cronbach alpha estimates given above. The results are shown in Table 10.

**Table 10: Standard error of measurements (SEM) (based on Cronbach alpha)**

|  | SA | LL | OPDCT | RP | RPSA | MCDCT | Cloze |
|---|---|---|---|---|---|---|---|
| SEM | 4.16 | 1.46 | 1.53 | 1.97 | 4.17 | 11.77 | 2.84 |

## CORRELATION COEFFICIENT BETWEEN PLUS AND MINUS VARIABLES

To explore the reliability issue further, correlation coefficients between plus and minus variables (plus and minus Degree of Imposition, Power, and Distance) for all six tests were calculated to determine the degree to which they were testing the same things across the three speech acts (see Table 16 in chapter 5, "Cell, attribute and situation with variable", adapted by Hudson et al.). Table 11 shows the descriptive statistics (means and standard deviation for each test with plus or minus variables), Table 12 presents the correlation coefficients, and Table 13 presents the squared values of correlation coefficients (also known as coefficients of determination).

## Table 11: Means and standard deviations for each test with plus or minus variables

| | Mean | SD | Difference between + and − | | Mean | SD | Difference between + and − |
|---|---|---|---|---|---|---|---|
| **SA** | | | | **RP** | | | |
| +Imposition | 33.90 | 9.80 | | +Imposition | 35.82 | 9.77 | |
| −Imposition | 45.52 | 7.84 | −11.62 | −Imposition | 36.96 | 10.06 | −1.14 |
| +Power | 41.24 | 8.52 | | +Power | 36.45 | 9.79 | |
| −Power | 38.17 | 8.60 | 3.07 | −Power | 36.33 | 10.20 | 0.12 |
| +Distance | 40.11 | 7.90 | | +Distance | 36.56 | 9.73 | |
| −Distance | 39.32 | 9.01 | 0.79 | −Distance | 36.22 | 10.14 | 0.34 |
| **LL** | | | | **RPSA** | | | |
| +Imposition | 43.84 | 9.47 | | +Imposition | 35.79 | 9.07 | |
| −Imposition | 49.73 | 7.19 | −5.89 | −Imposition | 37.74 | 9.52 | −1.95 |
| +Power | 48.51 | 7.24 | | +Power | 37.89 | 9.54 | |
| −Power | 45.06 | 9.35 | 3.45 | −Power | 35.64 | 9.05 | 2.25 |
| +Distance | 46.80 | 8.67 | | +Distance | 36.94 | 9.04 | |
| −Distance | 46.77 | 7.99 | 0.03 | −Distance | 36.60 | 9.33 | 0.34 |
| **OP** | | | | **MC** | | | |
| +Imposition | 44.02 | 7.77 | | +Imposition | 6.87 | 2.13 | |
| −Imposition | 48.29 | 5.63 | −4.27 | −Imposition | 7.00 | 1.97 | −0.13 |
| +Power | 46.69 | 6.30 | | +Power | 6.91 | 1.84 | |
| −Power | 45.62 | 6.71 | 1.07 | −Power | 6.96 | 2.08 | −0.05 |
| +Distance | 46.92 | 6.36 | | +Distance | 6.79 | 2.28 | |
| −Distance | 45.39 | 6.62 | 1.53 | −Distance | 7.09 | 2.10 | −0.30 |

Differences of means between plus variables (i.e., +Imposition, +Power, and +Distance) and minus variables (i.e., −Imposition, −Power, and −Distance) shown in Table 11 were calculated by subtracting the "minus" variable values from the "plus" variable values. The differences of all the six tests of "+Imposition" minus "−Imposition" had minus scores. This result is reasonable because the learners most likely have more difficulty in the situations where they have plus imposition (e.g., asking someone to do extra work or apologizing to someone for having destroyed his/her property) rather than minus imposition (e.g., asking to borrow a pen or apologizing for knocking over a cup but not destroying it). In other words, it was probably easier for the learners to perform in a situation with "−Imposition" in any of the six pragmatic tests, consequently, higher scores were given for "−Imposition" over "+Imposition," which showed minus scores for each of the differences presented in Table 11. Among the six tests, the SA test had the biggest single difference score (−11.62) which means that the learners assessed themselves as performing much less appropriately in the situations with "+Imposition." On the other hand, the learners may have less difficulty in realizing speech acts with "+Power" over "−Power" (e.g., a customer over a shop worker), thus higher scores were given for their realizations in situations with "+Power," which shows plus scores for the differences of all the six tests except the MCDCT in Table 11. Recall that the MCDCT had low reliability in the discussion above, so it is more dangerous to interpret the results on that test. In the case of plus or minus Distance, all of the differences were minimal (i.e., less than 1.00 for all the tests except the OPDCT, which had 1.53). This pattern may indicate that the variable of Distance has less affect on score variation than Power and/or Degree of Imposition (i.e., +Power or +Imposition may affect scores more strongly than +/−Distance).

**Table 12: Correlation coefficients between plus/minus variables for all six tests**

|        | Imposition | Power    | Distance |
|--------|------------|----------|----------|
| SA     | .7381**    | .8468**  | .8937**  |
| LL     | .9130**    | .9306**  | .9153**  |
| OPDCT  | .7821**    | .8961**  | .9057**  |
| RP     | .9846**    | .9535**  | .9769**  |
| RPSA   | .8448**    | .8385**  | .8895**  |
| MC     | .2332      | .3448*   | .0762    |

1-tailed significance: $*p<.01$ $**p<.001$

Table 12 indicates that the plus and minus variables correlated highly for all the six tests except the MCDCT. This overall result may indicate that one or more of these variables may not be necessary in designing pragmatic tests. Table 13 provides the squared values of each correlation coefficient presented in Table 12. These values, known as coefficients of determination, can be interpreted as the percent of overlapping variance between the two variables in question. For instance, the value of .5450 for Imposition on the SA (in Table 13) can be interpreted as indicating that the plus and minus items overlap about 54.5 percent on the SA.

Table 13 indicates that the highest amounts of overlap between plus and minus Imposition, Power, and Distance are on the RP test (i.e., all the coefficients were higher than .90). The next highest overlapping is found in the LL test (which had coefficients ranging from .83 and .87).

Table 13: Squared values of correlation coefficients between plus/minus
variables for all six tests presented in Table 12

|       | Imposition | Power | Distance |
|-------|------------|-------|----------|
| SA    | .5450      | .7171 | .7987    |
| LL    | .8336      | .8660 | .8378    |
| OPDCT | .6117      | .8030 | .8203    |
| RP    | .9694      | .9092 | .9543    |
| RPSA  | .7137      | .7031 | .7912    |
| MC    | .0544      | .1189 | .0058    |

## EQUIVALENCE OF THE FORMS

Research question 2 asked if forms A, B, and C of the pragmatics tests are parallel. All forms of the SA, LL, OPDCT, and MCDCT tests were examined. (Note: Different forms, A–C, were used for each test in order to avoid the learning effect. The RP and RPSA tests are not included here because they did not have multiple forms). For tests to be considered parallel, they must have approximately equal means, variances, and correlations with some outside measure. The means and standard deviations of each form are shown in Table 14.

Table 14: Variables of each form

| Tests/Forms  | Pos. scores | Mean    | SD      | Cases (n) |
|--------------|-------------|---------|---------|-----------|
| SA Form A    | 120         | 84.3750 | 17.1615 | 16        |
| SA Form B    | 120         | 82.8667 | 16.8348 | 15        |
| SA Form C    | 120         | 71.2500 | 12.7253 | 16        |
| LL Form A    | 120         | 88.8056 | 16.3656 | 14        |
| LL Form B    | 120         | 91.0556 | 17.8595 | 15        |
| LL Form C    | 120         | 98.8765 | 14.1051 | 18        |
| OPDCT Form A | 120         | 94.6632 | 11.6699 | 16        |
| OPDCT Form B | 120         | 87.4967 | 13.1289 | 17        |
| OPDCT Form C | 120         | 95.4960 | 11.7071 | 14        |
| MCDCT Form A | 120         | 64.7220 | 12.6575 | 18        |
| MCDCT Form B | 120         | 76.3335 | 15.7510 | 15        |
| MCDCT Form C | 120         | 67.8570 | 18.7815 | 14        |

While some fairly large differences in means appear within tests in Table 14, one-way ANOVAs were conducted, and no significant differences were found across forms for three of the tests (OPDCT $F=2.087$, $p=.136$; LL $F=1.782$, $p=.180$, and MCDCT $F=2.343$, $p=.108$). Thus, those differences that appear across forms for the three tests in Table 14 can only be interpreted as chance fluctuations. However, for the SA test, at least one significant difference was indicated by an $F$ value of 3.334 ($p=.045$). So the three forms of the SA cannot be said to be parallel because they do not appear to have equivalent means.

Table 15 shows the results of separate $F_{max}$ tests (using the $F$ table in Shavelson, 1981) which were conducted to see if the criterion of equal variances for each form is tenable.

### Table 15: Results of the $F_{max}$ tests

|        | $df$   | $F_{crit.}$ | $F_{obs.}$ | $p$ |
|--------|--------|-------------|------------|-----|
| SA     | 15, 15 | 2.43–2.39   | 1.82       | NS  |
| LL     | 14, 17 | 2.44–2.39   | 1.60       | NS  |
| OPDCT  | 16, 15 | 2.37–2.33   | 1.27       | NS  |
| MCDCT  | 13, 17 | 2.51–2.46   | 1.42       | NS  |

No forms of the four tests were found to be significantly different statistically (i.e., the variances can be considered approximately equivalent and the forms can be said to be parallel in terms of variance).

The last criterion for parallel forms is that they should have approximately equal correlations with some outside measure of the same trait. The correlations of the three forms of the SA (Forms A, B, and C) with the RP were .63, .64, and .54; the three forms of the LL with RP were .71, .82, and .84; and the three forms of the OPDCT with RP were .42, .57, and .74. So the three forms of each of these three tests appear to have similar correlations with an outside measure (RP in this case). However, the three forms of the MCDCT correlated at .58, −.14, .19, which are quite different and probably result from the low reliability of this test in general. The LL and OPDCT appeared to meet the three criteria for parallel forms of equal means, equal variances, and equal correlations with an outside measure. However, the SA appeared to have at least one significantly different mean, and the MCDCT had very different correlations with the RP as an outside measure (probably due to unreliability in the MCDCT), so these last two tests cannot be said to have strictly parallel froms.

## VALIDITY

Research question 3 asked what differences exist in *validity* between test formats for measuring the pragmatic competence of English speaking learners of Japanese. The question is further divided into three subtopics — (a) content validity, (b) criterion validity, and (c) construct validity.

CONTENT VALIDITY

Content validity is related to "whether the test is a representative sample of the content of whatever the test was designed to measure" (Brown, 1996, p. 233). The current tests were originally developed by Hudson, Detmer, and Brown (1992, 1995), and were modified for JSL/JFL learners (see chapter 3) with the same goals in mind. Table 16 shows the variable distribution across tests (Hudson et al. 1995, p. 6) used in this study. Frameworks for power, distance, and degree of imposition relationships were adapted from Hudson et al. (1995, p. 10–11) with minor changes being made for this study due to cultural differences (discussed in *Method* section in chapter 4). This kind of careful planning and matching of test items to a theoretical framework supports the content validity of a test.

**Table 16: Cell, attribute, and situation correspondences**
**(Hudson, Detmer, and Brown, 1995, pp. 6 and 10)**

| Speech acts | Cell number and attributes/corresponding situations | | | | | | | |
|---|---|---|---|---|---|---|---|---|
| Requests | | | | | | | | |
| cell | 1 | 2 | 3 | 4 | 5 | 6 | 7 | 8 |
| situation | 23 | 14 | 3 | 22 | 8 | 16 | 12 | 5 |
| Refusals | | | | | | | | |
| cell | 9 | 10 | 11 | 12 | 13 | 14 | 15 | 16 |
| situation | 10 | 9 | 15 | 17 | 21 | 20 | 24 | 4 |
| Apologies | | | | | | | | |
| cell | 17 | 18 | 19 | 20 | 21 | 22 | 23 | 24 |
| situation | 6 | 13 | 2 | 7 | 18 | 1 | 11 | 19 |
| Variables | | | | | | | | |
| Imposition | + | + | + | + | − | − | − | − |
| Power | + | + | − | − | + | + | − | − |
| Distance | + | − | + | − | + | − | + | − |

+ more; – less

CRITERION-RELATED VALIDITY

Criterion-related validity is usually estimated by calculating a correlation coefficient between a test and some criterion measure of the same thing. In this study the results of correlations of the six pragmatic measures were compared with each other and with the cloze test (Yamashita, 1994) as an established measure of overall Japanese language proficiency (for an overview on cloze testing, see Brown, 1980, or more recently, Ikeguchi, 1995) in order to investigate criterion-related validity. Table 17 shows the correlation coefficients.

Table 17: Correlation coefficients for variables SA to LL

|  | SA | RPSA | MCDCT | Cloze | OPDCT | RP |
|---|---|---|---|---|---|---|
| SA | 1.0000 | | | | | |
| RPSA | .6782** | 1.0000 | | | | |
| MCDCT | .1139 | .1846 | 1.0000 | | | |
| Cloze | .5090** | .4051* | .4136* | 1.0000 | | |
| OPDCT | .4907** | .4072* | .3811* | .6194** | 1.0000 | |
| RP | .6056** | .5253** | .2398 | .5543** | .5798** | 1.0000 |
| LL | .5561** | .4950** | .3608* | .6599** | .6565** | .7898** |

*$p<.01$ **$p<.001$

The SA test correlated significantly with five other tests (RPSA, cloze, OPDCT, RP, and LL) at $p<.001$. The RPSA test correlated significantly with the RP, LL (oral production), and SA at $p<.001$, and with the cloze and OPDCT (written production) at $p<.01$. The OPDCT correlated with the SA, RP, LL, and cloze significantly at $p<.001$ and the RPSA and MCDCT at $p<.01$ level. The RP test correlated significantly with the SA, RPSA, OPDCT, LL and cloze all at $p<.001$. The LL test correlated with the SA, RPSA, OPDCT, RP, and cloze significantly at $p<.001$ level, and with the MCDCT at $p<.01$. Among the six pragmatics measures and cloze test, the MCDCT correlated least well with the other tests. The MCDCT correlated with the OPDCT, LL, and cloze at the $p<.01$ level. On the other hand, the cloze test, which was used as a proficiency measure, correlated well with the SA, OPDCT, RP, LL at $p<.001$ level, and with the RPSA and MCDCT at $p<.01$ level. The squared values of these correlations are shown in Table 18. These statistics indicate the percentage of overlapping variance between whatever two tests are involved.

The RP test and the LL test, both oral production related-tests, overlapped most highly at .6238. Also, the SA test and the RPSA test, both self-assessment type tests, overlapped by .4600, which was the second highest level in the table. Taken altogether, these correlation coefficients do not provide very strong evidence for the criterion-related validity of any of the tests.

## Table 18: Squared correlation coefficients (% of overlapping variance)

| | SA | RPSA | MCDCT | Cloze | OPDCT | RP |
|---|---|---|---|---|---|---|
| SA | 1.0000 | | | | | |
| RPSA | .4600** | 1.0000 | | | | |
| MCDCT | .0130 | .0341 | 1.0000 | | | |
| Cloze | .2591** | .1641* | .1711* | 1.0000 | | |
| OPDCT | .2408** | .1658* | .1452* | .3837** | 1.0000 | |
| RP | .3668** | .2760** | .0575 | .3073** | .3362** | 1.0000 |
| LL | .3092** | .2450** | .1302* | .4355** | .4310** | .6238** |

*$p<.01$ **$p<.001$

## CONSTRUCT VALIDITY: FACTOR ANALYSIS

Construct validity will first be discussed based on the factor analysis shown in Table 19 (loadings over .30 are marked with an asterisk) and Table 20 (highest loadings for each variable are marked with a double asterisk). Varimax rotation converged in three iterations.

### Table 19: Factor analysis (*loadings over .30)

| | FACTOR 1 | FACTOR 2 |
|---|---|---|
| SA | .88125* | .08538 |
| RPSA | .81428* | .06732 |
| MCDCT | −.06665 | .87421* |
| OPDCT | .52741* | .62454* |
| RP | .76187* | .37751* |
| LL | .67759* | .55950* |
| Cloze | .50954* | .65270* |

According to Table 20, the SA, RPSA, RP and LL tests load highest on factor 1, while the MCDCT, cloze, and OPDCT load highest on factor 2. Factor 1 appears to be some sort of oral production factor, while factor 2 may be a paper-and-pencil factor. These factors, which seem to be test method factors, will be discussed in more depth in the next chapter.

### Table 20: Factor analysis (**highest loadings for each variable)

|        | FACTOR 1   | FACTOR 2   |
|--------|------------|------------|
| SA     | .88125**   | .08538     |
| RPSA   | .81428**   | .06732     |
| RP     | .76187**   | .37751     |
| LL     | .67759**   | .55950     |
| MCDCT  | –.06665    | .87421**   |
| OPDCT  | .52741     | .62454**   |
| Cloze  | .50954     | .65270**   |

## CONSTRUCT VALIDITY: DIFFERENTIAL GROUPS

The part of research question 3 on construct validity further asked if there are differences in the differential groups' construct validity of the six tests of pragmatic ability. More specifically, what are differences in the differential groups' construct validity of the six tests when comparing the pragmatic competence of: (a) the different levels of the English learners of Japanese (between Beginning, Intermediate, and Advanced levels) and (b) the different lengths of exposure to Japanese culture (JFL vs. JSL)?

In order to find answers to the above questions, two-way multivariate analysis of variance MANOVA procedures were run with six dependent variables (scores on the SA, RPSA, MCDCT, OPDCT, RP, and LL tests), and two independent variables (CULTURE [the amount of exposure of Japanese culture or JSL vs. JFL], and LEVEL [Beginning, Intermediate, and Advanced]). However, first it was necessary to examine the assumptions underlying MANOVA.

## MANOVA ASSUMPTIONS

Because the design of the multivariate analysis in this study had unequal cell sizes, it was especially important to check the assumptions that underlie MANOVA. The MANOVA assumptions were checked as follows.

Univariate outliers were checked using the SPSS EXAMINE command. Box plots for all cells in the design for each of the dependent variables indicated that there were no extreme cases or outliers.

Multivariate outliers were checked using Mahalanobis distance in SPSS REGRESSION. Each cell was examined for multivariate outliers separately. SPSS indicated that there were no outliers found, so casewise plots were not even produced by SPSS.

Normality was checked with the SPSS EXAMINE command. Out of the 36 distributions in the cells of this design (2 levels of CULTURE X 3 levels of LEVEL X 6 dependent variables = 36), only three had skewedness statistics higher than 1.00 in magnitude (positive or negative). Tabachnick and Fidell (1989) said:

> The central limit theorem proves that, with large sample sizes, sampling distributions of means are normally distributed regardless of the shapes of the distributions of variables. For example, if there are at least 20 degrees of freedom for error in a univariate ANOVA, the $F$ test is said to be robust to violations of normality of variables (provided that there are no outliers). The degree to which robustness extends to multivariate analyses is not yet clear, but the larger the sample size the less effect nonnormality of variables is likely to have on your conclusion. With grouped data with large samples, transformation of variables is less imperative. (p. 71).

While the sample in this study is not huge, 47 surpasses the 20 degrees of freedom mentioned above by Tabachnick and Fidell (1989).

Homogeneity of variance-covariance matrices was tested using the Box M statistics in SPSS MANOVA. The result was Box M=22.08, with an approximate $F$ (21, 2056)=.7815, $p$=.745 indicating that there is no problem in this study with homogeneity of variance-covariance matrices.

The linearity of relationships among all pairs of dependent variables was examined using SPSS PLOT for each pair. While the relationships were sometime weak, none appeared to be non-linear.

Multicollinearity was checked by examining the Pearson product-moment correlation matrix of all dependent variables with each other (see Table 17). Most of those correlations were fairly low. However, even the highest was .7898 (considerably higher than all the others), which is below the .80 that Tabachnick and Fidell (1989) set as the problematic level of collinearity. Therefore, multicollinearity does not appear to be a major problem in this study.

In sum, there were no worrisome violations of the assumptions of MANOVA in this study.

### THE MANOVA RESULTS

The Pillais, Hottelings, and Wilks statistics all indicated that there were no significant multivariate effects for the interaction of the independent variables (the lowest $p$ value was .941). However, significant multivariate differences were found for CULTURE and LEVEL separately (at $p<.01$). Hence, univariate follow-up statistics were calculated for CULTURE as shown in Table 21 and LEVEL as shown in Table 22. The more conservative $p<.01$ was chosen for these statistics because of the number of univariate comparisons being made here.

#### Table 21: Univariate F-tests for CULTURE (JSL vs. JFL)

| Variable | Hyp.SS | Error SS | Hyp.MS | Error MS | F | p |
|---|---|---|---|---|---|---|
| SA | 1018.95 | 8812.97 | 1018.95 | 214.95 | 4.74 | .035 |
| RPSA | 396.60 | 11748.62 | 396.60 | 286.55 | 1.38 | .246 |
| MCDCT | 3.56 | 403.86 | 3.56 | 9.85 | .36 | .551 |
| OPDCT | 38.92 | 4215.89 | 38.92 | 102.83 | .38 | .542 |
| RP | 1392.09 | 8018.11 | 1392.09 | 195.56 | 7.12 | .011* |
| LL | 1100.33 | 3944.18 | 1100.33 | 96.20 | 11.44 | .002* |

* $p<.01$

The two groups (JSL vs. JFL) turned out to be significantly different (at .01 as indicated by the asterisks) on two tests of pragmatics, the RP and LL, both of which dealt with oral production. These results lend evidence for the differential-groups construct validity of the RP and LL in terms of differences in pragmatics between those who have and have not lived in the culture.

#### Table 22: Univariate F-tests for LEVEL (Beginning, Intermediate, and Advanced)

| Variable | Hyp.SS | Error SS | Hyp.MS | Error MS | F | p |
|---|---|---|---|---|---|---|
| SA | 1073.79 | 8812.97 | 536.90 | 214.95 | 2.50 | .095 |
| RPSA | 1146.46 | 11748.62 | 573.23 | 286.55 | 2.00 | .148 |
| MCDCT | 43.40 | 403.86 | 21.70 | 9.85 | 2.20 | .123 |
| OPDCT | 1694.03 | 4215.89 | 847.01 | 102.83 | 8.24 | .001* |
| RP | 4375.88 | 8018.11 | 2187.94 | 195.56 | 11.19 | .000* |
| LL | 3932.28 | 3944.18 | 1966.14 | 96.20 | 20.44 | .000* |

* $p<.01$

Table 22 shows that the three groups (Beginning, Intermediate, and Advanced learners) turned out to be significantly different (at .01 as indicated by the asterisks) on three tests of pragmatics, the OPDCT, RP, and LL. These results provide evidence for the differential-groups construct validity of these three tests for separating levels of proficiency in pragmatic terms.

## Table 23: Variables related to practicality

| Variables | SA | RPSA | MCDCT | LL | OPDCT | RP |
|---|---|---|---|---|---|---|
| Language used[1] | E | J(e1) | J(e2) | J(e3) | J(e4) | J |
| Speech acts tested[2] | 24 | 24 | 24 | 24 | 24 | 24 |
| Average time (min.)[3] | 10 | 30RP+20 | 60~120 | 20 | 60~120 | 20 |
| Actual scoring pts.[4] | 120 | 120 | 24 | 720 | 720 | 120 |
| Rating | | | | | | |
|   By the participant | X[5] | X | X | | | |
|   By the raters | | | | X | X | X |
| Format[6] | | | | | | |
|   Read and marking | X | X | X | | | |
|   Written production | | | | | X | |
|   Oral production | | X | | X | | X |
| Equipment[7] | | | | | | |
|   Paper and pencil | X | | X | | X | |
|   Video-recording | | X | | | | |
|   Viewing video | | X | | | | X |
|   Tape-recording | | | | X | | |
| Interlocutor needed[8] | | X | | | | X |
| Room arrangement[9] | | X | | X | | |
| Transcription[10] | | | | (X) | (X) | (X) |

[1] The languages used in the tests are abbreviated with J (Japanese), E (English) or e (supplemental text in English accompanying the test)

  e1 = The roleplay scenarios and difficult vocabularies were supplemented by English, and the self-ssessment sheet was given in English

  e2 = Only the situations were supplemented by English but not for multiple-choice keys (i.e., the answer keys for multiple-choice questions were given in Japanese only)

  e3 = The situations were supplemented by English in written format

  e4 = The situations were supplemented by English

[2] Eight variations of three speech acts (requests, refusals, and apologies) make 24 situations for each test

[3] Average time being spent for each test is given in minutes. For the RPSA test, 30 minutes was spent for performing the eight roleplays and another 20 minutes was spent for assessment by viewing their own roleplays. The time spent for the OPDCT varied from average 60 minutes to 120 minutes according to the participants' self-reports.

[4] The SA test (5 points x 24 situations); the RPSA test (5 points x 24 speech acts); the MCDCT (1 point x 24 situations); the LL test (5 points x 6 categories x 24 situations); the OPDCT (5 points x 6 cateories x 24 situations); the RP test (5 points x 24 speech acts).

[5] "X" is used for marking existence

[6] The format of each test is categorized as "Read and marking" (read the description and mark on the Likert scale or choose the appropriate answer), "Written production" (the participants actually write the answer), and "Oral production" (the participants record [or audio-tape] their oral production).

[7] Equipment used for the tests is categorized as paper and pencil, video-recording, viewing video, and tape-recording.

[8] An interlocutor was involved for the RPSA test, and the RP test.

[9] Room arrangements were necessary for videotaping (the RPSA) and audio-taping (the LL test), but not for the RP (rating by raters at their own place).

[10] Transcription not required in this study

Research question 4 asked about differences in *practicality* between test formats for measuring pragmatic competence of English learners of Japanese. Table 23 shows a summary of variables related to practicality. The results presented in Table 23, indeed all of the results in this chapter, will be discussed in more depth in chapter 6.

# CHAPTER 6: DISCUSSION

The statistical results of this study were presented in the previous chapter in a fairly technical form. Here, I will discuss and analyze more closely the results as they relate to each of the research questions posed in chapter 3. Recall that the overall purpose of this study was to investigate whether or not there are differences among test formats for measuring the pragmatic competence of English speaking learners of Japanese.

## DESCRIPTIVE STATISTICS

The descriptive statistics (Table 3) showed that the means of the LL and OPDCT tests (production tests rated by the raters) were both high (93.38 and 92.32, respectively) compared to the other tests (which ranged from 69.35 to 79.43). Both the self-assessment and the RP tests had relatively low means. It is interesting that the overall mean of the RP test (rated by the raters) and the RPSA test (assessed by the ratees) were almost identical (72.78 and 73.66, respectively). Both ratings were based on participants' scoring for *appropriateness* on a five-point Likert scale. They were moderately correlated at .53 with $p<.001$ (see Table 17).

It is worth noting also that the SD of the RP test was the biggest (19.76) and that of the OPDCT the smallest (12.52). Also, the minimum score on the RP test was the second to lowest at 36.67 (second to the MCDCT at 20.00) and the minimum score of the OPDCT was the highest (67.56) of all the six tests. These results probably indicate that the RP test produced the most variance of all the tests, while the OPDCT produced the least. Perhaps the RP test produced more variance because the raters were required to base their scores on multiple variables such as the interactions with the interlocutor, tone of voice, facial expressions, and non-verbal gestures in addition to judging the participants' linguistic expression. In fact, in informal interviews with the researcher after the completion of the ratings for the RP test, the raters reported that they felt uncomfortable or awkward when the participants' non-verbal behavior did not appropriately accompany the language used in certain situations (as in one participant's not standing up when a manager of a company came in the room for an interview, or other participants' overuse of bowing in inappropriate situations). Such variables were factors only in the RP test and did not appear in the OPDCT or LL tests. Thus, the RP test might have had the biggest standard deviation (SD) among the tests because it was measuring more aspects of the speakers' behavior.

# RELIABILITY ISSUES

## CRONBACH ALPHA RELIABILITY ESTIMATES

The Cronbach alpha internal consistency estimates presented in Table 4 were all higher than .94 except for the MCDCT, which was considerably lower at .4652. It is especially noteworthy that the internal consistency reliability estimates for the two self-assessment tests, the SA and RPSA, were high. In previous self-assessment studies, there have been different opinions expressed by two groups of researchers — one group has found that self-assessment or rating tests were accurate and fairly reliable (Bachman and Palmer, 1989; LeBlanc and Painchaud, 1985; Oskarsson, 1978) and another group, especially Davidson and Henning (1985), saw self-rating as problematic. Bachman and Palmer (1989) strongly argued that the results for their self-assessment questionnaires (which were designed to test pragmatic ability) indicated that these self-asssessment tests can be reliable and valid measures of communicative language abilities. An example of the questions asked on the Bachman and Palmer test (1989) is: "How hard is it for you to use different kinds of English with different kinds of people? — for example, a child, a close friend, a teacher?" (1989, p. 27).

The present study also found that the self-ratings, both *imaginative* (referring to scores based on imagining oneself in a particular situation) self-ratings and *impressionistic* (referring to scores based on participants' impressions of their own performance) self-ratings, were equally reliable. An example of an *imaginative* self-rating is one that occurs before a roleplay begins, when the tester asks the participants how appropriately/satisfactorily they would respond in a particular situation such as "You live in a large apartment building. You are leaving to go to work. On your way out, you meet your next door neighbor, whom you haven't seen for a long time" (taken from the SA test in Hudson, Detmer, and Brown, 1995, p. 93). An example of an *impressionistic* self-rating is one in which the participants rate their own performances while watching their own roleplay video (as on the RPSA test).

Table 4 investigates the Cronbach's alpha reliability estimates for each form of each of the measures. Except for the MCDCT, the reliability estimates for all six pragmatics tests and the cloze test were high. Each form of the MCDCT was much lower in reliability than the other tests studied here, with Forms A, B, and C having reliabilities of .1671, .5017, and .6510, respectively. Since the choices (including correct answers and distractors) were originally written in English and based on the previous literature (most of the previous studies dealt with English or some other European language as the target language), the answer keys might not have been appropriate for this study. The problems with the MCDCT will be discussed next.

## PROBLEMS WITH THE MCDCT

There seem to be some strategies in speech act realization that are particular to Japanese speakers and not observed in the data reported in previous studies based on western languages (e.g., the CCSARP Project reported in Blum-Kulka, House, and Kasper, 1989).

Hudson, Detmer, and Brown (1995) reported that their Japanese ESL participants used the strategy of "dismay" when they had to apologize in English as in "Oh, I'm sorry. What shall I do?" (Hudson et al. 1995, p. 19). This strategy was never used by the American English speakers in the Hudson et al. pilot study which was conducted in English. Interestingly, in my data the "dismay" strategy was observed in all of the production tests (the LL, OPDCT, and RP) of the English speaking JSL participants (in Japanese as a target language) from Beginning to Advanced levels, although it was not observed in 100 percent of the cases. This strategy was used somewhat by the English speaking JFL participants (who had lived in Japan for less than two months). The dismay strategy was most apparent in such situations where the pragmatic variable combination was minus POWER and plus IMPOSITION (the DISTANCE was not relevant). Examples are: (a) that of a junior worker losing a valuable computer file borrowed from the boss; and (b) that in which the speaker, acting as a member of a volunteer group, failed to borrow a truck, thus failing to keep his promise to the president of the group. The English-speaking JSL participants' "dismay" expressions varied from very primitive expressions produced by a Beginning level JSL participant, *Nani shimasu ka?* (*What do I do?*, which is grammatically acceptable, but inappropriate in terms of expression in this context) to *Doo shitara yoroshiideshoo ka?*, (*What should I do* [to solve the problem]?), which was produced by an advanced JSL participant) with an IFID (illocutionary force indicating device) such as *sumimasen* (*I am sorry*) as a head act. Native Japanese speakers also used the "dismay" strategy in the pilot tests of all three production tests (but again, not ALL the native Japanese speakers used the dismay strategy). One such example is *Ikaga taisho sureba yoroshii deshoo ka?* (asking his senior what to do) meaning essentially the same as the expression uttered by the JSL Beginning level student (i.e., *What do I do?*), but expressed in a more sophisticated way.

The dismay strategy does not seem to be learned as formulaic expressions by the JSL learners, but rather seems to be learned from their observations or encounters where many Japanese people have displayed such expressions of dismay to show to a superior their feeling of *helplessness* or their *upset state* when they have to apologize (see Gass, 1987, 1990 for discussion about differences between SL and FL acquisition). Such dismay expressions were not included in the apology strategy options in the MCDCT because this study translated the options as they were in the original English MCDCT (because one of the eventual purposes of the study was to compare the testing measures cross-culturally with those developed in English).

Rose (1992a) suggested that another problem for the MCDCT occurred because of Japanese indirectness or "hinting" in requests. He pointed out that a Japanese hinting expression often contains *ga* or *kedo* (translated into English as *but*), but if it is rendered as "Ah, my hands are full but/so," the resulting utterance in English seems unnatural and is not likely to occur as a hint (Rose, 1992a, p. 72). The expression uttered in Japanese, "*Ano, te ga fusagatte irun desu ga...*" with a hinting ending, indicates that there is more to be said, but not by the speaker, so the hearer fills in the gap (Rose, 1992a, p. 72). In the MCDCT in the current study, there are eight situations in which a request is made. Many of these situations contained hinting expressions as keys which were translated from English. In all cases, the participants in the hinting situations were the speaker (in the first person singular) as in "Oh, I'd like to take some notes, but it seems that I have no pen with me" (in MCDCT Form A–5b in Hudson, Detmer, and Brown, 1995, p. 109). Eleven native Japanese speakers revealed interesting patterns on the Japanese OPDCT in the pilot study conducted by this researcher. In the same situation (i.e., OPDCT-Form A–5), nine NS Japanese speakers wrote (in Japanese), "Mr. Boss, I am sorry (*sumimasen*), but do *you* happen to have an extra pen?...If you do, could *you* lend me one?" One NS speaker wrote in Japanese, "I am sorry, but do *you* have an extra pen?" One last person explained, "I will not borrow a pen from my boss" (One of the intermediate JSL English speaking participants also said the same thing). None of the Japanese NS responses reflected the keys in the original English MCDCT (i.e., none of the NSs used the speaker as a subject of the action in the situation of hinting to his/her superior, but used their superior as a subject if there is such a relationship between the speaker and the hearer). This issue has been discussed by Blum-Kulka, House, and Kasper (1989a). They said that choice of perspective presents an important source of variation in requests (p. 19). They distinguished requests according to the speaker's perspective (e.g., "Can I...?"), the addressee's perspective (e.g., "Can you...?"), and the inclusive perspective (e.g., "Can we...?"). Niki and Tajika (1994) also found that the majority of English native speakers preferred the "Can I...?" strategy or *asking permission* while the preferences of Japanese students varied with the *requesting* strategy (i.e., "Can you...?) outnumbering the *asking permission* strategy. If the traits discussed above (such as *dismay* strategy, and Japanese way of "hinting") were not reflected in the answer key for the Japanese MCDCT, the participants would naturally be confused and would give wrong answers. Several of those Japanese native speakers who participated in the MCDCT pilot experiment reported to the researcher that they were very frustrated because there seemed to be no correct answer to select in many situations. Inappropriate options may have caused the low reliability of the Japanese version (or translation) of the MCDCT. It is apparently very difficult to make such a multiple-choice test reflect culturally-specific traits in the options if the test is made for cross-cultural use. If we are to use the MCDCT as a measure of Japanese pragmatics at all, extensive additional study of native speakers performing in Japanese will be needed.

One last comment about the MCDCT is that most of the current MCDCT options were very short sentences. In some situations (when the speaker is in minus POWER and plus IMPOSITION situations), a few long sentences were given in the LL and OPDCT samples, and naturally, more conversational exchanges were made in the RP situations. The current MCDCT did not reflect such a pattern and may have been designed to be too simple. The test needs to be revised accordingly.

## THE RATER RELIABILITY ISSUES

Table 5 showed the four native Japanese raters' Cronbach alpha internal consistency reliability estimates for the LL, OPDCT, and RP tests. The reliability estimates for the raters' scores were all very high. This study included participants from all proficiency levels ranging from those with no previous experience living in Japan (JFL learners) to those who had lived in Japan for more than twenty years (JSL learners). There was a great deal of variance in the participants' abilities (see Table 2), which is at least partly related to the high reliability estimates. Raters 1, 2, and 3 had previous Japanese language teaching experience, and Rater 4, a student majoring in Japanese, had no actual teaching experience but had just finished a course called "Teaching Japanese as a Foreign Language." All four raters were using the same rating scale (Appendixes D and I) for the first time. The instructions for rating each test were translated into Japanese from Hudson, Detmer, and Brown's rater's manual (1995) by the researcher, and then, proofread by another Japanese speaker before being given to the raters (Appendix L). The rater's internal consistency reliability estimates indicate the consistency of the rater's scores. The raters' reliability estimates in this study were all higher than .95, which indicates that if they were to rate the same data again, they would probably rate it with 95% similarity to their original ratings. This only indicates that the rater would rate with 95% consistency, but it does not measure the appropriateness of the level of their ratings. So the intraclass correlation coefficients were also calculated (also shown in Table 5).

Intraclass reliabilities indicated the extent to which the raters' scores correlated when considered together for each test. The intraclass correlation coefficients were .82 (for the LL test), .74 (for the OPDCT), and .88 (for the RP test). These statistics indicate that the ratings on the RP test were the most highly intercorrelated (i.e., the three raters' scores were correlated at 88% or with 12% error variance), and the OPDCT was the least correlated. In any case, all of the intraclass correlation coefficients were relatively high. It can be said that the RP test, which was rated based on the participants' oral and non-verbal performance on the video tape, had ratings which were the most highly correlated, and thus it was the most reliably scored, followed by the language lab oral performance test (LL), and then the written performance test (OPDCT).

Tables 6 to 8 indicate the interrater correlations for each test. The interrater correlations for all of the tests were significant at $p<.001$. The four raters (three raters were involved in each rating, but Rater 3 was replaced by Rater 4 on the LL test) came from different backgrounds (age, gender, teaching experiences, and social experiences). However, the interrater correlations were reasonably high (the highest at .8662 between Rater 1 and Rater 3 for the RP test, and the lowest at .7317 was between Rater 1 and Rater 2 on the OPDCT). Table 24 describes the raters according to several variables.

**Table 24: Rater descriptions**

| Rater | Gender | Age | Years of experience | Levels taught |
|-------|--------|-----|---------------------|---------------|
| Rater 1 | M | 60's | practicum* | beginning/intermed. |
| Rater 2 | F | 20's | 2 years | beginning |
| Rater 3 | F | 50's | 7 years | all levels |
| Rater 4 | F | 20's | methods** | none |

\* Rater 1 had worked for more than 35 years in an insurance company in Tokyo as a manager at the time he was retired.

\** Rater 4 was a senior at a university majoring Japanese. She took courses in Teaching Japanese as a Second Language.

The written raters' training manual (Hudson, Detmer, and Brown, 1995, p. 163–167, as translated into Japanese by the researcher) was given to each rater along with the data. An oral explanation was also given to each rater by the researcher as supplemental training. Hudson et al.'s manual clearly states (and the researcher emphasized) that "ungrammaticality is not an issue for the rating purposes," and further states that they should "not let errors in verb conjugation or article use influence your ratings" (Hudson et al. 1995, p. 164). However, Rater 3 reported to the researcher that even though she knew that ungrammaticality should not influence her ratings, she could not disregard ungrammaticality. Thus, participants with poor grammar skills, tended to receive lower scores from her. Raters 1 and 2 reported that participants with poor non-verbal behavior (e.g., one did not bow when it was necessary) also tended to receive lower scores on the RP test. It is understandable and expected that such factors might influence scores.

Some of the participants purposely avoided expressing speech acts. For example, one participant reported that, while at a meeting, she avoided requesting a memo paper from her boss. Another participant reported that he would accept an offer instead of refusing (which he was supposed to do according to the scenario) if the manager interviewing him for a new position asked him to take a tour of the inside of the company building, because, the participant said, he believed that Japanese would not refuse in such a case. The expected speech acts were omitted by the participants in both cases. Rater 1 reported that he gave lower scores when such speech acts were omitted even if the reasons were given by the participants (as explained in chapter 4, no missing speech act due to the participant's failure existed in the data, and it was explained to the raters by the researcher that there were cases in which the participants avoided certain speech acts on purpose). Also, Rater 1 reported that he thought that it was more natural in the case of a serious offense to a superior (where the speaker has to apologize) for the speaker to give an explanation and description of the offensive situation before using a head act expression such as *I am sorry* or *Forgive me*. Within the native Japanese OPDCT pilot data, there were several cases like that described by Rater 1. In situation 7 of Form A, an office worker lost a computer file which that worker borrowed from the boss. One NS

Japanese wrote (in Japanese), "Mr. Boss (*bucho*, a title), it seems that I lost your computer disk that I borrowed from you the other day. What should I do? I am very sorry." Another wrote, "Mr. Boss, I would like to talk to you for a while. Could you spend some time for me?" [literal translation]. Then, he continued, "(If the boss said *yes*, the participant wrote) I lost the floppy disk that I borrowed from you the other day. I am very sorry." A couple of other NSs even started their speeches with expressions of gratitude (thanking the boss for kindly letting him use the computer disk) and ended with a request, but used no apologetic expressions. One actual response went like this (literally translated): "Mr. Boss, thank you so much for the computer disk that you lent me last week. Well, to tell the truth, talking about the disk, it seems that it was misplaced somewhere and I can't find it. Could you please wait for a little while?" If a participant described the situation before the *western sense* of the head act (i.e., *I am sorry* in Japanese is not always a head act, but rather becomes a kind of *tail*-act, or comes at the end of the utterance especially in a seriously offensive situation), the Japanese production will be more acceptable and a higher score will be given, as in the case of Rater 1. Hudson et al.'s manual (1995, p. 166) instructed the raters to follow their intuition in case of difficulties and to always base their scores on the native-speaker norm. Even with a detailed rating instruction manual, there will still be variation among raters since each has different teaching and social experiences on which to base their ratings. Despite all the differences in raters' approaches described above, the interrater reliability estimates of this study were relatively high, and so it can be concluded that the ratings were fairly reliable, both in terms of internal consistency and in terms of interrater correlations.

## THE STANDARD ERROR OF MEASUREMENT

The SEM indicates "the consistency of a set of test scores...this statistic is used to determine a band around a student's score within which that the student's score would probably fall if the test were administered to him or her repeatedly" (Brown, 1996, p. 206). The formula in Brown (1996, p. 207) was applied to calculate the SEM of the six tests using the reliability estimates obtained from Table 3 and the SEMs were reported in Table 10. The SEM estimates of the pragmatics tests, except for the MCDCT, were relatively small, which indicates (along with the reliability estimates) that any chance fluctuations due to unreliability, at least for five of the pragmatics tests (the SA, LL, OPDCT, RP, the RPSA tests), were reasonably small.

## CORRELATION COEFFICIENTS BETWEEN PLUS AND MINUS VARIABLES

Table 12 shows that total scores for items testing plus and minus aspects of all variables (Degree of Imposition, Power, and Distance) were correlated significantly by $p < .001$ for all the tests except the MCDCT. The low correlations for the plus and minus variables in the MCDCT are probably due to the low reliability of that measure. Squared values of correlation between plus and minus variables for the six tests (Table 13) indicates that the plus and minus aspects of the production tests (i.e., the LL, OPDCT, and RP tests) overlapped most highly (all at more than .80 except for the .61 for Degree of Imposition on the OPDCT). Among those three tests, the RP overlapped most highly (higher than .90 on all variables). In contrast, the self-assessment tests (i.e., the SA and RPSA tests) overlapped somewhat less highly (less than .80). The MCDCT's pattern of overlapping looks problematic (lower than .12 for all variables) and is probably due to the reliability problems discussed above.

The above results indicate that at least for the three production tests, Degree of Imposition, Power, and Distance overlap considerably indicating that to a great extent, they are probably tapping some common feature. This interpretation, in turn, indicates that the tests could possibly be shortened by eliminating one or the other of these categories. However, it is difficult to say (from the Tables 11, 12, and 13) which variables, plus or minus, could be eliminated since the SDs presented in Table 11 are not consistent (e.g., SDs for +I, –P, and +D in the LL test were all larger than the SDs of the counterparts, or –I, +P, and –D, whereas SDs for –I, –P, and –D in the RP test were higher than the counterparts). More research in this area would be very useful for making decisions about test design.

## EQUIVALENCE OF THE FORMS

Research question 2 asked if forms A, B, and C of the pragmatics tests are parallel. Using ANOVA procedures to test the condition of equal means, the $F_{max}$ test to check the condition of equal variances, and Pearson product-moment correlation coefficients with the RP scores to test the condition of equal correlations with an outside measure, it was found that the three forms of the LL and the three forms of the OPDCT met the conditions of parallel forms. Significant differences in the three means of the three SA forms were found, so those forms cannot be said to meet all three conditions. In addition, large differences were found in the correlations of the scores on the three forms of the MCDCT with the RP scores.

One of the reasons for using three forms was to avoid the learning effect. However, relatively large differences between means on forms were found even where there were no statistically significant differences (e.g., in the SA test, the mean of the Form A was 84.38 whereas Form C was 71.25; on the LL test, Form A was 88.81 whereas Form C was 98.88; on the OPDCT, the highest mean was 95.50 on Form C whereas the lowest mean was 87.50 on Form B). Readers must take this into account when thinking about the degree to which the three forms on four of these tests are parallel.

## VALIDITY ISSUES

Research question 3 asked what the differences are in the *validity* between test formats for measuring the pragmatic competence of English speaking learners of Japanese. Validity is defined as "the degree to which a test measures what it claims, or purports, to be measuring" (Brown, 1996, p. 231) and is often discussed in terms of *content validity*, *criterion-related validity*, and *construct validity* (see Brown, 1996 for a discussion of this issue in language testing).

## CONTENT VALIDITY

The current tests were originally developed by Hudson, Detmer, and Brown (1992, 1995). They carefully studied item specifications based on both pragmatics and politeness theory (see Hudson et al. 1992, 1995) and designed the tests to meet these specifications (i.e., testing cross-cultural pragmatic competence). They specifically controlled variables of relative power, social distance and absolute ranking of impositions.

Conversational topics and situations are also a cognitive and a socially-situated construct, and they influence interlanguage interactions (Zuengler, 1993). One obstacle to designing a pragmatics test is the lack of representative situations needed to elicit the speech acts to be tested. In Hudson et al.'s framework, a variety of contexts are included, such as situations in an office, a club for a nation-wide activity such as a hiking club, a shop, a house which is rented, and so forth. Some situations might not be familiar to all of the participants, but there should always be some other situations which they know about and are able to respond to. The current tests were modified for JSL/JFL learners (see chapter 4) with the same goals in mind. The participants in this study varied from students to office workers and some other professionals (a lawyer, a judge, teachers, etc.), and provided considerable variance in the data.

In the pilot study in which 36 native Japanese speakers were asked to answer the translated Japanese version, Form A (*n*=12), Form B (*n*=10), and Form C (*n*=14) of the OPDCT, the participants made a number of comments about which of the situations they thought were not relevant or appropriate in the Japanese context. The following comments were given by some of the participants:

*In the request situation to your boss for lending you a pen at a meeting* [Form A–5] — it is not natural for the company worker (a) not to bring a pen to a meeting and (b) then to ask to borrow a pen from your superior or boss.

*You live in a large house, hold the lease to the house, and rent out the other rooms* [Form A–9, etc.] — it is not common in the Japanese society to rent a big house and rent out the other rooms.

*...you are responsible for mowing the lawn every week* [Form A–22] — it is not likely in Japanese society.

*The leader of the project asks you to give a message to your secretary* [Form B–4] — the leader should ask his/her own secretary to give a message to your secretary, instead of asking you directly.

*The mechanic promised to have your car ready tomorrow morning, but you found out that it was not true* [Form B–10] — it was not likely that the mechanic didn't tell the customer about the delay before the customer returned.

*The head of the department forgot to bring paper to write memos at a meeting* [Form B–16] — it is not likely that the head of the department would forgot to bring paper and a pencil to a meeting.

*You live in a large house, hold the lease to the house and rent out the other rooms. You are late for a meeting with one of your house-mates* [Form C–1] — I was unable to decide which form I should use for apologizing because the relationship (closeness, how long they have known each other, etc.) was not clear.

*Ordering a framed photograph of the office workers as a gift at a good-bye party* [Form C–10] — it is not common in Japan.

*You arranged to borrow your friend's truck to help move furniture...but you found this morning that you can't borrow it* [Form C–7] — it is strange that you won't know it until the morning.

*A friend's birthday party is planned at your house* [Form C–9] — it is not popular to have a home-party in Japan.

In the above list of comments, the second comment was given by several NSs and thus seemed the most problematic. Other comments were voiced by only a couple of NSs. Although some of the situations may not be common in Japanese society as some NS participants commented, the number of participants who commented about them was very small. The point is that even though some of the test's scenarios do seem highly unlikely within the context of the Japanese society, they will still give the participants a clear idea of the relationship between the speaker and hearer. Even the Japanese NSs were able to answer what they would say if the situations were real. So my decision was to use the translated version for surveying my American JSL participants and believe that its use would not jeopardize my method of testing. Some minor changes which would not affect the original frameworks for Power, Distance, and Degree of Imposition relationships were made, as already reported in chapter 4 (such as a family picture on an office desk being changed to a small table calendar, a drug store being changed to a "convenience" store, a store's 10th anniversary "party" being changed to an anniversary "sale," etc.).

## CRITERION-RELATED VALIDITY

Basically, criterion-related validity investigates how strongly a test is correlated to a well-established measure of the construct involved (Brown, 1996). In this study, the cloze test was used as a general proficiency test. In Table 17, the SA, OPDCT, RP and LL tests were all correlated with the cloze test fairly highly at $p<.001$ level, and the RPSA and MCDCT were correlated with the cloze test a little less highly at $p<.01$ level. In other words, all of the pragmatics tests in this study correlated with the cloze test at a level well beyond chance correlations (at least at $p<.01$) and the magnitudes were reasonably high indicating that they are criterion-related valid in terms of overall proficiency.

Among the six pragmatics tests, the MCDCT seems to be correlated the least with all the other tests probably because of the unreliability of this test. However, the MCDCT also seems to be measuring different things from the other tests as indicated by the problems with options discussed in a previous section of this chapter.

Another way of looking at the data is through the *coefficient of determination* (Table 18), the squared value of the validity coefficient, which can be directly interpreted as the percentage of overlapping variance between the two measures (Brown, 1988, p. 104). Notice that the SA test was correlated with all other tests at the $p<.001$ level, and overlapped about 46% with the RPSA test. This result is striking because (a) the participants were not required to produce any pragmatic performance on the SA test, (b) the situations on the SA test are explained in the participant's mother tongue, English, and (c) the test only asks the participants to think about the situation in their head and to rate how well they would be able to respond in the foreign or second language (in this case, Japanese). Moreover, it took only about ten minutes to complete all 24 of the SA test situations. The SA test appears to be a fairly strong tool for testing pragmatics, especially for placement test or diagnostic purposes, or perhaps for purposes of doing needs analysis in curriculum development. The results showed that the learners' own judgments (on the SA) correlated well with other time-consuming tests, both oral or written (e.g., the LL, OPDCT, or RP tests), and that it is also a very reliable measure in terms of internal consistency (.9359 in Table 3). In actuality, the self-assessment is not very different from the estimation of professional teachers, just as Oscarson (1989) claimed. In addition to the testing purposes discussed above, the SA might serve as a source of motivation for students if it were given when they first start studying a new language.

The LL test was also moderately correlated with all other tests at $p<.001$ except the MCDCT at $p<.01$. The LL test overlapped about 62% with the RP, which sounds reasonable because the scores of both tests were based on the participants' oral production. The tape-recorded LL oral production was correlated most highly with the RP test, which was based on video-taped performances. This researcher was concerned about the LL test possibly being unnatural because participants were asked to produce language orally without a live interlocutor, and the participants were expected to respond differently from in an authentic conversation. However, the results of the statistical analyses indicate that the two tests (the RP in which an interlocutor was involved and the LL which involved no interlocutor) were fairly strongly correlated with each other with 62% overlapping variance.

Nonetheless, it is worth noting that some inherent differences between the LL and RP tests have been detected in qualitative analysis, and are presented here in Extracts 1 through 4, which were taken from the LL and RP tests of the same participants (Beginning JSL and Advanced JFL learners).

## THE 'JOB APPLICATION' CASE

Situation [Apology] — You accidentally knock over something.

LL [Form B–2]: You accidentally knock over a vase on the desk of a manager with whom you were talking about a job application. (Without interlocutor)

RP [RP #5]: You visit a company for a job interview, accidentally startle the manager, and he drops some papers on the floor. (With interlocutor)

### Extract 1: LL

*S1 = Beginning level JSL Male*

> S1: Hontoni gomennasai. Sumimasen.
> 'I am really sorry. I am sorry (forgive me)'

### Extract 2: RP

*IL = the Interlocutor (native Japanese speaker)*

> S1: A, sumimasen!
> 'Oh, I am sorry!'

> IL: A, ie ie, daijoobu desu.
> 'Oh, no, no, that's OK.'

> S1: Ano, a…
> 'Well,…ah…'

> IL: A, ie ie, daijoobu desu.
> 'Oh, no, no, that's OK.'

> S1: Daijoobu desu ka? Ano…
> 'Is it OK? Ah…'

> IL: Hai.
> 'Yes (it's OK).'

### Extract 3: LL

*S2 = Advanced level JFL Male*

> S2: Ano, ano…sumimasen deshita. A…
> 'Ah…ah…I am sorry. Ah…' [sounding upset]

*Extract 4: RP*

S2: Konnichiwa. A, suimasen.
'Hello. Oh, I am sorry!'

IL: A, ie ie, a, doomo arigatoo gozaimasu
'Oh, no, no..Oh, thank you very much' *[after NN2 picked it up]*.
Daijoobu desu.
'It's OK.'

S2: Sumimasen…
'I am sorry.'

In both cases (S1 in Extracts 1 and 2, and S2 in Extracts 3 and 4), the utterances in the LL test (i.e., Extracts 1 and 3) were short. The IFID (illocutionary force indicating device), *I am sorry*, was used directly. In the RP situations (i.e., extracts 2 and 4), on the other hand, there were a few exchanges with the interlocutor along with emotional expressions/exclamations like *ah* (*o h*) or *ano…* (*umm…*) (as discussed in Blum-Kulka, House, and Kasper, 1989a). Participant S1 showed his embarrassment about the problem that he caused, and asked the interlocutor whether it was "OK." Participant S2's non-verbal behavior, picking up the papers scattered on the floor, also lead to the interlocutor's expression of gratitude in Extract 4.

There are cases of many other combinations of variables, other than differences between the LL and RP test types, which result in either shorter or longer utterances. For instance, when the Degree of Imposition became larger in a minus Power situation, utterances tended to be longer regardless of the test type (i.e., both the LL test and the RP test).

Also, it was observed that in the RP test, the native Japanese interlocutor constantly supplied the necessary words and expressions in the sequence of conversation with a very poor beginner (JFL), so that the conversation could flow. As a result, the roleplays, even those of beginners, sounded as if the conversation went smoothly. Examples of the interlocutor supplying words in the roleplay appear in the following example:

## THE 'AT THE CAR GARAGE' CASE

Situation [Request/Apology: RP #1] — You want to ask a mechanic to have a company van ready by early tomorrow morning, which is one day earlier than it is supposed to be ready. After the mechanic leaves to talk with another mechanic, you accidentally knock over his coffee and it spills over some papers on the desk. The speaker or the subject is a customer (+Power).

*Extract 5*

*S3 = Beginning level JFL male (ten days after arrival in Japan)*

S3:  Suimasen.
'Excuse me.'

IL:  A, doomo irasshaimase.
'Welcome.'

S3:  Etto, senshuu boku no kuruma ga motte kimashita.
'Umm..last week, I brought in my car.'

IL:  A, hai, ja suwatte kudasai.
'Oh, yes, please sit down.' *[IL asked S3's name]*

IL:  E..XX-san no kuruma wa asatte dekirun desukedo.
'Um..your (name) car will be ready the day after tomorrow.'

S3:  Demo, eetto, ashita…
'Well, but, tomorrow…'

IL:  Ashita hoshii desu ka?
'You want it tomorrow?'

S3:  Ashita hoshii desu.
'I want it tomorrow.'

IL:  Ashita hoshii desu ka. hai, wakarimashita.
'You want it tomorrow, I see. Yes, I understand.'
*[IL left to check with other mechanic/S3 knocked over a cup]*

S3:  Gomennasai. etto, *coffee* o…
'I am sorry. Um..the coffee..'

IL:  Koborechai mashita ka?
'Has it (the coffee) spilled?'

S3:  Hai.
'Yes.'

IL:  Daijoobu desu, daijoobu desu.
'It's OK, it's OK.'

S3:  Ee..tto, kami ga…ee…tto..
'Well..um..paper..um…'

IL:  Kami nureteru kedo daijoobu desu.
'The paper is wet, but it's all right.'

S3:  A, soo desu ka. Suimasen.
'Is that so? I am sorry.'

In the above example, the interlocutor tried hard to understand what the participant was attempting to tell him. In the process, the interlocutor supplied words, which appears to be a characteristic of roleplays — a characteristic that did not appear in the other test types. Perhaps this word-supplying tendency occurs in the RP and not the others because the RP is most like real conversation where such an effect between NS and NNS may occur often.

## CONSTRUCT VALIDITY

*Factor analysis.* Construct validity was first investigated based on a factor analysis (Table 19 and Table 20). The SA, RPSA, RP, and LL tests loaded highest on factor 1 in Table 20 (after VARIMAX rotation). This pattern may indicate that factor 1 is related to oral performance (RP and LL) and to self-assessments (SA and RPSA). Since the SA test is a self-assessment of the participants' anticipated oral pragmatic competence, and the RPSA a self-assessment of the participants' actual oral production (i.e., roleplays), it seems reasonable to conclude that all four tests under factor 1 are related to oral performance. On the other hand, the MCDCT, cloze, and OPDCT loaded highest on factor 2. This may indicate that factor 2 represents paper-and-pencil type tests, in which reading and writing skills are involved. The above findings indicate that there may be a strong method effect which would mean that the oral tests would be testing somewhat differently from the paper-and-pencil tests based on the different formats of the tests.

*The differential groups study.* Research question 3 also asked whether there are differences in the differential groups construct validity of the six tests of pragmatic ability. Hence, in part, this part of the investigation can be called a "differential-groups study" (Brown, 1996, p. 240). In a differential-groups study, the purpose is to discover if the test in question differentiates between people who have little of the construct under investigation and people who have more of it. If it turns out that the test does differentiate in this way between the two groups, it can be inferred that the test is measuring the construct that it was designed to measure. In this study, three participant groups were formed based on (a) their levels of Japanese (including three levels: Beginning, Intermediate, and Advanced levels) or LEVEL, and (b) their length of exposure to Japanese culture (including two levels: the JSL and JFL groups) or CULTURE.

Significant multivariate differences were found for CULTURE and LEVEL ($p<.01$), and thus univariate follow-up statistics were calculated for the CULTURE and LEVEL.

The CULTURE groups consisted of two groups (JFL vs. JFL), which turned out to be significantly different ($p<.01$) on two tests of pragmatics, the RP and LL (both of which dealt with oral production). These results indicate that pragmatic oral production may be associated with the experience of living in a target culture. To illustrate the above claim, here are extracts from two Beginning level (JFL and JSL) roleplays:

Situation [Refusal: RP #3]: You hold a lease to a house and rent out the other rooms. One of your housemates wanted to hold a party on the weekend, but you have already scheduled painters to come over the weekend.

## Extract 6

*S4 = Beginning level JFL female (ten days in Japan)*

IL: Ano, I san ni tanomitai koto ga arun desu keredomo iidesu ka? Konshuu no doyoobi ni koko de *party* o shitai no desu kedo…
'I would like to ask you something. Is it OK? I want to plan a party here this Saturday…'

S4: Doyoobini mada aa…
'On Saturday…still…'

IL: Hai.
'Yes?…'

S4: Penkiya no…
'The painter…'

IL: A, penkiya san ga kurun desu ka?
'Oh, is a painter coming?'

S4: Hai.
'Yes.'

IL: A, soonan desu ka. Ja, ano raishuu no doyoobi wa doo desu ka?
'Oh, is that so? Then, how about next Saturday?'

S4: Etto…raishuu no doyoobi wa… anata no heya *carpet*…
'Aa…next Saturday… your room…carpet…'

IL: A, *carpet*-ya san. Hai, wakari mashita. Jaa, nichiyoobi.
'Oh, a carpet worker. Yes, I understand. Then Sunday.'

## Extract 7

*S5 = Beginning level JSL male (2 years experiences living and working in Japan)*

IL: Ee, konshuu no doyoobi ni desu
'Um..this coming Saturday,

Ne, koko de *party* o shitai no desu kedo iidesu ka?
I would like to plan a party here. Is it OK?'

S5: Chotto…raishuu desu ka?
'Well [hedge]..next week?

[*repetition of Request*]

IL: Konshuu.
'This week.'

S5: Konshuu no doyoobi wa chotto… muzukashii to omoimasu kedo… *painter* to *carpet* ya san, koko ni kimasu.
'This Saturday.. "*chotto*" [*hedge*] I think [*subjectivizer*] it is difficult [*roundabout*] because a painter and a carpet worker will come here. [*grounder*]'

IL: A, soo nan desuka…
'Oh, I see.'

Both S4 and S5 were in the same beginning Japanese course at ICU, where they were placed strictly on the basis of their placement test scores (a three-hour aural comprehension, grammar, vocabulary, and reading including KANJI tests). Their speech act realizations (for Refusals) seem to be strikingly different. S4 (JFL) was not able to use clear refusal strategies (except for supplying words) and depended totally on oral interpretation by the interlocutor. On the other hand, S5 (JSL) used head acts (e.g., repetition of part of request *Raishuu desu ka?*, hedging or *chotto*, grounder or giving the reason of his refusal, *painter to carpet ya san, kokoni kimasu*), modification (subjectivizer, *…to omoimasu…*, or *I think* and *kedo…* or *but*), and explanation of state of difficulty of accepting the interlocutor's request (i.e., S5 said *…muzukashii…* or *it is difficult* upon the interlocutor's request *…iidesuka?* or *May I…/Can I…?*). He did not answer using a strict word such as *No* in refusing the interlocutor's request for permission, but rather avoided it and used a roundabout strategy with the expression *muzukashii*, or *difficult*. He rather successfully refused the interlocutor's request in a sophisticated way, or very indirect way, as most native Japanese would do as reported by Clancy (1986) and Beebe and Takahashi (1989). S5 had worked at a local municipal office in the countryside of Japan for two years. Even though his general Japanese proficiency was labeled *Beginning*, based on his placement test scores, his pragmatic ability certainly made him different from JFL beginners who had had little or no experience living in Japan.

The above examples indicate that the experience of living in a target culture may affect the pragmatic oral production competence. It also coincides with the claim of Wagner-Gough and Hatch (1975) that it is the interactions that learners engage in which shape their language and determine their language development.

The three LEVEL groups were Beginning, Intermediate, and Advanced learners, which turned out to be significantly different ($p<.01$) on three tests of pragmatics: the OPDCT, RP, and LL. These three tests were the only production tests of the six pragmatics tests, and were also those scored by native raters. These results may indicate that the pragmatic production tests, either oral (the RP and LL tests) or written (the OPDCT), may tend to be related to general level of language proficiency. There are two interpretations of the above claim (i.e., that the three proficiency level groups were significantly different on the three pragmatics tests of production). First, this result may indicate that the raters' scores tend to correspond closely to a participants' linguistic skills even though the raters' manual suggested they overlook grammatical errors and usage. Actually, a couple of raters confessed to the researcher that they rated those participants lower who performed poorly in grammar even though they were told not to count the grammatical errors in their rating. This coincides with Bachman and Palmer's (1982) suggestion that the language components of grammatical and pragmatic competence are closely associated with each other.

Second, the overall proficiency level of the participants may fundamentally affect their acquisition of pragmatic competence. Most of the beginners may have difficulty in formulating sophisticated syntax and expressions which affect the rating on such categories as expressions, formality, and politeness (see rating sheet in Hudson, Detmer, and Brown, 1995, p. 169, or the Japanese translation version in Appendixes M and L respectively). Figure 3 shows the mean scores of each level on the three pragmatic production tests.

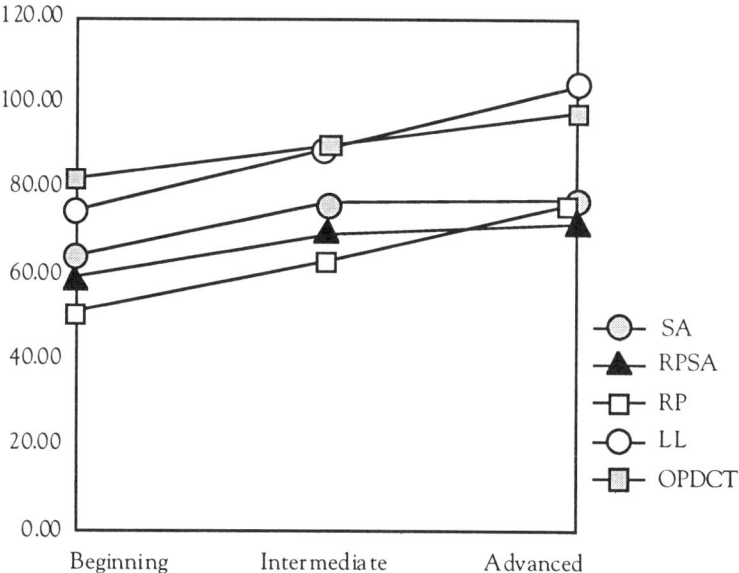

Figure 3: Means by levels for the SA, RPSA, RP, LL, and OPDCT

Notice that the lines in Figure 3 for the LL test and the RP test are parallel, with the LL test score means for each level about 20 points higher. However, the line for the OPDCT crosses the line for the LL test (i.e., the mean score of Beginning level on the OPDCT was the highest of all the tests, but the OPDCT scores for the Intermediate and Advanced levels were second highest — in fact, the LL test scores were the highest in both Intermediate and Advanced levels). It may be difficult for the participants to describe delicate pragmatic expressions in a paper-and-pencil format. For instance, one rater (Rater 2) reported that she found that the same expression may give a different impression to the hearer. She had the impression that one participant was being rude because a written expression on the OPDCT was too blunt. But afterward, she recognized that the same expression in one of the tapes (on the LL test) sounded very emotional and polite with appropriate intonation. (Although, she did not know if the expressions on the LL and OPDCT tests were produced by the same participant since all the names on the OPDCT given to the raters were anonymous). She further reported that there were also occasions when the reverse was true (i.e., the OPDCT made a good impression, but the same expression sounded inappropriate to the rater when it was said poorly on the tape in the LL test).

Moreover, the non-significance of differences on the two self-assessment tests (i.e., the SA, and RPSA) is not surprising. This result may indicate that the learners were able to assess themselves regardless of their levels of proficiency. (Thus there would be no significant differences by LEVEL or CULTURE.) Figure 3 further shows the relationship of means for the SA, RPSA, and the RP test at each level. Note that the RP test scores were given by raters, whereas the SA and RPSA test scores were given by the participants themselves and that both the RPSA and RP scores were based on the same roleplay performances.

It is interesting that the participants' self-assessment SA and the RPSA test scores are so parallel (the SA test scores were higher for every level group). What is also interesting is that the RP scores given to Advanced level participants were highest of all whereas the RP scores given to Beginning and Intermediate were the lowest of all tests (i.e., the SA and RPSA tests rated by participants). There are two possible reasons for this interaction: (a) the advanced level learners may have high expectations or goals to achieve, so they were not satisfied with their own performances and underrated themselves on both the SA and RPSA tests, and/or (b) learners of Japanese may become modest like the Japanese themselves as their levels of Japanese language increase (i.e., they may have picked up the Japanese tendency to be modest about their own performance skills), and tend to underrate their own performances (see Yamashita, 1996a, 1996b). If case (a) is true, it would be interesting to find out what advanced level learners of other foreign languages, especially western languages, would say in the same situations. If advanced learners of other foreign languages also underrate their performance, it could be said that advanced language learners are likely to underrate their performance in any target language. The reason might be that their expectations are too high. In fact, Blanche (1988) also reported the same phenomenon (see chapter 2, *Self-assessment and Roleplay self-assessment*). On the other hand, if (b) is true, it would be interesting to find out whether or not Japanese native speakers really are significantly more modest about their skills when compared to the self-assessments of other native speakers (i.e., Do they underrate their ability in foreign language competence, as well as their skills in sports, etc.?). Also, it would be helpful to get the results of a questionnaire which asks participants if there were occasions when they felt they should be modest in Japanese society or culture, and whether they have actually done so in practice.

The non-significant results for mean differences on the MCDCT present a different problem. These results indicate either (a) all learners could tell the differences of levels of different speech acts at least receptively, or (b) the formats of the questions or options were not appropriate. The latter seems to be more likely in light of the low internal consistency reliability estimates presented in Table 3. As pointed out earlier in this chapter, culture-specific strategies such as "dismay" when apologizing, or "implying" (e.g., "it is difficult...") when refusing seem to be used often in such speech acts in Japanese, but such options were not included in the multiple-choice items of the MCDCT. Also, as the raters reported, the tone, intonation, pauses between utterances, and non-verbal behaviors all played important parts in the realization of the speech acts studied here. Even in the paper-and-pencil OPDCT, some participants implied the inclusion of hesitation in their speech by adding ellipses as in refusing, *chotto isogashii...sumimasenga...* or *I am a little bit busy... Sorry...* (Intermediate JSL-Male), or apologizing, *ano... sumimasen... chotto iinikui kotoga arundesuga...* "[omit the rest]" or *Umm... I am sorry... it's a little bit hard to say, but...* (Advanced JSL-Male). The multiple-choice options on the current MCDCT were written in a much more straightforward manner, with direct, flowing sentences which lacked such elements.

## PRACTICALITY ISSUES

Research question 4 focused on differences in *practicality* between test formats for measuring the pragmatic competence of English learners of Japanese. Table 23 in chapter 5 shows a summary of variables related to practicality.

The SA and RPSA tests can be administered in the learner's native language (in this case, English), requiring relatively little testing time. Both tests can also be administered in a paper-and-pencil format, and no preparation or rater scoring are necessary. In contrast, learners spent more than an hour completing the MCDCT and an equal amount of time finishing the OPDCT. While the SA and MCDCT require only marking answers on a sheet and the RPSA only requires marking a sheet while watching their own roleplays, the OPDCT, LL and RP tests elicit actual language production and thus necessitate that raters judge the participants' productive language performances. These last three tests require making the arrangements necessary to get ratings, that is, scheduling, training, or instructing the raters on how to rate the data. The rating process may also involve paying money to raters.

Another consideration is that the LL and RP tests require audio equipment (a tape-recorder and tapes for the LL test, and a video camera and a VCR for the RP test). Moreover, the RP test requires an interlocutor to interact with each participant, which also involves the scheduling of both the participant and the interlocutor, and payment for the interlocutor. In addition, transcription of the LL and RP data is helpful for analysis (although not indispensable).

To conclude this discussion, if all other variables (such as reliability, validity, and so forth) are held constant, the most practical test seems to be the SA test. However, it is important to remember that, in this study, the SA test was presented to the participants as a "task" as a part of the research study, so the conditions may change if it was given as a "test." For instance, if the SA test was given as a placement test, or one of the tests which would be used for a course grade, the results might be completely different. However, the SA test probably could be used for diagnostic purposes or to increase students' attention or motivation with regard to pragmatics issues in the second or foreign language learning.

The least practical test seems to be the RP test because it takes time, and it requires an interlocutor and raters, as well as equipment such as a video camera, videotape, and so forth and a room for videotaping. However, the RP test elicited the results closest to natural and authentic interactions. The reliability of the RP in this study was very high and the variance was large (which indicates that the RP test differentiates beginners well from the advanced learners). Hence, the RP could be used for proficiency testing of pragmatics or could function as part of instructional materials for students by giving them opportunities to watch their own performances and get feedback and guidance.

The LL test seemed to provide similar results to those found on the RP, at least in this study. In addition, the LL is easier to administer because it does not require an interlocutor. However, the language produced on the LL is probably not as natural as that produced on the RP.

The OPDCT is basically a written version of the LL test. This test is also easy to administer because of its paper-and-pencil format and because it requires no special equipment or interlocutor. Perhaps this ease of administration is why so many previous studies used this method.

However, we have to be careful in deciding which test is the most appropriate one. The decision should be based on the purpose of the test and the conditions under which it will be administered, as well as the considerations of reliability, parallel forms, and validity discussed above.

# CHAPTER 7: CONCLUSION

## SUMMARY OF FINDINGS

This study investigated whether there were differences among test formats for measuring the cross-cultural pragmatic competence of English speaking learners of Japanese. A total of six direct and indirect, and open-response and selected-response type tests were studied using the data of forty-seven North American English speaking learners of Japanese as a second or foreign language (JSL and JFL respectively). All of the six tests except for the multiple-choice discourse completion test (MCDCT) were found to be reasonably reliable and valid in one way or another. The results indicate that cross-cultural pragmatic measures (excluding the MCDCT) developed originally in English by Hudson, Detmer, and Brown (1992, 1995) for testing cross-cultural pragmatics of learners of English as a second or foreign language can also be used with other populations to study other target languages (i.e., Japanese in this study) with a few minor adjustments in some of the situations.

Moreover, the participants' length of exposure to the target culture appears to be associated with performance on two of the pragmatic oral production tests (the LL and the RP). The participants' levels of proficiency seem to be more closely associated with the three production tests (the OPDCT, LL, and RP tests). Practicality was discussed from various angles. It was suggested that each test has strengths and weaknesses, and that the decision as to which test to use should be based on the purpose of the test along with the desired levels of reliability and validity.

## LIMITATIONS

### TEST ITEMS

The tests in this study were developed as prototype measures of cross-cultural pragmatics. Three speech acts (requests, apologies, and refusals) were selected, and the test items were carefully specified and developed. However, as Austin (1962) estimated, there are somewhere between 1,000 and 10,000 illocutionary forces or speech acts in English. Flowerdew (1990) provides another theoretical overview on the issue, but whatever the number of speech act possibilities in the overall taxonomy, they will most certainly not merge into three speech acts. Thus, even though the current tests were designed to be a basic model for cross-cultural pragmatic measures, the area which these tests can cover is limited.

Also, all of the six tests investigated in this study dealt with assessment or production of the participants' own pragmatic performances based on their understanding of the cross-cultural pragmatics of a target language including what they would say in the situation. These tests do not test perception or comprehension of the cross-cultural pragmatics of the target language or culture. Perception of the pragmatics of a target culture or getting an understanding of what a native speaker is saying is another important facet of pragmatics, since a serious discrepancy would occur in communication if the participants failed to understand the correct meaning or pragmatic function of a native speaker's utterances. Hence, development of some sort of test to measure perception of cross-cultural pragmatics is as important as the present development of measures of pragmatic production.

## PARTICIPANTS

Another limitation of this study is that it had a variety of participants (see chapter 4), who were all volunteers for the study. As a result, their reasons for participation might have been varied. For instance, some may have been interested in participating in the research even though they were not told what the research was about or what it was for; others may have expected to learn something new in Japanese and improve their Japanese skills; others may have wanted to show good will and help their Japanese teacher (this researcher); while still others may only have been interested in the money that they were being paid. In any case, it would have been extremely difficult to use random samples for this study because the cooperation of the participants was essential since the tests were complex and time-consuming. Reasonably, educational institutions are typically not willing to sacrifice too many class hours for an individual's research.

Another problem with the participants was that an imbalance in the numbers of JFL and JSL participants developed (13 vs. 34, respectively). It was more difficult to find the JFL participants in Japan because the JFL group was defined for this study as participants who had lived in Japan in less than a month after their arrival in Japan for the first time. Such people are relatively rare compared to the JSL type.

## DATA

The pilot study (which involved administering the LL, RP, and OPDCT tests to native Japanese speakers) indicated some mismatches in the Japanese speech act strategies and situations from the original English scenarios. However, the number of mismatches was limited, and the decision was made to basically use a translated version of the English pragmatic measures. Five of the pragmatics tests (i.e., the SA, LL, OPDCT, RP, and RPSA) worked well under these conditions. However, the MCDCT was problematic as already pointed out in previous chapters. One of the problems was that strategies that were not represented in the MCDCT were used in the LL, OPDCT, and RP tests not only by JSL participants from all levels but also by the native Japanese speakers. Authentic Japanese language data should have been studied, and the MCDCT should have been adapted or revised based on both the pilot data and authentic data.

Also, this study would have been stronger if retrospective interviews had been conducted with the participants. Given that the self-assessment tests were found to be highly reliable, it would probably have been informative and interesting to find out how the participants went about assessing the appropriateness of their own pragmatic performances. Such interviews, however, were not possible in this study because the participants were already required to take six time-consuming pragmatics tests and a cloze proficiency test.

# STRENGTHS OF THE STUDY

## PARTICIPANTS

Participants in many existing cross-cultural pragmatics studies were university students. Since pragmatic comprehension and production are related to pragmalinguistic (i.e., "how learners understand nonliteral utterances, both in terms of propositional content and illocutionary force assignment, and how they assess the politeness value of conventions of means and form," according to Kasper, in press) and sociopragmatic (i.e., "how learners perceive variables in the social context and in the linguistic act itself," Kasper, in press) issues, experience with social interactions is important even for native speakers to perform pragmatics appropriately. This issue is taken so seriously in Japanese society that many companies send their new young employees (who have entered their company right after finishing university education) to special training camps where the young employees learn social conventions such as how to speak properly to their seniors or outsiders, how to talk on the phone, and so forth. Thus, university students may not be the best sample for a pragmatics studies because they may lack social experience. In contrast with many other studies, the research reported here included many professions besides university students. The range of ages was wide (between 18 and 49), and the length of stay in the target culture was also varied as was the participants' levels of proficiency (from beginners to near-native advanced learners). Additionally, the numbers of each gender were fairly balanced in this study (25 males and 22 females). Naturally, people who were older, and had lived or had work experience in the target culture longer, and so forth had more chances to learn or acquire pragmatic competence in the target language. A sample like the one in this study which generates high variance on a variety of variables is very unique among the pragmatics studies to date. Overall, the variables and participants in this study may well represent the real world more than previous studies.

## DATA COLLECTION

Although seven participants were eliminated from the final analysis due to missing data (tests that they did not take), the data of the remaining 47 participants were almost perfectly complete. Each participant had twenty-four situations in each test which had a total of 144 speech act variations (24 x 6 tests) and 72 speech act production samples (24 x 3 production tests, i.e., the LL, OPDCT, and RP tests) per participant. Since there were 47 participants in this study, the total speech act samples produced by the participants which were available for investigation were 3,384 (72 x 47). Of the 3,384 samples, only two samples were missing from the formal data collection sessions. One was missing from a roleplay video by one participant. However, an audio-tape backup had been made, so the missing speech act was recovered (it happened to be *sumimasen* or *I'm sorry*). Also, one participant skipped one speech act from his LL test recorded on audio-tape. Since he had already gone back to San Francisco at the time this error was discovered, the researcher made a long-distance telephone call, and recorded the sample once again on the telephone.

The examples above are a couple of unique cases which needed follow-up. Overall, the data collection was well-planned, largely because of much appreciated advice from the original group of researchers at the University of Hawai'i at Mānoa (Hudson et al. 1995). Both the variety of participants and the richness of the data contributed to the effectiveness of the statistical results and the success of this research project.

# PEDAGOGICAL IMPLICATIONS

## HOW CAN THESE TESTS BE USED IN THE CLASSROOM?

When we discuss the application of pragmatics tests in the classroom, we have to be careful to match appropriate tests to different types of decisions that we make for different purposes. In order to do that, we should understand what kinds of tests are available for classroom level decisions like diagnosis and achievement as well as for institution level decisions like proficiency and placement. Brown (1996) discussed four types of decisions for language tests (i.e., proficiency test, placement test, achievement test, and diagnostic test). He first presented two categories of tests: (a) norm-referenced tests, or NRTs (in which the interpretations are relative, general language abilities are measured, normal distributions of scores around a mean are expected, a variety of question contents are used, and the content of the test is not predictable), and (b) criterion-referenced tests, or CRTs (in which interpretations are absolute, specific objectives-based language points are measured, the amount of material learned by each student is assessed, non-normal distributions may be expected, the tests may consist of a series of short, well-defined subtests, and students know what content to expect in test questions). According to Brown (1996), proficiency tests and placement tests are categorized as NRTs, and achievement tests and diagnostic tests are categorized as CRTs. Proficiency tests are used to assess the students' general levels of language proficiency or skills prerequisite to entry or exit from an institution, or for administrative decisions like admissions decisions. According to Brown (1996, pp. 9–15), placement tests are used for grouping students of similar ability levels together. In contrast, achievement tests are usually administered at the end of a course to determine how effectively students have mastered the instructional objectives, while diagnostic tests are aimed at assessing the strengths and weaknesses of each individual student in order to determine the degree to which the specific instructional objectives of the course have been accomplished, or needing more work.

Table 25 summarizes this researcher's suggestions for matching each type of pragmatics test with the four types of decisions discussed above. Each of the six pragmatics tests will now be discussed in more detail. The self-assessment, the one in which participants answer with how well they think they would say whatever is required in each situation, only took about 10 minutes on average, which is a short period of time in comparison with the other tests. The participants did not produce any sentences, yet the results were very reliable. This sort of test may well be useful for formative evaluation or placement test purposes within JSL/JFL programs. The SA test also raises the learners awareness about issues related to pragmatics. For instance, if a question asks how students would rate their L2 competence in a situation where they have lost a book borrowed from the boss, the students may be seriously thinking about such a situation in the target language for the first time.

### Table 25: Matching tests

| Tests of pragmatics | Norm Referenced | | Criterion Referenced | |
|---|---|---|---|---|
| | Proficiency | Placement | Achievement | Diagnostic |
| SA | – | – | – | X+ |
| LL[1] | X | X | X | X+ |
| OPDCT[2] | X | X | X | X+ |
| RP[3] | X | X | X | X+ |
| RPSA | – | – | – | X+ |
| MCDCT[4] | X | X | X | X |

– : not recommended
X+: recommended
X: usable with care, but not the best choice for reasons presented below and referenced in the table:
  [1] time consuming for scoring; raters necessary; equipment necessary
  [2] time consuming for scoring; raters necessary; not oral
  [3] time consuming for scoring; raters necessary; interlocutor necessary; equipment necessary
  [4] not oral; not actual production; reported problematic in this study in terms of reliability

The RPSA test is another self-assessment test, but in this case the participants rate their actual performance in a roleplay. The scores on the RPSA were systematically lower than the SA at all three levels of proficiency. Hopefully, knowing about and watching their own performances will motivate students to learn about pragmatics or at least to integrate pragmatics goals into their language learning processes.

The production tests (the LL, OPDCT, and RP tests) also more or less revealed the participants' actual performances. The results of these tests could be used for placement or diagnostic purposes as well as for research purposes. These tests also could also be used to help learners to become more aware of pragmatic language use. Moreover, such tests could be used for communicative classroom activities by applying pair-work or group-work in the classroom. They could even contribute to other aspects of language learning as sources for new language information.

My only concern about the further application of the current tests is that all the tests were introduced to the participants as "tasks" which were described as being used by the researcher, a doctoral candidate, to study American students learning Japanese in Japan. In other words, the participants did the tests voluntarily as part of a research project, not as tests for diagnostic or placement purposes. The results may have been somewhat different if the students had felt that the scores might be used to make decisions about their placement, about their grades, and so forth. For instance, if the SA test were used as, say, a placement test, it is not known whether the same results (i.e., high reliability, etc.) would be obtained because the participants might respond differently.

## CAN PRAGMATICS BE TAUGHT?

One issue that has been raised in the literature is whether the second language learner needs to possess speech acts equivalent to those which a native speaker possesses (Flowerdew, 1988). If speech acts were universal (Fraser, Rintell, and Walters, 1980), learning speech acts in a target language would be easy — the learners would simply learn the form needed to express a given speech act in the target language. However, it is not simply a matter of knowing the correct *form*. Although the CCSARP project coding scheme (Blum-Kulka, House, and Kasper, 1989b) gives almost the whole picture of request and apology strategies which are regarded as being universal, it has been pointed out in this study and elsewhere (Hudson, Detmer, and Brown, 1995; Ikoma and Shimura, 1993; Rose, 1992a; Wierzbicka, 1985, 1991) that there are also culture-specific speech act realization strategies which are not included in that coding scheme. It is important for the learner to be aware of the differences between universal speech acts and language specific speech acts if such differences exist. The necessity for teaching speech acts, especially culture- or language-specific speech acts will be discussed next in relation to the *pragmatic failure* issue.

The issue of pragmatic failure has been discussed at length (Thomas, 1983). Thomas (1983) defined *pragmatic failure* as "the inability to understand 'what is meant by what is said'." She argued that pragmalinguistic features, or highly conventionalized usage, can be taught straightforwardly as "part of the grammar." In other words, *pragmalinguistic failure* is a "linguistic problem caused by differences in the linguistic encoding of pragmatic force." Thus, such failures should be relatively easy to overcome.

In contrast, *sociopragmatics failure* is difficult to overcome because "it involves the student's system of beliefs, or cross-culturally different perceptions of what constitutes appropriate linguistic behavior" (Thomas, 1983). Communication breakdown due to pragmatics failure (both pragmalinguistic and sociopragmatics failures) may occur in both comprehension and production. Focusing on aspects of pragmatic knowledge through consciousness-raising activities and communicative practice would seem to facilitate language learning (Kasper and Schmidt, in press).

One strong tool for promoting consciousness-raising activities (and also for research purposes) is the use of audiovisual media. For instance, the National Language Research Institute of Japan recently developed a video series collection of short conversational exchanges which is very useful for studying certain aspects of the pragmatics of Japanese (Nishihara, 1996). A group of the National Language Research Institute showed the video to native speakers of Japanese and foreigners (from different cultural backgrounds who were studying the Japanese language) without the sound and compared how each conversational exchange was comprehended and how NSs and NNSs said they would react linguistically (Nishihara, 1996). For example, in one scene, a young woman bumped into a middle-aged woman in a passage in an apartment building. The middle-aged woman said something (it looked like she criticized the young woman in the video) to the back of the young woman when the young woman left after bowing to the middle-aged woman. The questions given to the viewers were about what they think each woman said to the other, what they (the viewers) would have said if they were in the same situation, and so forth. Such a video could be used both for research purposes to study cross-cultural pragmatics and also for classroom activities that raise learners' consciousness about issues of pragmatics in the target culture.

## CAN PRAGMATICS BE ACQUIRED?

The essential issue here is whether or not pragmatic competence has an acquirable hierarchy of difficulty (in the way that some SLA studies claim to have found an order of acquisition for grammatical morphemes). Most of the interlanguage pragmatics studies focus on non-native speakers' second language use rather than second language learning based on native speaker norm (or how native speakers perform) (Kasper and Schmidt, in press).

There are actually three different conditions under which learners may have to deal with target language pragmatics: (a) the learner's native language does not have a pragmatic strategy similar to that found in the target language, (b) the learner's language does have an equivalent pragmatic strategy, but the function is different, or (c) the learner's language has exactly the same pragmatic strategy and function.

In the first case (a), the learner needs to be made aware of and acquire the strategy of the target language, and then learn the vocabulary and correct grammatical forms necessary to correctly realize the speech act. Such would be the case in learning to use the *dismay* strategy reported earlier in this study. The novice beginner who was reported in chapter 6 to have noticed the *dismay* strategy during her stay in the target culture (i.e., she learned the concept first), used it in the correct situation, although not with quite the right grammatical form. Some intermediate and advanced participants also used the *dismay* strategy correctly and did so in the correct form.

The second case (b) might be a potential case of negative transfer. An example is reported in Ikoma (1993) in which Japanese learners of English often say *I'm sorry* to express gratitude because a formulaic expression *sumimasen* is often used in such a case in Japanese and interpreted as apologetic "sorry."

In contrast, in the third case (c), where learners already have the same strategy and function (or repertoire for making the speech act realization) in their native language, they should easily learn the form and match the function. In this case, it really is just a simple matter of acquiring the form. In terms of the question addressed by this section (Can pragmatics be acquired?), it could be said that in cases (a) and (b) above, such cultural-specific strategies can possibly be taught after considerable investigation of the pragmatic differences between the two languages, and then those strategies may be acquired.

## SUGGESTIONS FOR FURTHER RESEARCH

### USING THE CURRENT DATA

Since the current study collected data using six pragmatic measures, various further investigation could be carried out.

*Combination of variables:* The current tests were constructed with three variables (Degree of Imposition, Power, and Distance) for three speech acts (requests, refusals, and apologies). In the analysis, correlation coefficients of plus and minus of each variable were studied. It was found that the plus and minus aspects of variables on each test were highly correlated. Further research might therefore be useful on what combinations of variables, such as that +Imposition and –Power together, or –Imposition and –Power are most effective.

*Item analysis:* Each test has 24 situations. There may be some situations which may not discriminate between beginners and advanced students, or between people who have pragmatic competence as opposed to people who do not. Such items could be eliminated and the test could be tailored to be more efficient.

*Study of raters' scoring:* Even though the rating sheet and the rating manual were used in order to conduct the study as objectively as possible, there still might be a possibility that the gender or age of raters and ratees may affect the resulting scores. Such relationships between raters and ratees based on gender, age, and so forth would be worth investigating.

*Qualitative study:* The three production tests (the LL, OPDCT, RP tests) provide rich data for qualitative study. Some possibilities are comparative studies of strategies (or politeness, or grammatical forms, etc.) of each speech act in terms of gender, level, age, differences between JSL and JFL, and so forth.

## FUTURE DIRECTIONS

Whether or not the cross-cultural pragmatics or interlanguage pragmatics are universal is still a big issue that researchers are investigating. While there seems to be variation in culture-specific speech act strategies, the majority of the speech acts still seem to be universal as the CCSARP suggested. Much further study is definitely needed in this area to clarify the issue once and for all.

Also, the use of correct speech acts in a target culture is very important for second language learners because the incorrect use of speech acts may cause serious problems of misunderstanding. Thus studying differences between the speech acts of different cultures and teaching speech acts in a target language both become very important. Various methods and media can be used for studying and teaching pragmatics. The author hopes that the pragmatics tests created and studied here will prove useful in the future for researchers, teachers, and testers in both Japanese as a second language and Japanese as a foreign language situations.

# REFERENCES

Austin, J. L. (1962). *How to do things with words*. Oxford: Oxford University Press.

Bachman, L. (1982). The trait structure of cloze test scores. *TESOL Quarterly 16*, 61–70.

Bachman, L. (1990). *Fundamental considerations in language testing*. Oxford: Oxford University Press.

Bachman, L. F., & Palmer, A. S. (1981). A multitrait-multimethod investigation into the construct validity of six tests of speaking and reading. In A. S. Palmer, P. J. M. Groot, & G. A. Trosper (Eds.), *The construct validation of tests of communicative competence* (pp. 149–165). Washington: TESOL.

Bachman, L. F., & Palmer, A. S. (1982). The construct validation of some components of communicative proficiency. *TESOL Quarterly, 16*, 449–466.

Bachman, L. F., & Palmer, A. S. (1989). The construct validity of self-ratings of communicative language ability. *Language Testing, 6*, 15–29.

Beebe, L. M., & Takahashi, T. (1989). Sociolinguistic variation in face-threatening speech acts: Chastisement and disagreement. In M. R. Eisenstein (Ed.), *The dynamic interlanguage: Empirical studies in second language variation* (pp. 199–218). New York: Plenum.

Beebe, L. M., Takahashi, T., & Uliss-Weltz, R. (1990). Pragmatic transfer in ESL refusals. In R. C. Scarcella, E. Andersen, & S. D. Krashen (Eds.), *Developing communicative competence in a second language* (pp. 55–73). Rowley, MA: Newbury House.

Bergman, M. L., & Kasper, G. (1993). Perception and performance in native and nonnative apology. In G. Kasper, & S. Blum-Kulka (Eds.), *Interlanguage pragmatics* (pp. 82–107). Oxford: Oxford University Press.

Bialystok, E. (1993). Symbolic representation and attentional control in pragmatics competence. In G. Kasper, & S. Blum-Kulka (Eds.), *Interlanguage Pragmatics* (pp. 43–58). Oxford: Oxford University Press.

Blanche, P. (1988). Self-assessment of foreign language skills: implications for teachers and researchers. *RELC Journal, 19* (1), 75–96.

Blum-Kulka, S. (1982). Learning to say what you mean in a second language: A study of speech act performance of learners of Hebrew as a second language. *Applied Linguistics, 3* (1), 29–59.

Blum-Kulka, S. (1983). Interpreting and performing speech acts in a second language: A cross-cultural study of Hebrew and English. In N. Wolfson, & E. Judd (Eds.), *Sociolinguistics and second language acquisition* (pp. 36–55). Rawley, MA: Newbury House.

Blum-Kulka, S. (1989). Playing it safe: The role of conventionality in indirectness. In S. Blum-Kulka, J. House, & G. Kasper (Eds.), *Cross-cultural pragmatics: Requests and apologies* (pp. 37–70). Norwood, NJ: Ablex.

Blum-Kulka, S. (1991). Interlanguage pragmatics: The case of request. In R. Phillipson, E. Kellerman, L. Selinker, M. Sharwood Smith, & M. Swain (Eds.), *Foreign and second language pedagogy research* (pp. 255–272). Clevedon, UK: Multilingual Matters.

Blum-Kulka, S., & House, J. (1989). Variation in requesting behavior. In S. Blum-Kulka, J. House, & G. Kasper (Eds.), *Cross-cultural Pragmatics: Requests and apologies* (pp. 123–154). Norwood, NJ: Ablex.

Blum-Kulka, S., House, J., & Kasper, G. (1989a). Investigating cross-cultural pragmatics: An introductory overview. In S. Blum-Kulka, J. House, & G. Kasper (Eds.), *Cross-cultural Pragmatics: Requests and apologies* (pp. 1–34). Norwood, NJ: Ablex.

Blum-Kulka, S., House, J., & Kasper, G. (1989s). (Eds.), *Cross-cultural Pragmatics: Requests and apologies*. Norwood, NJ: Ablex.

Blum-Kulka, S., & Olshtain, E. (1985). Degree of approximation: Nonnative reactions to native speech act behavior. In S. M. Gass, & C. G. Madden (Eds.), *Input in second language acquisition* (pp. 303–325). Rowley, MA: Newbury House.

Blum-Kulka, S., & Olshtain, E. (1986). Too many words: Length of utterance and pragmatic failure. *Studies in Second Language Acquisition, 8,* 47–61.

Brown, J. D. (1980). Relative merits of four methods for scoring cloze tests. *Modern Language Journal, 64,* 311–317.

Brown, J. D. (1983). A closer look at cloze: Validity and reliability. In J. W. Oller, Jr. (Ed.), *Issues in language testing* (pp. 237–250). Cambridge, MA: Newbury House.

Brown, J. D. (1988). *Understanding research in second language learning: A teacher's guide to statistics and research design.* London: Cambridge University Press.

Brown, J. D. (1996). *Testing in language programs.* Upper Saddle River, NJ: Prentice Hall Regents.

Brown, P., & Levinson, S. (1987). *Politeness: Some universals in language usage.* Cambridge: Cambridge University Press.

Campbell, D. T., & Fiske, D. W. (1959). Convergent and discriminant validation by the multitrait-multimethod matrix. *Psychological Bulletin, 56,* 81–105.

Campbell, R., & Wales, R. (1970). The study of language acquisition. In J. Lyons (Ed.), *New horizons in linguistics.* Harmondsworth: Penguin Books.

Canale, M. (1988). From communicative competence to communicative language pedagogy. In J. C. Richards, & R. W. Schmidt (Eds.), *Language and communication* (pp. 2–28). London: Longman.

Canale, M., & Swain, M. (1980). Theoretical bases of communicative approaches to second language teaching and testing. *Applied Linguistics, 1,* 1–47.

Chavez-Oller, M.A., Chihara, T., Weaver, K., & Oller, Jr., J. W. (1985). When are cloze items sensitive to constraints across sentences? *Language Learning, 35* (1), 181–206.

Chomsky, N. (1965). *Aspects of the theory of syntax.* Cambridge, MA: MIT Press.

Clancy, P. (1986). The acquisition of communicative style in Japanese. In B. Schieffelin, & E. Ochs (Eds.), *Language socialization across cultures* (pp. 213–250). Cambridge: Cambridge University Press.

Cohen, A. D., & Olshtain, E. (1981). Developing a measure of sociocultural competence: The case of apology. *Language Learning, 31* (1), 113–134.

Cohen, A. D., & Olshtain, E. (1993). The production of speech acts by EFL learners. *TESOL Quarterly, 27* (1), 33–56.

Cohen, A. D., & Olshtain, E. (1994). Researching the production of second-language speech acts. In E. Tarone, S. Gass, & A. Cohen (Eds.), *Research methodology in second-language acquisition* (pp. 143–156). Hillsdale, NJ: Lawrence Erlbaum Associations.

Cohen, A. D., Olshtain, E., & Rosenstein, D. (1986). Advanced EFL apologies: What remains to be learned? *International Journal of the Sociology and Language, 62,* 51–74.

Davidson, F., & Henning, G. (1985). A self-rating scale of English difficulty. *Language Testing, 2,* 164–179.

Eckard, R., & Kearny, M. A. (1981). Teaching conversation skills in ESL. *Language education: Theory and practice, 38.* Washington, DC: Center for Applied Linguistics.

Edmondson, W., & House, J. (1991). Do learners talk too much? The waffle phenomenon in interlanguage pragmatics. In R. Phillipson, E. Kellerman, L. Selinker, M. Sharwood Smith, & M. Swain (Eds.), *Foreign/second language pedagogy research* (pp. 273–286). Clevedon, UK: Multilingual Matters.

Edmondson, W., House, J., Kasper, G., & Stemmer, B. (1984). Learning the pragmatics of discourse, *Applied Linguistics, 5,* 113–127.

Eisenstein, M., & Bodman, J. (1993). Expressing gratitude in American English. In G. Kasper, & S. Blum-Kulka (Eds.), *Interlanguage pragmatics* (pp. 64–81). Oxford: Oxford University Press.

Faerch, C., & Kasper, G. (1986). The role of comprehension in second-language learning. *Applied Linguistics 7* (3), 257–274.

Faerch, C., & Kasper, G. (1989). Internal and external modification in interlanguage request realization. In S. Blum-Kulka, J. House, & G. Kasper (Eds.), *Cross-cultural pragmatics: Requests and apologies* (pp. 221–247). Norwood, NJ: Ablex.

Fiksdal, S. (1989). Framing uncomfortable moments in cross-cultural gatekeeping interviews. In S. Gass, C. Madden, D. Preston, & L. Selinker (Eds.), *Variation in second language acquisition: Discourse and pragmatics* (pp. 190–207). Clevedon, UK: Multilingual Matters.

Flowerdew, J. (1988). Speech acts and language teaching. *Language Teaching, 21* (2), 69–82.

Flowerdew, J. (1990). Problems of speech act theory from an applied perspective. *Language Learning, 40* (1), 79–105.

Fraser, B. (1990). Perspectives on politeness. *Journal of Pragmatics, 14,* 219–236.

Fraser, B., Rintell, E., & Walters, J. (1980). An approach to conducting research on the acquisition of pragmatic competence in a second language. In D. Larsen-Freeman (Ed.), *Discourse analysis in second language research* (pp. 75–91). Rowley, MA: Newbury House.

Gass, S. (1987). The resolution of conflicts among competing systems: A bidirectional perspective. *Applied Psycholinguistics, 8*, 329–350.

Gass, S. (1990). Second and foreign language learning: Same, different or none of the above? In B. Van Patten, & J. F. Lee (Eds.), *Second language acquisition/Foreign language learning* (pp. 34–44). Clevedon, UK: Multilingual Matters.

Gumperz, J. J. (1972). Introduction. In J. J. Gumperz, & D. Hymes (Eds.), *Directions in Sociolinguistics* (pp. 1–25). New York: Holt, Rinehart and Winston.

Gumperz, J. J. (1978). The conversational analysis of interethnic communication. In E. L. Ross (Ed.), *Interethnic communication: Proceedings of the Southern anthropological society*. In R. C. Scarcella, E. S. Andersen, & S. D. Krashen (Eds.), (pp. 223–238). New York: Newbury House.

Hartford, B. S., & Bardovi-Harlig, K. (1992). Experimental and observational data in the study of interlanguage pragmatics. *Pragmatics and Language Learning Monograph Series, 3*. 33–52.

Hartford, B. S., & Bardovi-Harlig, K. (1996). "At your earliest convenience:" A study of written student requests to faculty. *Pragmatics and Language Learning Monograph Series, 7*. 55–69.

House, J. (1989). Politeness in English and German: The functions of please and *bitte*. In S. Blum-Kulka, J. House, & G. Kasper (Eds.), *Cross-cultural Pragmatics: Requests and apologies* (pp. 96–119). Norwood, NJ: Ablex.

House, J., & Kasper, G. (1987). Interlanguage pragmatics: Requesting in a foreign language. In W. Lorscher, & R. Schulze (Ed.), *Perspectives on language and performance* (pp. 250–88). Tubingen, Germany: Narr.

Hudson, T., Detmer, E., & Brown, J. D. (1992). *A framework for testing cross-cultural pragmatics*. Technical Report (2). Honolulu: University of Hawai'i, Second Language Teaching and Curriculum Center.

Hudson, T., Detmer, E., & Brown, J. D. (1995). *Developing prototypic measures of cross-cultural pragmatics*. Technical Report (7). Honolulu: University of Hawai'i, Second Language Teaching and Curriculum Center.

Hymes, D. (1972). On communicative competence. In J. B. Pride, & J. Holmes (Eds.), *Sociolinguistics* (pp. 269–93). Harmondsworth: Penguin.

Ide, S. (1989). Formal forms and discernment: Two neglected aspects of universals of linguistic politeness. *Multilingua, 8*, 223–248.

Ikeguchi, C. (1995). Cloze testing options in the classroom. In J. D. Brown, & S. O. Yamashita (Eds.), *Language testing in Japan* (pp. 166–178). Tokyo: The Japan Association for Language Teaching.

Ikoma, T. (1993). *Sorry for giving me a ride: The use of apologetic expressions to show gratitude in Japanese.* Unpublished master's thesis, the University of Hawai'i at Mānoa, Honolulu.

Ikoma, T., & Shimura, A. (1993). Eigo kara nihongo eno *pragmatic transfer:* "Kotowari" to iu hatsuwa kooi ni tsuite [Pragmatic transfer from English to Japanese: The speech act of refusals]. *Nihongo Kyoiku [Japanese Language Education], 79,* 41–52.

Johnston, B., Kasper, G., & Ross, S. (1993a). Effect of rejoinders in production questionnaires. University of Hawai'i Working Paper in ESL, 13–1, University of Hawai'i at Mānoa, Honolulu.

Johnston, B., Kasper, G., & Ross, S. (1993b, August). Questionnaires as data collecting instruments in interlanguage pragmatics. Paper presented at the meeting of AILA, Amsterdam, Holland.

Jonz, J. (1987). Textual cohesion and second-language comprehension. *Language Learning, 37,* 409–438.

Jonz, J. (1990). Another turn in the conversation: What does cloze measure? *TESOL Quarterly, 24* (1), 61–83.

Kashiwazaki, H. (1993). Hanashikake Kodo no danwabunseki: Irai [Conversational analysis of starting to talk: Request]. *Nihongo Kyoiku [Japanese Language Education], 79,* 53–63.

Kasper, G. (1984). Pragmatic comprehension in learner-native speaker discourse. *Language Learning, 34,* 1–20.

Kasper, G. (1989). Variation in interlanguage speech act realisation. S. Gass, C. Madden, D. Preston, & L. Selinker (Eds.), *Variation in second language acquisition: Discourse and pragmatics* (pp. 37–58). Clevedon, UK: Multilingual Matters.

Kasper, G. (Ed.). (1992). *Pragmatics of Japanese as native and target language.* Technical Report (3). Honolulu: University of Hawai'i, Second Language Teaching and Curriculum Center.

Kasper, G. (in press). Interlanguage pragmatics. In H. Byrnes (Ed.). *Perspectives on research and scholarship in second language learning.* Modern Language Association.

Kasper, G., & Blum-Kulka, S. (Eds.). (1993). *Interlanguage pragmatics.* New York: Oxford University Press.

Kasper, G., & Dahl, M. (1991). Research methods in interlanguage pragmatics. *Studies in Second Language Acquisition, 13,* 215–247.

Kasper, G., & Schmidt, R. (in press). Developmental issues in interlanguage pragmatics. *Studies in Second Language Acquisition, 18* (2).

LeBlanc, R., & Painchaud, G. (1985). Self-assessment as a second language placement instrument. *TESOL Quarterly, 19* (4), 673–687.

Lebra, T. (1976). *Japanese patterns of behavior.* Honolulu: University of Hawai'i Press.

Leech, G. (1983). *Principles of Pragmatics*. Harlow: Longman.

Niki, H., & Tajika, H. (1994). Asking for permission vs. making requests: Strategies chosen by Japanese speakers of English. *Pragmatics and Language Learning Monograph Series, 5,* 110–124.

Nishihara, S. (1996, February). *Research frameworks for cross-cultural, cross-lingual contact*. Paper read for the 18th research meeting, The Research Center for Japanese Language Education and the Japanese Language Program, International Christian University, Tokyo.

Olshtain, E. (1983). Sociocultural competence and language transfer: The case of apology. In S. Gass & L. Selinker (Eds.), *Language transfer in language learning* (pp. 232–249). Rowley, MA: Newbury House.

Olshtain, E. (1989). Apologies across languages. In S. Blum-Kulka, J. House, & G. Kasper (Eds.), *Cross-cultural Pragmatics: Requests and apologies* (pp. 155–173). Norwood, NJ: Ablex.

Olshtain, E. (1996, February). Lecture delivered in the Distinguished Lecture Series at the Temple University Japan, Tokyo.

Olshtain, E., & Blum-Kulka, S. (1985). Cross-cultural pragmatics and the testing of communicative competence. *Language Testing, 2,* 16–30.

Olshtain, E., & Cohen, A. (1983). Apology: A speech-act set. In N. Wolfson, & E. Judd (Eds.), *Sociolinguistics and language acquisition* (pp. 18–35). Rowley, MA: Newbury House.

Olshtain, E., & Weinbach, L. (1987). Complaints: A study of speech act behavior among native and nonnative speakers of Hebrew. In M. Papi & J. Vershueren (Eds.), *The pragmatic perspective* (pp. 195–208). Amsterdam: Benjamin.

Oskarsson, M. (1978). *Approaches to self-assessment in foreign language learning*. Oxford: Pergamon Press.

Oscarson (Oskarsson), M. (1989). Self-assessment of language proficiency: rationale and applications. *Language Testing, 6* (1), 1–13.

Oshima-Takane, Y., & MacWhinney, B. (1995). *CHILDES manual for Japanese*. Montreal: McGill University.

Phillipson, R., Kellerman, E., Selinker, L., Sharwood Smith, M., & Swain, M. (1991). *Foreign and Second language pedagogy research*. Clevedon, UK: Multilingual Matters.

Rintell, E. M., & Mitchel, C. J. (1989). Studying requests and apologies: An inquiry into method. In S. Blum-Kulka, J. House, & G. Kasper (Eds.), *Cross-cultural Pragmatics: Requests and apologies* (pp. 248–272). Norwood, NJ: Ablex.

Rose, K. R. (1992a). *Method and scope in cross cultural speech act research: A contrastive study of requests in Japanese and English*. Unpublished doctoral dissertation, University of Illinois at Urbana-Champaign.

Rose, K. R. (1992b). Speech acts and questionnaires: The affect of hearer response. *Journal of Pragmatics, 17,* 49–62.

Rose, K. R. (1994). On the validity of discourse completion tests in non-Western contexts. *Applied linguistics, 15,* 1–14.

Sasaki, M. (1995a, March). *Assessing Japanese students' pragmatic competence in English as a foreign language: A comparison of production questionnaires and roleplays.* Paper presented at the meeting of the American Association for Applied Linguistics, Long Beach, CA.

Sasaki, M. (1995b). *Assessing Japanese students' pragmatic competence in English as a foreign language: A comparison of production questionnaires and roleplays.* Unpublished manuscript.

Scarcella, R., & Brunak, J. (1981). On speaking politely in a second language. *International Journal of the Sociology of Language, 27*, 59–75.

Searle, J. R. (1965). What is a speech act? In S. Davis (Ed.), *Pragmatics: A reader* (pp. 254–264), New York: Oxford University Press.

Searle, J. R., Kiefer, F., & Bierwisch, M. (1980). *Speech act theory and pragmatics.* Dordrecht, Holland: D. Reidel.

Shavelson, R. J. (1981). *Statistical reasoning for the behavioral sciences.* Boston: Allyn and Bacon, Inc.

Shimamura, K. (1993). *Judgment of request strategies and contextual factors by Americans and Japanese EFL learners.* Unpublished master's thesis, the University of Hawai'i at Mānoa, Honolulu.

Shimura, A. (1993, May). *"Kotowari" toiu hatsuwa kouiniokeru taigu hyogen toshiteno shoryakuno hindo, kouzouni kansuru chukan gengo goyou-ron kenkyu.* [Interlanguage pragmatics of omission of refusals in honorific expressions]. Paper presented at the meeting of the Society for Teaching Japanese as a Foreign Language, Tokyo, Japan.

SPSS Incorporated. (1988). SPSS/PC+ Statistics 4.0.1. Chicago, IL.

Tabachnick, B. G., & Fidell, L. S. (1989). *Using multivariate statistics.* New York: Harper Collins.

Takahashi, T., & Beebe, L. M. (1987). The development of pragmatic competence by Japanese learners of English. *JALT Journal, 8*, 131–155.

Takahashi, T., & Beebe, L. M. (1993). Cross-linguistic influence in the speech act of correction. In G. Kasper & S. Blum-Kulka (Eds.), *Interlanguage pragmatics* (pp. 138–158). Oxford: Oxford University Press.

Tanaka, N. (1988). Politeness: Some problems for Japanese speakers of English. *JALT Journal, 8*, 81–102.

Tanaka, S., & Kawade, S. (1982). Politeness strategies and second language acquisition. *Studies in Second Language Acquisition, 5*, 18–33.

Thomas, J. (1983). Cross-cultural pragmatic failure. *Applied Linguistics, 4*, 91–112.

Trosborg, A. (1987). Apology strategies in natives/non-natives. *Journal of Pragmatics, 11*, 147–167.

Verschueren, J., Ostman, J., & Blommaert, J. (1995). (Eds.). *Handbook of Pragmatics: Manual.* Amsterdam: John Benjamins.

Wagner-Gough, J., & Hatch, E. (1975). The importance of input data in second language acquisition studies. *Language Learning, 25*, 297–307.

Wierzbicka, A. (1985). A semantic metalanguage for a cross-cultural comparison of speech acts and speech genres. *Language in Society, 14,* 491–514.

Wierzbicka, A. (1991). *Cross-cultural pragmatics: The semantics of human interaction.* Berlin: Mouton de Gruyter.

Wolfson, N. (1989). *Perspectives: Sociolinguistics and TESOL.* Cambridge, MA: Newbury House.

Wolfson, N., & Judd, E. (Ed.). (1983). *Sociolinguistics and language acquisition.* Rowley, MA: Newbury House.

Wolfson, N., Marmor, T., & Jones, S. (1989). Problems in the comparison of speech acts across cultures. In S. Blum-Kulka, J. House, & G. Kasper (Eds.), *Cross-cultural pragmatics: requests and apologies* (pp. 174–196). Norwood, NJ: Ablex.

Yamashita, S. (1994). Is the reading comprehension performance of learners of Japanese as a second language the same as that of Japanese children? — An analysis using a cloze test. *Japanese Language Education Around the Globe, 4,* 133–146.

Yamashita, S. (1996a, March). *Comparing JSL roleplays and self-assessments.* Paper presented at the meeting of the Tenth Annual International Conference on Pragmatics and Language Learning at University of Illinois, Urbana-Champagne.

Yamashita, S. (1996b, April). *Assessing pragmatic competence in Japanese as a second language.* Paper presented at the meeting of the National Foreign Language Research Center, University of Hawai'i at Mānoa, Honolulu.

Yamashita, S., & Ogawa, S. (1994). *Interview project: Interviewing, understanding, and appreciating the Japanese.* Tokyo: Kuroshio Shuppan.

Yokoyama, K. (1993). *Nihongo ni okeru, "Nihonjin no nihonjin ni taisuru kotowari" to "Nihonjin no Amerika jin ni taisuru kotowari" no hikaku: Shakaigengogaku no level deno foreigner talk* [Comparison of refusals in Japanese between Japanese refusing to Japanese and Japanese refusing to American: "Foreigner talk" on a sociolinguistic level]. *Nihongo Kyooiku, 81,* 141–151.

Yoshinaga, N., Maeshiba, N., & Takahashi, S. (1992). Bibliography on Japanese pragmatics. In G. Kasper (Ed.), *Pragmatics of Japanese as native and target language* (pp. 1–26). Honolulu: University of Hawai'i, Second Language Teaching and Curriculum Center.

Zuengler, J. (1993). Explaining NNS interactional behavior: The effect of conversational topic. In G. Kasper, & S. Blum-Kulka (Eds.), *Interlanguage Pragmatics* (pp. 184–195). New York: Oxford University Press.

# APPENDIX A: ANNOUNCEMENT FOR PARTICIPANTS

DEAR STUDENTS:

I am teaching Japanese in the Japanese Language Program at International Christian University, and currently working on my Ph. D. As part of my dissertation research, I am working on a joint research project with scholars at the University of Hawaii at Manoa. The scholars in Hawaii are studying Japanese students studying English in America, and I am studying American students studying Japanese in Japan. We will analyze the data cross-culturally when we finish collecting them.

I would like to ask you to help me to make this project a success.

What you would need to do to help me:
1) Questionnaire A (in English)-->take home
2) Oral production-->[time will be arranged]
3) Questionnaire B (in Japanese with Engl. suppl.)--->take home
4) Roleplay with a Japanese-->to be videotaped
5) Interview with me
6) Questionnaire C (in Japanese with Engl. suppl.)-->take home

While you are doing all those tasks for me (from 1 to 6), you will not only learn practical Japanese, but you will also get telephone cards equivalent to ¥2,000, and a special feedback session if you wish. Please take this opportunity to polish your Japanese before you return to your country!

Please contact:
Sayoko Yamashita
Home tel/fax: 0422-36-1786 or 0422-55-3515
ICU Office tel: 0422-33-3344
-------------------------------------------------------------------
Please check:  (     )I will be a participant.

YOUR NAME:

YOUR LEVEL:

YOUR CONTACT TELEPHONE NUMBER:

AVAILABLE TIME AND DAY: please fill
in the box on the right with (     ).

DO YOU WANT TO HAVE A FEEDBACK
SESSION?  (     )YES/(     )NO

DO YOU WANT MONEY INSTEAD OF
TELEPHONE CARDS? (     )YES/(     )NO

# APPENDIX B: PARTICIPANT DATA SHEET

To participants in Yamashita's research project.

Thank you for participating in this project. The six tasks will each be given separately. You are now receiving the first task involves some take-home questions. Please mail your sheet to my address (please use the self-addressed stamped envelope) when you finish it. When you return it to me, we will arrange a time and day for the second task--a production task which will be tape-recorded at your school with me.

We need certain background information for this cross-cultural research. Please let us know about you and your language study by answering the following questions:

==============================cut here================================

1. YOUR NAME:                          2. AGE:              3. M / F

4. YOUR MAJOR:

5. WHERE WERE YOU BORN (WHICH STATE)?:

6. HOW LONG HAVE YOU BEEN STUDYING JAPANESE/WHERE/HOW MANY HOURS
   A WEEK?
   (Example)                        [month/year]
   North Central College (CA)  9.1993-5.1994  3 hrs/week


7. HAVE YOU LIVED IN JAPAN BEFORE?  (   )YES-(   )NO-->HOW LONG?
   (Example)    [year]    [length]          [purpose]
   Yokohama  1987-1988   14 mos    high school exchange program


8. IF YOU HAVE LIVED IN A FOREIGN COUNTRY, PLEASE LIST THE NAME
   AND YEAR.
   (Example)    [year]         [total length]
   Korea      1987-1988           8 mos

# APPENDIX C: SELF-ASSESSMENT TEST (FORM A, B, AND C)

## (HUDSON ET AL. 1995)

Name: _____     Age: _____
Native language: _____     Sex: _____
Years of Japanese study: _____

**Directions:** Read each of the situations on the following pages.
It is expected that you would say something IN JAPANESE in each
of the situations. After thinking about what you would say, give
yourself a general rating on your ability to speak JAPANESE
appropriately in each situation. Circle the corresponding number
(1, 2, 3, 4, or 5) on the sheet. For example, if you think what
you would say IN JAPANESE would be completely appropriate, you
would circle the number 5. If you think it would be very unsatisfactory, you would circle 1. [*But remember that you are NOT
asked to produce or write any sentence on the sheet. Just think
about it in your head and rate it*].

While rating yourself consider your general JAPANESE ability to:
  - recognize what you should say
  - use appropriate expressions
  - use the appropriate amount of speech
  - use the appropriate levels of politeness, directness, and
    formality

Example:
Situation: You live in a large apartment building. You are
leaving to go to work. On your way out, you meet your next door
neighbor, whom you haven't seen for a long time.

You might think you would say:

> あ、お早うございます。しばらくお会いしませんでしたが、
> ずっとお元気でしたか。

In this case you might circle 5.

>      very  1  2  3  4 ⑤  completely
>  unsatisfactory             appropriate

You might think you would say:

> はじめまして。どこへ行くんですか。今日は元気ですね。
> 家族はどうですか。

In this case you might circle 2 because there are some inappropriate expressions, and too many expressions over all.

>      very  1 ②  3  4  5  completely
>  unsatisfactory             appropriate

IT'S THE END OF THE EXAMPLE.

NOW, LET'S BEGIN. SUPPOSE YOU ARE LIVING IN JAPAN AND SPEAK
JAPANESE IN EACH SITUATION (FROM 1 TO 24)...

**Situation 1**: You live in a large house. You hold the lease to the house and rent out the other rooms. You are in the room of one of your house-mates collecting the rent. You reach to take the rent check when you accidentally knock over a small, empty vase on the desk. It doesn't break.

**Rating:** I think what I would say in this situation would be

very
unsatisfactory   1 - - - 2 - - - 3 - - - 4 - - - 5   completely
appropriate

**Situation 2**: You work in a small shop that repairs jewelry. A valued customer comes into the shop to pick up an antique watch that you know is to be a present. It is not ready yet, even though you promised it would be.

**Rating:** I think what I would say in this situation would be

very
unsatisfactory   1 - - - 2 - - - 3 - - - 4 - - - 5   completely
appropriate

**Situation 3**: You are applying for a new job in a small company and want to make an appointment for an interview. You know the manager is very busy and only schedules interviews in the afternoon from one to four o'clock. However, you currently work in the afternoon. You want to schedule an interview in the morning. You go into the office this morning to turn in your application form when you see the manager.

**Rating:** I think what I would say in this situation would be

very
unsatisfactory   1 - - - 2 - - - 3 - - - 4 - - - 5   completely
appropriate

**Situation 4**: You are a member of the local chapter of a national ski club. Every month the club goes on a ski trip. You are in a club meeting now helping to plan this month's trip. The club president is sitting next to you and asks to borrow a pen. You cannot lend your pen because you only have one and need it to take notes yourself.

**Rating:** I think what I would say in this situation would be

very
unsatisfactory   1 - - - 2 - - - 3 - - - 4 - - - 5   completely
appropriate

**Situation 5**: You work in a small department of a large office. You are in a department meeting now. You need to borrow a pen in order to take some notes. The head of your department is sitting next to you and might have an extra pen.

**Rating:** I think what I would say in this situation would be

very
unsatisfactory        1 - - - 2 - - - 3 - - - 4 - - - 5        completely appropriate

**Situation 6**: You are an office manager and are interviewing to fill a position that is open. You are interviewing someone now. You walk over to the filing cabinet to get the applicant's application when you accidentally step on a small shopping bag belonging to the applicant. You hear a distinct crunching. You are certain you have broken whatever is in the small bag.

**Rating:** I think what I would say in this situation would be

very
unsatisfactory        1 - - - 2 - - - 3 - - - 4 - - - 5        completely appropriate

**Situation 7**: You work in a small department of a large office. Last week the head of the department loaned you a computer program on disk. You can't find the disk, and think you have lost it. You have just finished a meeting with your department when the head of the department passes near you.

**Rating:** I think what I would say in this situation would be

very
unsatisfactory        1 - - - 2 - - - 3 - - - 4 - - - 5        completely appropriate

**Situation 8**: You are shopping for your friend's birthday and see something in a display case. You want to look at it more closely. A salesclerk comes over to you.

**Rating:** I think what I would say in this situation would be

very
unsatisfactory        1 - - - 2 - - - 3 - - - 4 - - - 5        completely appropriate

**Situation 9**: You live in a large house. You hold the lease to the house and rent out the other rooms. Each person in the house is responsible for a few hours of chores every week. One of your house-mates asks if you can do extra chores this week because your house-mate is going out of town. You cannot do your house-mate's chores this week because you are very busy at work this week and do not have any extra time.

**Rating:** I think what I would say in this situation would be

very 1 - - - 2 - - - 3 - - - 4 - - - 5 completely
unsatisfactory appropriate

**Situation 10:** You are the manager in an office that is now hiring new employees. Last week an applicant came into the office and scheduled an interview for tomorrow. Now, that same person is in the office asking to reschedule the interview because of a family funeral. You cannot reschedule because you are about to leave the country for two weeks, your schedule is completely full, and you need to hire before you leave.

**Rating:** I think what I would say in this situation would be

very 1 - - - 2 - - - 3 - - - 4 - - - 5 completely
unsatisfactory appropriate

**Situation 11:** You work in a small shop. You are working in the back room when you hear the bell that tells you there is a customer in the front room. You are on the phone making an important business call. You finish the call as quickly as you can and go out to help the waiting customer.

**Rating:** I think what I would say in this situation would be

very 1 - - - 2 - - - 3 - - - 4 - - - 5 completely
unsatisfactory appropriate

**Situation 12:** You want to apply for a job in a small office. You want to get an application form. You go to the office and see the office manager sitting behind a desk.

**Rating:** I think what I would say in this situation would be

very 1 - - - 2 - - - 3 - - - 4 - - - 5 completely
unsatisfactory appropriate

**Situation 13:** You are the president of the local chapter of a national hiking club. Every month the club goes on a hiking trip and you are responsible for organizing it. You are on this month's trip and have borrowed another member's hiking book. You are hiking by a river and stop to look at the book. The book slips from your hand, falls in the river and washes away. You hike on to the rest stop where you meet up with the owner of the book.

**Rating:** I think what I would say in this situation would be

very 1 - - - 2 - - - 3 - - - 4 - - - 5 completely
unsatisfactory appropriate

**Situation 14**: You have worked in a small department of a large office for a number of years and are the head of the department. You have just been given an extra heavy work assignment to do. You know that one of your co-workers in the department is especially skilled in the area of this assignment. However, you also know that this person is very busy. You want your co-worker to help with the assignment. You go to the desk of your co-worker.

**Rating:** I think what I would say in this situation would be

very     1 - - - 2 - - - 3 - - - 4 - - - 5     completely
unsatisfactory                                 appropriate

**Situation 15**: You work in a repair shop. One of your valued customers comes in with an antique that is to be a present for a fiftieth wedding anniversary. The customer asks that it be repaired for the party tomorrow. You look at the antique and realize that you cannot do the job in one day. It will take you at least two weeks to finish.

**Rating:** I think what I would say in this situation would be

very     1 - - - 2 - - - 3 - - - 4 - - - 5     completely
unsatisfactory                                 appropriate

**Situation 16**: You are the president of the local chapter of a national book club. The club reads and discusses a new book every month. You are at this month's meeting, talking with a member of the book club. You need to get the phone number of Sue Lee, another member of the club. You think this person has Sue's number.

**Rating:** I think what I would say in this situation would be

very     1 - - - 2 - - - 3 - - - 4 - - - 5     completely
unsatisfactory                                 appropriate

**Situation 17**: You are a teacher at a large school. You see the lead teacher on campus. The lead teacher asks you to call all of the other teachers tonight and tell them that there will be a meeting tomorrow. You cannot do it because you know that it will take hours and you have friends coming over to your house tonight.

**Rating:** I think what I would say in this situation would be

very     1 - - - 2 - - - 3 - - - 4 - - - 5     completely
unsatisfactory                                 appropriate

**Situation 18**: You are in a small bank buying traveler's checks. You move to take the checks when you accidentally knock over a small ceramic figure on the clerk's desk. It doesn't break.

**Rating:** I think what I would say in this situation would be

$$\text{very unsatisfactory} \quad 1 - - - 2 - - - 3 - - - 4 - - - 5 \quad \text{completely appropriate}$$

**Situation 19:** You work in a bookstore. You are scheduled to start work at noon today. You will take over for your supervisor who is working the morning shift. You go to work and arrive at the bookstore a few minutes after noon. You see your supervisor.

**Rating:** I think what I would say in this situation would be

$$\text{very unsatisfactory} \quad 1 - - - 2 - - - 3 - - - 4 - - - 5 \quad \text{completely appropriate}$$

**Situation 20:** You and a few of your co-workers are working on a special project. You have been appointed the project leader. You are walking in the hallway when another co-worker also working on the project asks you to give a message to Mary when you see her at a meeting you and Mary have scheduled this afternoon. You cannot deliver the message because you will not be seeing her. Mary has canceled the meeting.

**Rating:** I think what I would say in this situation would be

$$\text{very unsatisfactory} \quad 1 - - - 2 - - - 3 - - - 4 - - - 5 \quad \text{completely appropriate}$$

**Situation 21:** You are walking through a department store. As you walk past a display, a salesclerk asks you to watch a short video demonstration for a new product. You cannot stop because you are on your way to meet someone for lunch.

**Rating:** I think what I would say in this situation would be

$$\text{very unsatisfactory} \quad 1 - - - 2 - - - 3 - - - 4 - - - 5 \quad \text{completely appropriate}$$

**Situation 22:** You rent a room in a large house. The person who holds the lease lives in the house as well. You are responsible for mowing the lawn every week, a job that takes you about two hours to do. You want the lease-holder to mow the lawn for you this week because you are going out of town. You are in the living room when the lease-holder walks in.

**Rating:** I think what I would say in this situation would be

$$\text{very unsatisfactory} \quad 1 - - - 2 - - - 3 - - - 4 - - - 5 \quad \text{completely appropriate}$$

**Situation 23**: You are an office manager and are hiring to fill a position that has just opened up. Yesterday, many people filled out application forms for the job. The form is very long and takes most people many hours to complete. You are getting ready to interview an applicant, but cannot find the completed application in the files. You want the applicant to resubmit the application. The applicant is now here for the interview.

**Rating**: I think what I would say in this situation would be

very
unsatisfactory      1 - - - 2 - - - 3 - - - 4 - - - 5      completely
appropriate

**Situation 24**: You work as a sales clerk in a department store. A customer is paying for an item and should get three dollars back in change. The customer asks that the three dollars be given in quarters, not dollar bills. You cannot give the change because you do not have enough quarters to spare.

**Rating**: I think what I would say in this situation would be

very
unsatisfactory      1 - - - 2 - - - 3 - - - 4 - - - 5      completely
appropriate

**Situation 1**: You work in a small department of a large office. You have worked here for a number of years and are the head of the department. You are in the office of another member of the department in a meeting. You accidentally knock over a framed picture on the desk. It doesn't break.

**Rating:** I think what I would say in this situation would be

very
unsatisfactory    1 - - - 2 - - - 3 - - - 4 - - - 5    completely
appropriate

**Situation 2**: You are applying for a job in a company. You go into the office to turn in your application form to the manager. You talk to the manager for a few minutes. When you move to give the manager your form, you accidentally knock over a vase on the desk and spill water over a pile of papers.

**Rating:** I think what I would say in this situation would be

very
unsatisfactory    1 - - - 2 - - - 3 - - - 4 - - - 5    completely
appropriate

**Situation 3**: You are applying for a student loan at a small bank. You are now meeting with the loan officer. The loan officer is the only person who reviews the applications at this bank. The loan officer tells you that there are many other applicants and that it should take two weeks to review your application. However, you want the loan to be processed as soon as possible in order to pay your tuition by the deadline.

**Rating:** I think what I would say in this situation would be

very
unsatisfactory    1 - - - 2 - - - 3 - - - 4 - - - 5    completely
appropriate

**Situation 4**: You work for a large company. You and a few of your co-workers are working on a special project. You are just finishing a meeting with the group. The leader of the project asks you to give a message to your secretary. You cannot deliver the message because you are going directly to a meeting scheduled at one of the branch offices.

**Rating:** I think what I would say in this situation would be

very
unsatisfactory    1 - - - 2 - - - 3 - - - 4 - - - 5    completely
appropriate

**Situation 5**: You are a member of the local chapter of a national ski club. Every month the club goes on a ski trip. You are in a meeting with the club president, helping plan this month's. You want to borrow some paper in order to take some notes.

**Rating**: I think what I would say in this situation would be

very
unsatisfactory      1 - - - 2 - - - 3 - - - 4 - - - 5      completely
appropriate

**Situation 6**: You are shopping in a store that sells handmade crafts. You have shopped here a number of times before and usually make a substantial purchase. Today you are looking for a present for your mother's birthday. You are browsing near a clerk. You pick up a small statuette to get a better look at it and drop it on the floor. It breaks.

**Rating**: I think what I would say in this situation would be

very
unsatisfactory      1 - - - 2 - - - 3 - - - 4 - - - 5      completely
appropriate

**Situation 7**: You rent a room in a large house. The person who holds the lease lives in the house as well. Each person in the house is responsible for a few hours of chores every week. Your chore is to vacuum the house. This morning when you were using the lease-holder's vacuum you accidentally dropped it and now it does not work. You are now in the living room and the lease-holder walks in.

**Rating**: I think what I would say in this situation would be

very
unsatisfactory      1 - - - 2 - - - 3 - - - 4 - - - 5      completely
appropriate

**Situation 8**: You are on an airplane. It is dinner time. The flight attendant sets your food on your tray. You need a napkin.

**Rating**: I think what I would say in this situation would be

very
unsatisfactory      1 - - - 2 - - - 3 - - - 4 - - - 5      completely
appropriate

**Situation 9**: You work in a small department of a large office. You have worked here for a number of years and are the head of the department. You have an important meeting scheduled with another member of your department this afternoon. You are in your office when the member stops in and asks to cancel the meeting in order to work on a special project that is due tomorrow. You cannot schedule the meeting for later because you have to report the information to others at a meeting tomorrow.

**Rating:** I think what I would say in this situation would be

very
unsatisfactory      1 - - - 2 - - - 3 - - - 4 - - - 5      completely
appropriate

**Situation 10**: Last week you had trouble with your company car and took it to a company mechanic. The mechanic promised to have it ready tomorrow morning. You are going on a business trip tomorrow afternoon and need the car. You stop by the repair shop to make sure the repairs will be finished in time. Now the mechanic tells you the shop is very busy and asks if you can wait an extra day for your car. You cannot delay your trip.

**Rating:** I think what I would say in this situation would be

very
unsatisfactory      1 - - - 2 - - - 3 - - - 4 - - - 5      completely
appropriate

**Situation 11**: You are in the airport going through customs after a trip to a foreign country. It is your turn, but when the customs officer asks you for your papers, you realize you do not know where they are. You look in your bag for a little while, find them, and give them to the waiting officer.

**Rating:** I think what I would say in this situation would be

very
unsatisfactory      1 - - - 2 - - - 3 - - - 4 - - - 5      completely
appropriate

**Situation 12**: You work in a restaurant. You have just taken a customer's order and are ready to leave the table. The customer is still holding the menu and you need it for another table.

**Rating:** I think what I would say in this situation would be

very
unsatisfactory      1 - - - 2 - - - 3 - - - 4 - - - 5      completely
appropriate

**Situation 13**: You are the president of the local chapter of a national camping club. Every month the club goes on a camping trip and you are responsible for organizing it. Last week you were supposed to meet with another member of the club to plan this month's trip. You had to reschedule because you were too busy. The rescheduled meeting was for 7:30 this morning, but you got caught in heavy traffic and just now arrive at the club headquarters. It is 9:00 a.m.

**Rating:** I think what I would say in this situation would be

very
unsatisfactory      1 - - - 2 - - - 3 - - - 4 - - - 5      completely
appropriate

**Situation 14**: You live in a large house. You hold the lease to the house and rent out the other rooms. The washing machine is broken. It is Saturday and the repair person is scheduled to fix it this morning. However, you will not be home because you have to pick up your parents at the airport. You want one of your house-mates to stay home this morning. You are in the kitchen when a house-mate walks in.

**Rating:** I think what I would say in this situation would be

very
unsatisfactory    1 - - - 2 - - - 3 - - - 4 - - - 5    completely
                                                         appropriate

**Situation 15**: You work in a small printing shop. It is late afternoon and a valued customer comes in to ask if you can print 1500 copies of a new advertisement by tomorrow morning. To do this you would have to work into the night. You are tired after a long day and cannot stay late.

**Rating:** I think what I would say in this situation would be

very
unsatisfactory    1 - - - 2 - - - 3 - - - 4 - - - 5    completely
                                                         appropriate

**Situation 16**: You work in a small department of a large office. You have worked here for a number of years and are the head of the department.  You are in a meeting with the other members of your department. You need to write some notes, but realize you do not have any paper. You turn to the person sitting next to you.

**Rating:** I think what I would say in this situation would be

very
unsatisfactory    1 - - - 2 - - - 3 - - - 4 - - - 5    completely
                                                         appropriate

**Situation 17**: You are a member of the local chapter of a national camping club. Every month the club goes on a camping trip. The president of the club is responsible for organizing the trips, a job that takes a number of hours. You are on this month's trip talking to the president of the club. The president is going to be out of town for a week and asks you to plan the next trip. You cannot plan the trip because you are going to be very busy with work.

**Rating:** I think what I would say in this situation would be

very
unsatisfactory    1 - - - 2 - - - 3 - - - 4 - - - 5    completely
                                                         appropriate

**Situation 18:** You are in a small family-owned restaurant. You go up to the counter to pay your bill. When you reach to hand your check to the restaurant worker you accidentally knock a few of the menus on the floor.

**Rating:** I think what I would say in this situation would be

very
unsatisfactory $\quad$ 1 – – – 2 – – – 3 – – – 4 – – – 5 $\quad$ completely appropriate

**Situation 19:** You teach in a small school. You have a meeting with the lead teacher for your grade at two o'clock today. When you show up at the meeting it is a few minutes after two.

**Rating:** I think what I would say in this situation would be

very
unsatisfactory $\quad$ 1 – – – 2 – – – 3 – – – 4 – – – 5 $\quad$ completely appropriate

**Situation 20:** You live in a large house. You hold the lease to the house and rent out the other rooms. You are in the living room when one of your house-mates asks to talk to you. Your house-mate explains that it will only take a few minutes and is not important. However, you cannot talk now because you are on your way out.

**Rating:** I think what I would say in this situation would be

very
unsatisfactory $\quad$ 1 – – – 2 – – – 3 – – – 4 – – – 5 $\quad$ completely appropriate

**Situation 21:** You are on your lunch hour. You go into a small shop to look for a present for your friend's birthday. You find something you like and buy it. As you are ready to leave the clerk asks to borrow your pen. You cannot lend your pen because you have to hurry back to work.

**Rating:** I think what I would say in this situation would be

very
unsatisfactory $\quad$ 1 – – – 2 – – – 3 – – – 4 – – – 5 $\quad$ completely appropriate

**Situation 22:** You work for a small department in a large office. The assistant manager of the office gave you a packet of materials to summarize for tomorrow. However, when you start working on the assignment, you realize that you do not have all of the information. You know that the head of the department has the information. You need to get the information, but you know it will take the head of your department about an hour and a half to locate it. You see the head of the department.

**Rating:** I think what I would say in this situation would be

very
unsatisfactory $\quad$ 1 – – – 2 – – – 3 – – – 4 – – – 5 $\quad$ completely appropriate

**Situation 23:** You are the personnel officer in an office that is now hiring new employees. The application form is quite long and takes most applicants several hours to complete. The form must be typed. An applicant comes in and gives you a completed form. However, it has been typed with a very faint ribbon. The application needs to be retyped.

**Rating:** I think what I would say in this situation would be

very
unsatisfactory    1 - - - 2 - - - 3 - - - 4 - - - 5    completely
appropriate

**Situation 24:** You work in a small store. A customer comes into the store and asks for change for a ten dollar bill. You cannot give the change because you don't have it in the register.

**Rating:** I think what I would say in this situation would be

very
unsatisfactory    1 - - - 2 - - - 3 - - - 4 - - - 5    completely
appropriate

**Situation 1:** You live in a large house. You hold the lease to the house and rent out the other rooms. You and one of your house-mates had planned to meet at 6:00 this evening to talk about house rules. However, you were late leaving work. It is a few minutes after 6:00 and as you enter the house you see your house-mate waiting in the living room.

**Rating:** I think what I would say in this situation would be

very
unsatisfactory  1 - - - 2 - - - 3 - - - 4 - - - 5  completely
appropriate

**Situation 2:** You are a professional photographer. Last month you took many pictures at a company party. You promised that the prints would be ready for the next company newsletter. The editor of the newsletter comes into your office to pick up the prints, but they are not ready now.

**Rating:** I think what I would say in this situation would be

very
unsatisfactory  1 - - - 2 - - - 3 - - - 4 - - - 5  completely
appropriate

**Situation 3:** You have recently moved to a new city and are looking for an apartment to rent. You are looking at a place now. You like it a lot. The landlord explains that you seem like a good person for the apartment, but that there are a few more people who are interested. The landlord says that you will be called next week and told if you have the place. However, you need the landlord to tell you within the next three days.

**Rating:** I think what I would say in this situation would be

very
unsatisfactory  1 - - - 2 - - - 3 - - - 4 - - - 5  completely
appropriate

**Situation 4:** You are a member of the local chapter of a national hiking club. You are on a hike now. You and a few other hikers have just stopped for a rest. The president of the club sits next to you, takes out a bottle of water to share with everyone. The president offers the bottle to you first. You have brought your own water.

**Rating:** I think what I would say in this situation would be

very
unsatisfactory  1 - - - 2 - - - 3 - - - 4 - - - 5  completely
appropriate

**Situation 5**: You are a member of the local chapter of a national ski club. You are on the club bus and have just arrived at the mountain. You are sitting near the club president. You see that the president is applying sun screen lotion. You want to use the president's lotion because you have forgotten to bring your own. You turn to the club president.

**Rating**: I think what I would say in this situation would be

very
unsatisfactory   1 - - - 2 - - - 3 - - - 4 - - - 5   completely
appropriate

**Situation 6**: You are in a computer store sitting at the desk of a salesperson. You have decided to buy several computers for your business and are handing the payment to the salesperson when you accidentally knock over a cup of coffee on the desk. The coffee spills across the desk and onto the salesperson.

**Rating**: I think what I would say in this situation would be

very
unsatisfactory   1 - - - 2 - - - 3 - - - 4 - - - 5   completely
appropriate

**Situation 7**: You are a member of a local charitable organization. Last week you promised the president of the organization that you would borrow your friend's truck to help move furniture from one office to the another today. However, you found out this morning that you cannot borrow the truck. You are now at the office and see the president.

**Rating**: I think what I would say in this situation would be

very
unsatisfactory   1 - - - 2 - - - 3 - - - 4 - - - 5   completely
appropriate

**Situation 8**: You are shopping in the drug store. You need to buy some envelopes, but cannot find them. You see a salesclerk nearby.

**Rating**: I think what I would say in this situation would be

very
unsatisfactory   1 - - - 2 - - - 3 - - - 4 - - - 5   completely
appropriate

**Situation 9**: You live in a large house. You hold the lease to the house and rent out the other rooms. One of your house-mates is talking with you and mentions that it would be a good idea to have a party next weekend. In fact, your house-mate says that the invitations have already been sent out. You cannot allow a party next weekend because you have already scheduled for painters to come and paint the inside of the house that same weekend.

**Rating:** I think what I would say in this situation would be

very
unsatisfactory    1 - - - 2 - - - 3 - - - 4 - - - 5    completely
appropriate

**Situation 10:** You have organized a good-bye party for a co-worker. Everyone in the office has contributed money to have a photograph of all of the office workers framed. The frame store promised that it would be ready today. You go into the store and the clerk tells you that they are very busy now and asks if you can wait another day. You cannot wait because the good-bye party is this evening.

**Rating:** I think what I would say in this situation would be

very
unsatisfactory    1 - - - 2 - - - 3 - - - 4 - - - 5    completely
appropriate

**Situation 11:** You are applying for a loan at a small bank. You have filled out all of the forms and are reaching over the desk to hand them to the loan officer when you accidentally knock over the loan officer's desk calendar.

**Rating:** I think what I would say in this situation would be

very
unsatisfactory    1 - - - 2 - - - 3 - - - 4 - - - 5    completely
appropriate

**Situation 12:** You are a salesperson in a gift shop. You need to get something out of a display case now. However, you are unable to get into the case because a customer is standing in the way and blocking your path.

**Rating:** I think what I would say in this situation would be

very
unsatisfactory    1 - - - 2 - - - 3 - - - 4 - - - 5    completely
appropriate

**Situation 13:** You work in a small department of a large office. You have worked there for a number of years and are the head of the department. Last weekend you borrowed a co-worker's portable computer because you had a lot of extra work to do and were going out of town. However, you accidentally erased some important information that was stored on the computer. It is Monday morning and you see your co-worker.

**Rating:** I think what I would say in this situation would be

very
unsatisfactory    1 - - - 2 - - - 3 - - - 4 - - - 5    completely
appropriate

**Situation 14:** You live in a large house. You hold the lease to the house and rent out the other rooms. This weekend you are going to put new carpeting in all of the bedrooms. Thus, all of the furniture needs to be moved out of your house-mate's bedroom. You are sitting in the kitchen when your house-mate enters the room.

**Rating:** I think what I would say in this situation would be

very
unsatisfactory　1 - - - 2 - - - 3 - - - 4 - - - 5　completely
appropriate

**Situation 15:** You are applying for a job in a large company. You have just finished an interview with the manager and are getting ready to leave the office when the manager explains that it is time for a tour of the company. You cannot go on the tour because you did not know about it and have another meeting scheduled in twenty minutes.

**Rating:** I think what I would say in this situation would be

very
unsatisfactory　1 - - - 2 - - - 3 - - - 4 - - - 5　completely
appropriate

**Situation 16:** You and a few of your co-workers are working on a special project. You have been appointed the project leader. You are working on the project now and are making a few copies on the Xerox machine. One of your co-workers on the project enters the room. You need a paper clip. You notice that your co-worker has a box of paper clips.

**Rating:** I think what I would say in this situation would be

very
unsatisfactory　1 - - - 2 - - - 3 - - - 4 - - - 5　completely
appropriate

**Situation 17:** You rent a room in a large house. The person who holds the lease lives in the house as well. Each person in the house is responsible for a few hours of chores every week. Your chore is to vacuum the house. The lease holder asks if you can vacuum the house tomorrow afternoon because the lease-holder is having visitors tomorrow night. You cannot vacuum tomorrow afternoon because you are going to be very busy all day.

**Rating:** I think what I would say in this situation would be

very
unsatisfactory　1 - - - 2 - - - 3 - - - 4 - - - 5　completely
appropriate

**Situation 18:** You are buying four tickets to a movie. You have a coupon for a free ticket. You tell the ticket clerk about the coupon, but when you look for it you can't find it right away. After a little while you find the coupon. You hand it to the clerk.

**Rating:** I think what I would say in this situation would be

very
unsatisfactory     1 - - - 2 - - - 3 - - - 4 - - - 5     completely
appropriate

**Situation 19:** You and a few of your co-workers are working on a special project. You are at a meeting in the office of the project leader. As you are reaching for your briefcase you accidentally knock over the project leader's umbrella which was leaning against the desk.

**Rating:** I think what I would say in this situation would be

very
unsatisfactory     1 - - - 2 - - - 3 - - - 4 - - - 5     completely
appropriate

**Situation 20:** You are the president of the local chapter of a national camping club. You are on a camping trip now. One of the club members is putting on mosquito repellent and offers some to you. You do not need to use the repellent because you have your own.

**Rating:** I think what I would say in this situation would be

very
unsatisfactory     1 - - - 2 - - - 3 - - - 4 - - - 5     completely
appropriate

**Situation 21:** You are a tourist in a large city. You have taken your film to a photo shop. When you go into the shop to pick up the pictures, the salesperson asks if you would like some coupons for more film developing. You do not need the coupons because you are leaving the city today.

**Rating:** I think what I would say in this situation would be

very
unsatisfactory     1 - - - 2 - - - 3 - - - 4 - - - 5     completely
appropriate

**Situation 22:** You work in a small department of a large office. You had an important meeting with the head of your department last week, but you had to cancel it because you got sick. The rescheduled meeting is for this afternoon. You came into the office this morning and felt okay. However, it is now lunch-hour and you are feeling sick again. You want to postpone today's meeting. You go to the office of the department head.

**Rating:** I think what I would say in this situation would be

very
unsatisfactory     1 - - - 2 - - - 3 - - - 4 - - - 5     completely
appropriate

**Situation 23:** Last week you had trouble with your company car. You took it to a company mechanic. You need the car tomorrow for an out of town meeting. It is Monday morning and the mechanic said your car would be ready this afternoon. However, you have another meeting this afternoon and do not think that you will get out of the meeting until after the shop closes. You go to the shop now. You want someone to stay late this afternoon in order for you to pick up your car.

**Rating:** I think what I would say in this situation would be

very
unsatisfactory       1 - - - 2 - - - 3 - - - 4 - - - 5       completely
appropriate

**Situation 24:** You work as a travel agent in a large department store. You are helping a customer at your desk. The customer gets out a packet of bubble-gum, takes a piece, and offers you a piece. You do not like bubble-gum.

**Rating:** I think what I would say in this situation would be

very
unsatisfactory       1 - - - 2 - - - 3 - - - 4 - - - 5       completely
appropriate

# APPENDIX D: RATING SHEET FOR DCT/LANG LAB

(HUDSON ET AL. 1995)

| very unsatisfactory | 1 - - - 2 - - - 3 - - - 4 - - - 5 | completely appropriate |
|---|---|---|

| SITUATION | | | | | | |
|---|---|---|---|---|---|---|

| **Response #** _____ | | | **Response #** _____ | | | |
|---|---|---|---|---|---|---|
| speech act | 1-2-3-4-5 | | | speech act | 1-2-3-4-5 | |
| expressions | 1-2-3-4-5 | | | expressions | 1-2-3-4-5 | |
| amount/info | 1-2-3-4-5 | − + | | amount/info | 1-2-3-4-5 | − + |
| formality | 1-2-3-4-5 | − + | | formality | 1-2-3-4-5 | − + |
| directness | 1-2-3-4-5 | − + | | directness | 1-2-3-4-5 | − + |
| politeness | 1-2-3-4-5 | − + | | politeness | 1-2-3-4-5 | − + |

| **Response #** _____ | | | **Response #** _____ | | | |
|---|---|---|---|---|---|---|
| speech act | 1-2-3-4-5 | | | speech act | 1-2-3-4-5 | |
| expressions | 1-2-3-4-5 | | | expressions | 1-2-3-4-5 | |
| amount/info | 1-2-3-4-5 | − + | | amount/info | 1-2-3-4-5 | − + |
| formality | 1-2-3-4-5 | − + | | formality | 1-2-3-4-5 | − + |
| directness | 1-2-3-4-5 | − + | | directness | 1-2-3-4-5 | − + |
| politeness | 1-2-3-4-5 | − + | | politeness | 1-2-3-4-5 | − + |

| **Response #** _____ | | | **Response #** _____ | | | |
|---|---|---|---|---|---|---|
| speech act | 1-2-3-4-5 | | | speech act | 1-2-3-4-5 | |
| expressions | 1-2-3-4-5 | | | expressions | 1-2-3-4-5 | |
| amount/info | 1-2-3-4-5 | − + | | amount/info | 1-2-3-4-5 | − + |
| formality | 1-2-3-4-5 | − + | | formality | 1-2-3-4-5 | − + |
| directness | 1-2-3-4-5 | − + | | directness | 1-2-3-4-5 | − + |
| politeness | 1-2-3-4-5 | − + | | politeness | 1-2-3-4-5 | − + |

| **Response #** _____ | | | **Response #** _____ | | | |
|---|---|---|---|---|---|---|
| speech act | 1-2-3-4-5 | | | speech act | 1-2-3-4-5 | |
| expressions | 1-2-3-4-5 | | | expressions | 1-2-3-4-5 | |
| amount/info | 1-2-3-4-5 | − + | | amount/info | 1-2-3-4-5 | − + |
| formality | 1-2-3-4-5 | − + | | formality | 1-2-3-4-5 | − + |
| directness | 1-2-3-4-5 | − + | | directness | 1-2-3-4-5 | − + |
| politeness | 1-2-3-4-5 | − + | | politeness | 1-2-3-4-5 | − + |

| **Response #** _____ | | | **Response #** _____ | | | |
|---|---|---|---|---|---|---|
| speech act | 1-2-3-4-5 | | | speech act | 1-2-3-4-5 | |
| expressions | 1-2-3-4-5 | | | expressions | 1-2-3-4-5 | |
| amount/info | 1-2-3-4-5 | − + | | amount/info | 1-2-3-4-5 | − + |
| formality | 1-2-3-4-5 | − + | | formality | 1-2-3-4-5 | − + |
| directness | 1-2-3-4-5 | − + | | directness | 1-2-3-4-5 | − + |
| politeness | 1-2-3-4-5 | − + | | politeness | 1-2-3-4-5 | − + |

---
| ＴＡＳＫ３の答え方 |
---

**Directions**

Read each situation in Japanese with English supplement if it is
necessary.  After each situation write what you would say in a normal
conversation <u>in Japanese</u>.  You may use any Japanese writing system such
as HIRAGANA, KANJI or Roman characters.  You may also use a dictionary
if you wish.  But please do not use English!  Never ask Japanese people
about what they would say in each situation.

　つぎのページからつづく２４の場面を読んで下さい。そしてそれぞれの場面について、ふつうの会話であなたならどう言うかを書いて下さい。ひらがな、かんじ、ローマ字など何で書いてもいいです。わからない場面は、英語の説明を読んでいいです。じしょでしらべてもかまいません。でも、ぜったい日本人に聞かないで下さい。

［注意！！！］
　このＴＡＳＫはテストではありません。言い方は人によっていろいろです。場面の説明のあとで、「あなた」がどういうかを書いて下さい。この研究はみなさがどう言うかを知るためのものなので、ぜったいに言い方や表現を日本人に聞いたり、本で調べないで下さい。（じしょは使ってもいいです）。上のやくそくをまもって下さる方は、下の名前のところにサインをお願いします。

---
　わたしはこの場面の答を、自分の力だけで考えました。
　わたしは日本人に答え方や表現などについて聞きませんでした。
　わたしは答を書くとき、表現について本などをみませんでした。

　１９９５年　　月　　日　名前：
---

○場面全部を答えるのにどのくらい時間がかかりましたか？

　　　　　　　　　　　　　　　　　　　　　　時間　　　分

Name:_____     Age:_____

Native Language:_____     Sex:_____

Years of Japanese study:_____

Directions:

Read each of the situations on the following pages.  After each
situation write what you would say in the situation in a normal
conversation.

Example:
場面　例

　あなたは大きなアパートに住んでいます。仕事に出かけるところです。
部屋を出たとき、となりの人に会いました。その人とは長い間会っていません。

あなたはそのとき何と言いますか。

_____

_____

_____

English supplement:

You live in a large apartment building.  You are leaving to go to work.
On your way out, you meet your next door neighbor, whom you haven't seen
for a long time.

場面 1

あなたは大きな家を借りて住んでいます。そして空いている部屋を他の人に貸しています。今、あなたはある部屋に部屋代をもらいに来ました。お金を受け取ろうとしたとき、つくえの上にあった小さい花びんをたおしてしまいました。その花びんには何も入っていませんでした。花びんはこわれませんでした。

あなたはそのとき何と言いますか。

_____
_____
_____

場面 2

あなたは宝石の修理をする小さい店で働いています。今大切な客が店に品物を取りに来ました。おくりものにする骨董品の時計です。本当は今日出来上がっているはずでしたが、まだ出来ていません。

あなたはそのとき何と言いますか。

_____
_____
_____

場面 3

あなたはある小さい会社に就職したいと思っています。面接の日時を決めたいのですが、人事部長はとても忙しく、午後1時〜4時の間しか面接をしてくれません。しかしあなたは今、午後仕事をしているので、午前中に面接をしてほしいと思っています。けさその会社に応募書類を出しに行くと、そこにちょうど人事部長がいました。

あなたはそのとき何と言いますか。

_____
_____
_____

場面 4
　あなたは全国組織のスキー・クラブの、地方支部の会員です。そのクラブでは、毎月スキー旅行に行きます。あなたは今、今月のスキー旅行を決めるミーティングに出ています。クラブの会長があなたのとなりにすわっていて、ペンを貸してほしいと言いました。しかし、あなたは1本しか持っていません。そのペンはあなたが自分でノートを取るのに必要です。

あなたはそのとき何と言いますか。

_____

_____


場面 5
　あなたは大きな会社の小さな部で働いています。今その部の会議に出席していますが、ノートを取るのにペンを借りる必要があります。となりにすわっている部長が一本よぶんに持っているかもしれません。

あなたはそのとき何と言いますか。

_____

_____

_____


場面 6
　あなたはある会社の部長です。社員を採用するために面接をしています。今あなたは、ある人と面接中です。その人の書類を取りにたなのところへ行こうとしたとき、うっかりその人の紙袋をふんでしまいました。ガシャっという音がはっきり聞こえました。

あなたはそのとき何と言いますか。

_____

_____

_____

場面 7
　あなたは大きな会社の小さな部で働いています。先週あなたは部長からコンピューター・ソフトのフロッピー・ディスクを借りました。そのディスクが見つかりません。どうもなくしてしまったようです。今ちょうど部の会議が終わったところです。そのとき部長があなたのそばを通りかかりました。

あなたはそのとき何と言いますか。

_____
_____
_____


場面 8
　あなたは友達のために誕生日のプレゼントをさがしています。ショーケースの中のものをよく見たいと思っているところへ店員がやって来ました。

あなたはそのとき何と言いますか。

_____
_____
_____


場面 9
　あなたは大きな家を借りて住んでいます。そして空いている部屋をほかの人に貸しています。この家では、みんなが毎週数時間ずつ家事をすることになっています。さてそのうちの一人が、旅行するためあなたに今週かわりに家事をやってもらえるかどうかたずねて来ました。あなたは今週仕事がとても忙しく、空いた時間がぜんぜんないので、かわってあげることができません。

あなたはそのとき何と言いますか。

_____
_____
_____

場面 10
　あなたはある会社の部長です。あなたの会社では今社員を募集しています。先週一人応募者が来て、明日面接をすることにしました。ところがその応募者がまた会社に来て、身内の葬式のため、面接の日時を変更してほしいと言いました。
　あなたはまもなく2週間ほど海外に行くことになっており、スケジュールもぎっしりつまっているため、日程を変えることができません。しかし、あなたは出かける前に雇う人を決めなくてはなりません。

あなたはそのとき何と言いますか。

_____
_____
_____

場面 11
　あなたは小さな店の店員です。奥の部屋で大事な仕事の電話をしているとき、表にお客がきてドアのベルを鳴らしました。あなたは急いで電話を終え、待っているお客のところへ出て行きました。

あなたはそのとき何と言いますか。

_____
_____
_____

場面 12
　あなたはある小さい会社の求人募集に応募しようと思っています。応募書類を取りに行くと、部長が席に座っています。

あなたはそのとき何と言いますか。

_____
_____
_____

場面 13
　あなたは全国組織のハイキング・クラブの、地方支部の会長です。クラブでは
毎月ハイキングに行きますが、あなたがその企画の責任者です。
　さて、あなたは今、今月のハイキングをしているところです。ある会員からハ
イキングの本を借りました。ところが、川べりのところで立ち止まってその本を
見ようとしたところ、手がすべって本は川に落ちて流れて行ってしまいました。
あなたが休憩地点まで来ると、ちょうどそこにあなたに本を貸してくれた会員が
いました。

　あなたはそのとき何と言いますか。

_____
_____
_____


場面 14
　あなたは大きな会社の小さな部で長年働いていて、今部長です。あなたは今回
とても大事な仕事を与えられました。その分野の仕事が特によく出来る同僚が同
じ部にいます。この人はとても忙しいのですが、あなたはこの人にぜひ仕事を手
伝ってほしいと思っています。あなたはその人の机のところに行きます。

　あなたはそのとき何と言いますか。

_____
_____
_____


場面 15
　あなたは修理屋で働いています。お得意さんの一人が結婚50周年のお祝いに
するため、骨董品を持って店に来ました。あしたのパーティまでになおしてほし
いということです。品物を見てみると、1日でなおすのはとても無理で、少なく
とも2週間はかかりそうです。

　あなたはそのとき何と言いますか。

_____
_____
_____

場面 16
　あなたは全国組織の読書クラブの、支部の会長です。このクラブでは、毎月新しい本を読み、話し合います。今、あなたは今月の集まりに出ているところで、クラブの会員と話をしています。あなたは鈴木マリという会員の電話番号が必要ですが、この会員が鈴木さんの電話番号を知っているかもしれません。

あなたはそのとき何と言いますか。

_____
_____
_____


場面 17
　あなたは大きな学校の先生です。学校で主任の先生に会った時、明日会議があるので、今夜他の先生全員に電話をし、そのことを伝えるように頼まれました。しかしそれは非常に時間のかかることで、おまけに、今夜は家に友達が来るのでできません。

あなたはそのとき何と言いますか。

_____
_____
_____


場面 18
　あなたは小さな銀行でトラベラーズ・チェックを買いました。チェックを受け取ろうとしたとき、机の上にあった陶器の小さい人形を倒してしまいました。人形は壊れませんでした。

あなたはそのとき何と言いますか。

_____
_____
_____

場面 19

あなたは本屋の店員です。今日は昼の１２時から仕事に出ることになっていました。あなたの上司が午前のシフトで、あなたはそのあとを引継ぎます。あなたが店に着いたとき、１２時を何分か過ぎていました。入って行くとあなたの上司がいます。

あなたはそのとき何と言いますか。

_____
_____
_____


場面 20

あなたは同僚何人かと特別のプロジェクトに係わっています。あなたはそのプロジェクトのリーダーです。今日は同僚の加藤さんと会議をするはずでしたが、加藤さんはその会議を中止しました。

さて、廊下を歩いていると、同じプロジェクトの同僚に午後の会議で加藤さんに会ったら伝えるよう伝言を頼まれました。しかしあなたは加藤さんに会わないので、伝言を伝えることはできません。

あなたはそのとき何と言いますか。

_____
_____
_____


場面 21

あなたはデバートでショッピングをしています。ある品物を買うことにし、支払をしようとしました。すると、店員が新製品の特別サービスの説明をし、短いデモンストレーションを見せたいと言いました。あなたは人と昼食の約束があるので、それを見ることはできません。

あなたはそのとき何と言いますか。

_____
_____
_____

場面 22
　あなたは大きな家を借りている人から、空いている部屋を一部屋借りています。その人もやはりその家に住んでいます。あなたは毎週芝かりをすることになっていて、それには大体2時間かかります。あなたは今週旅行に出かけるので、その人に芝かりをかわってほしいと思っています。あなたが居間にいるところへ、その人が入って来ました。

あなたはそのとき何と言いますか。

_____
_____
_____
_____


場面 23
　あなたはある会社の部長です。あなたの会社では、ちょうど社員が一人欠員になり、今募集をはじめたところです。昨日はたくさんの応募者が応募書類を書いて行きました。応募書類はとても長いもので、書くのにかなりの時間を要します。さて、あなたは一人の応募者と面接する用意をしていますが、その人の応募書類がファイルの中に見つかりません。そこで書類を再提出してもらおうと思っています。今、その応募者が面接のためにここに来ました。

あなたはそのとき何と言いますか。

_____
_____
_____
_____


場面 24
　あなたはデパートの店員です。あるお客が買い物をして、おつりが千円でした。そのお客に千円札ではなく、100円玉でおつりがほしいと言われましたが、100円玉が余分にないのであげることができません。

あなたはそのとき何と言いますか。

_____
_____
_____
_____

場面 1

あなたは大きな会社の小さな部で長年働いており、部長をしています。今同じ部の社員の机のところで話をしていて、その人の机の上にあった湯呑み茶碗をうっかりたおしてしまいました。茶碗にはお茶は入っていませんでしたし、こわれませんでした。

あなたはそのとき何と言いますか。

_____
_____
_____

場面 2

あなたはある会社に就職したいと思っています。あなたはその会社の部長のところに応募書類を提出しに行きました。そして部長と数分話をしました。さて、書類を渡そうとした時、あなたはうっかり机の上の花びんをたおしてしまいました。そしてつんであった書類に水をこぼし、ぬらしてしまいました。

あなたはそのとき何と言いますか。

_____
_____
_____

場面 3

あなたは大学に、学資の貸付申請に来ています。今、あなたは学生部の担当者と会っているところです。貸付申請の書類を調べるのは、ここの大学ではこの人だけです。この人の話では、ほかにも申請した人がたくさんいて、あなたの申請の結果が出るのは2週間後だということです。しかしあなたは今後の予定もあるのでできるだけ早く手続きをすすめて、結果を知らせてほしいと思っています。

あなたはそのとき何と言いますか。

_____
_____
_____

場面 4
　あなたは大きな会社の社員で、同僚何人かと特別なプロジェクトに係わっています。今、ちょうどそのグループのミーティングが終わるところです。プロジェクトのリーダーからあなたの秘書への伝言を頼まれましたが、あなたはこれからすぐに支社での会議に向かうので、伝言を伝えることができません。

あなたはそのとき何と言いますか。

_____
_____
_____

場面 5
　あなたは全国組織のスキー・クラブの、地方支部の会員です。そのクラブでは、毎月スキー旅行に行きます。あなたは今、クラブの会長と今月の旅行のための相談をしています。あなたはメモをとるために紙を少しもらいたいと思っています。

あなたはそのとき何と言いますか。

_____
_____
_____

場面 6
　あなたは手作りの工芸品を売る店で買い物をしています。あなたはここに何回も来たことがあり、いつもかなりの値段の買い物をしています。今日はお母さんの誕生日のプレゼントを探していて、店員のそばで品ものをみています。小さい人形を手に取ってよく見ようとしたら、落としてこわしてしまいました。

あなたはそのとき何と言いますか。

_____
_____
_____

場面 7
　あなたは大きい家を借りている人から空いている部屋を一部屋借りています。その人もやはりその家に住んでいます。この家では、住んでいる人が全員毎週決まった仕事をすることになっていて、あなたの係りは掃除です。
　今朝、あなたはこの家を借りている人から電気掃除機を貸してもらったのですが、落としてしまい、そのあと、この掃除機は動かなくなってしまいました。今、あなたは居間にいます。そこへ、掃除機の持ち主が入って来ました。

あなたはそのとき何と言いますか。

_____

_____

_____


場面 8
　あなたは飛行機に乗っています。夕食の時間になり、乗務員がおぼんに食事の用意をしてくれました。あとはナプキンが必要です。

あなたはそのとき何と言いますか。

_____

_____

_____


場面 9
　あなたは大きい会社の小さな部で長年働いていて、今部長です。今日の午後、同じ部の社員と大事な会議をする予定になっています。あなたが部屋にいると、その人が会議を取りやめてほしいとたのみにきました。あしたが期限の特別なプロジェクトの仕事をするためです。あなたはあしたの会議で、今日の会議の報告をしなければならないので、延期することはできません。

あなたはそのとき何と言いますか。

_____

_____

_____

場面 10
　先週、会社の車の調子が悪かったので、あなたは車を会社の修理工のところへ持って行きました。修理工は、必ずあしたの朝までに直すと約束しました。あなたはあしたの午後、車を使うことになったので、確認するために修理工のところへ来ました。修理工にきくと、工場がとても忙しいので、もう一日待ってほしいと言いました。あなたはどうしてもあしたの午後、車が必要です。

あなたはそのとき何と言いますか。

_____
_____
_____


場面 11
　あなたは海外旅行から帰ってきて、今税関を通っているところです。あなたの番になり、係り官に書類を出そうとしましたが、しまった場所がわかりません。かばんの中をしばらくさがすと見つかったので、待っている係官に出しました。

あなたはそのとき何と言いますか。

_____
_____
_____


場面 12
　あなたはレストランで働いています。注文を取ったので、もどろうと思いますが、お客さんはまだメニューを手に持っています。メニューはほかのテーブルに持って行かなくてはなりません。

あなたはそのとき何と言いますか。

_____
_____
_____

場面 13

あなたは全国組織のキャンピング・クラブの、地方支部長です。クラブでは毎月キャンプ旅行に行きますが、あなたがその企画の責任者です。先週あなたはクラブの会員の一人と、今月の旅行の打ち合わせをするはずでしたが、忙しくて都合がつかず、日にちを変えてもらいました。今朝の7時半ということになったのですが、渋滞に巻き込まれ、クラブの本部に、やっと着きました。今9時です。

あなたはそのとき何と言いますか。

_____
_____
_____

場面 14

あなたは大きな家に住んでいて、空いている部屋を他の人に貸しています。今、洗濯機がこわれていて、今日、土曜日の午前中に修理の人が来ることになっています。あなたは空港に両親を迎えに行かなければならないので、家にいられません。そこでだれかほかの人に、午前中家にいてもらいたいと思います。あなたが台所にいるところへ、だれか入ってきました。

あなたはそのとき何と言いますか。

_____
_____
_____

場面 15

あなたは小さな印刷屋で働いています。夕方おとくいさんが来て、明日の朝までに新しい広告を1500枚印刷できるかどうか聞きました。その仕事をするためには夜遅くまで働かなくてはなりません。あなたは朝からずっと働いて疲れているので、夜遅くまで仕事をすることはできません。

あなたはそのとき何と言いますか。

_____
_____
_____

場面 16
　　あなたは大きい会社の小さな部で長年働いていて、今部長です。今、そこの
会議をしているところです。ノートを取らなければならないのですが、紙をもっ
ていないのに気がつきました。あなたはとなりにすわっている人の方を向きます。

あなたはそのとき何と言いますか。

_____
_____
_____


場面 17
　　あなたは全国組織のキャンピング・クラブの、地方支部の会員です。クラブで
は毎月キャンプ旅行に行きますが、クラブの会長がその企画の責任者です。企画
をねるのには何時間もかかります。
　　さて、あなたは今月の旅行に参加しているところです。会長が一週間家を空け
るので、あなたに次の旅行の計画を立ててほしいと言います。あなたは仕事がと
ても忙しくなるのでそれはできません。

あなたはそのとき何と言いますか。

_____
_____
_____


場面 18
　　あなたは家族でやっている小さなレストランにいます。カウンターのところへ
勘定を払いに行きました。店員にお金を渡そうと手をのばしたら、メニューにぶ
つかって何枚か床に落としてしまいました。

あなたはそのとき何と言いますか。

_____
_____
_____

場面 19
　あなたは小さい学校で教えています。今日の２時から学年主任の先生との会議があります。あなたが会議の場に着くと、２時を何分か過ぎていました。

あなたはそのとき何と言いますか。

---
---
---

場面 20
　あなたは大きな家を借りて住んでいて、空いた部屋を他の人に貸しています。あなたが居間にいたところ、一人が話があるといってやってきました。話は短くてすむし、それほど大事ではないということです。　あなたはちょうど外出するところなので、話はできません。

あなたはそのとき何と言いますか。

---
---
---

場面 21
　今昼休みです。小さい店に友達の誕生日プレゼントを探しに行き、気に入ったものが見つかったのでそれを買いました。帰ろうとすると、店員が、お客についての調査をしたいので、質問表に記入してほしいと言いました。あなたは急いで仕事にもどらなければならないので、記入することはできません。

あなたはそのとき何と言いますか。

---
---
---

場面 22
　あなたは大きい会社の小さな部で働いています。副部長があなたのところへ資料を1たば持ってきて、明日までにまとめるように言いました。しかしその仕事をはじめてみると、資料が全部そろっていないことに気がつきました。部長が残りの資料を持っているのです。その資料が必要ですが、それを部長に探してもらうのに1時間半くらいはかかってしまいそうです。ちょうどそこへ部長がやって来ました。

あなたはそのとき何と言いますか。

_____
_____
_____

場面 23
　あなたはある会社の人事担当者です。あなたの会社では今社員を募集しています。応募書類はとても長く、書くのに数時間はかかります。おまけに、タイプで打っていなければなりません。応募者の一人が書類を提出しに来ましたが、タイプの字がうすいのでもう一度打ちなおしてもらわなければなりません。

あなたはそのとき何と言いますか。

_____
_____
_____

場面 24
　あなたは小さな店の店員です。入ってきたお客に千円札をくずしてほしいと言われましたが、レジに小銭がないのでくずすことができません。

あなたはそのとき何と言いますか。

_____
_____
_____

場面 1

　あなたは大きな家を借りて住んでいます。空いている部屋を他の人に貸しています。あなたはそのうちの一人と、今夜6時に会って、家のことで話をすることになっていました。けれども、あなたは仕事から帰るのが遅くなってしまいました。今6時を何分か過ぎたところです。家に着いてみると相手の人は居間で待っていました。

　あなたはそのとき何と言いますか。

_____
_____
_____

場面 2

　あなたはプロの写真家です。先月あなたはある会社のパーティで、たくさんの写真を撮りました。あなたは会社の次の社内報に間に合うように写真を現像しておくと約束しました。今、その社内報の編集者が写真を取りに来ていますが、まだできていません。

　あなたはそのとき何と言いますか。

_____
_____
_____

場面 3

　あなたは最近引越をしました。アパートを探していて、今一軒見ているところです。あなたはそのアパートがとても気に入りました。大家さんによれば、あなたに貸してもよいのですが、他にも何人か借りたい人がいるとのことでした。大家さんは、そのアパートが借りられるかどうか、来週電話をくれると言っています。しかし、あなたは3日以内にどうしても連絡が欲しいのです。

　あなたはそのとき何と言いますか。

_____
_____
_____

場面 4
　あなたは全国組織のハイキング・クラブの、地方支部の会員です。あなたは今ハイキングをしているところです。他の会員何人かと一緒に休むことにしました。クラブの会長が、あなたのとなりに座って、水筒を出して皆に水をすすめています。会長はあなたに一番先にすすめてくれましたが、あなたは自分の水筒を持ってきています。

あなたはそのとき何と言いますか。

_____
_____
_____

場面 5
　あなたは全国組織のスキー・クラブの、地方支部の会員です。あなたは今クラブのバスに乗っていて、山に着いたところです。あなたはクラブの会長のそばに座っています。会長は日焼け止めを塗っています。あなたは自分のを忘れてきたので、会長のを借りたいと思います。

あなたはそのとき何と言いますか。

_____
_____
_____

場面 6
　あなたはコンピューターを売っている店で、店員と話をしています。あなたは会社で使うコンピューターを何台か買うことにしました。店員にお金を渡そうとしたとき、うっかり机の上のコーヒーカップをひっくり返してしまいました。コーヒーは机にこぼれて、店員の服にもかかってしまいました。

あなたはそのとき何と言いますか。

_____
_____
_____

場面 7

あなたは地元のボランティア団体のメンバーです。先週あなたは、事務所の品物を他の事務所に移すために友達のトラックを借りてくる、とその団体の会長に約束しました。今日が移動の日ですが、今朝、トラックが借りられないことがわかりました。あなたが事務所に来てみると、会長がいました。

あなたはそのとき何と言いますか。

_____
_____
_____

場面 8

あなたはコンビニエンスストアで買い物をしています。封筒が欲しいのですが、見つかりません。近くに店員がいます。

あなたはそのとき何と言いますか。

_____
_____
_____

場面 9

あなたは大きな家を借りて住んでいます。あいている部屋を他の人に貸しています。そのうちのひとりが、今週の土曜日は友達の誕生日で、あなたの家でパーティをする予定になっていると言いました。しかし、その日はもうペンキ屋さんに家の中を塗ってもらうように頼んであるので、パーティをすることはできません。

あなたはそのとき何と言いますか。

_____
_____
_____

場面 10
　あなたは同僚の送別会の幹事です。会社のみながお金を出して社員全員の写真を額に入れてもらうようにしました。額縁店は今日でき上がるといっていました。お店に行ってみると、店員が、今とても忙しいので、もう1日待ってほしいと言いました。送別会は今夜なので、待つことはできません。

あなたはそのとき何と言いますか。

_____

_____

_____


場面 11
　あなたは小さな銀行で、融資を申し込んでいるところです。あなたは書類を全部書き終わりました。融資の担当者に渡そうと手をのばしたら、その人の卓上カレンダーをうっかり倒してしまいました。

あなたはそのとき何と言いますか。

_____

_____

_____


場面 12
　あなたはギフトショップの店員です。ショーケースから出すものがあるのですが、お客さんがその前に立っているので出すことができません。

あなたはそのとき何と言いますか。

_____

_____

_____

場面 13
　あなたは大きい会社の小さな部で長年働いています。今はそこの部長をしています。先週末、たくさん仕事が残っていて、旅行もすることになっていました。そこであなたは同僚からポータブルコンピューターを借りました。ところがあなたはコンピューターに入っていた大事なデータをうっかり消してしまいました。今日は月曜日で、その同僚に会いました。

あなたはそのとき何と言いますか。

---
---
---

場面 14
　あなたは大きな家を借りて住んでいます。空いている部屋を他の人に貸しています。来週の週末、あなたは全部の部屋に新しいカーペットを入れる予定です。そのため、来週の週末には全員の部屋から家具を出してもらわなければなりません。あなたが台所にいると、だれかが入ってきました。

あなたはそのとき何と言いますか。

---
---
---

場面 15
　あなたはある大きな会社に就職口を求めています。今、人事部長との面接が終わったところです。面接はうまく行きましたが、思ったよりずっと時間がかかりました。帰ろうとすると、人事部長が、これから会社の中を案内すると言いました。あなたは次の約束があるので、ついて行くことができません。

あなたはそのとき何と言いますか。

---
---
---

場面 16
　あなたは同僚何人かと特別なプロジェクトに関わっています。あなたはそのプロジェクトのリーダーです。ちょうど今あなたはその仕事をしていて、書類のコピーをしています。プロジェクトのメンバーがひとり部屋に入ってきました。あなたはペーパークリップが必要ですが、見るとその人が1箱持っています。

あなたはそのとき何と言いますか。

_____
_____
_____


場面 17
　あなたは大きな家を借りている人から、空いている一部屋を借りています。その人もやはりその家に住んでいます。この家では、みな毎週数時間ずつ家事をすることになっています。あなたの係りは掃除機をかけることです。大家さんが、明日の午後掃除をしてくれるかどうかあなたに尋ねてきました。明日の晩、お客さんが来るからです。あなたは明日は一日とても忙しいので、午後掃除をすることはできません。

あなたはそのとき何と言いますか。

_____
_____
_____


場面 18
　あなたは映画のチケットを4枚買うところです。1枚分は無料の券を持っています。あなたは窓口でそう言いましたが、なかなかその券が見つかりません。しばらく探すと見つかったので、窓口の人に渡しました。

あなたはそのとき何と言いますか。

_____
_____
_____

場面 19
　あなたは同僚何人かと特別なプロジェクトに関わっています。今、プロジェクトのリーダーの部屋で打ち合わせをしています。ブリーフケースを取ろうと手をのばしたら、机に立てかけてあったリーダーの傘をうっかり倒してしまいました。

　あなたはそのとき何と言いますか。

_____
_____
_____


場面 20
　あなたは全国組織のキャンピングクラブの地方支部の部長です。今、キャンプ旅行に来ています。メンバーのひとりが虫よけの薬をつけていて、あなたにもすすめてくれました。しかし、あなたは自分のを持ってきているので、必要ありません。

　あなたはそのとき何と言いますか。

_____
_____
_____


場面 21
　あなたは大きな都市に旅行に来ています。写真屋さんにフィルムの現像を頼んでありました。写真を受け取りに来ると、店員が、また今度フィルムを出すときのために、割引券はいりますか、と聞きました。あなたは今日帰ってしまうので、割引券はいりません。

　あなたはそのとき何と言いますか。

_____
_____
_____

場面 22
　あなたは大きな会社の小さな部で働いています。先週あなたは部長と重要な打ち合わせの予定がありました。しかし、あなたは具合が悪くなったので、キャンセルしなければなりませんでした。打ち合わせは、今日の午後に予定が変わりました。あなたは、今朝出勤したときは元気でした。しかし、今昼休みで、また具合が悪くなってしまいました。今日の打ち合わせも延期したいと思います。あなたは部長の部屋に行きました。

あなたはそのとき何と言いますか。

_____
_____
_____

場面 23
　先週、会社の車の調子が悪くなりました。そこであなたは車を会社の修理工のところへ持って行きました。あなたは明日出張があるので、車が必要です。工場に車を取りに行くと、修理工は、今日の午後にならないとできない、と言いました。しかし、今日の午後は別の会議があって、工場が閉まるまでに来られそうもありません。車が受け取れるように、だれかに今日の夕方遅くまで工場に残っていてほしいと思います。

あなたはそのとき何と言いますか。

_____
_____
_____

場面 24
　あなたはある大きなデパートの旅行カウンターで働いています。今お客さんの相手をしているところです。お客さんが、チューイングガムを出して、1枚すすめてくれました。しかし、あなたはガムは嫌いなのです。

あなたはそのとき何と言いますか。

_____
_____
_____

# APPENDIX F: ENGLISH SUPPLEMENT (FORM A, B, AND C)

## (HUDSON ET AL. 1995)

English supplement                                                    Form A

**Situation 1**: You live in a large house. You hold the lease to the house and rent out the other rooms. You are in the room of one of your house-mates collecting the rent. You reach to take the rent check when you accidentally knock over a small, empty vase on the desk. It doesn't break.

**Situation 2**: You work in a small shop that repairs jewelry. A valued customer comes into the shop to pick up an antique watch that you know is to be a present. It is not ready yet, even though you promised it would be.

**Situation 3**: You are applying for a new job in a small company and want to make an appointment for an interview. You know the manager is very busy and only schedules interviews in the afternoon from one to four o'clock. However, you currently work in the afternoon. You want to schedule an interview in the morning. You go into the office this morning to turn in your application form when you see the manager.

**Situation 4**: You are a member of the local chapter of a national ski club. Every month the club goes on a ski trip. You are in a club meeting now helping to plan this month's trip. The club president is sitting next to you and asks to borrow a pen. You cannot lend your pen because you only have one and need it to take notes yourself.

**Situation 5**: You work in a small department of a large office. You are in a department meeting now. You need to borrow a pen in order to take some notes. The head of your department is sitting next to you and might have an extra pen.

**Situation 6**: You are an office manager and are interviewing to fill a position that is open. You are interviewing someone now. You walk over to the filing cabinet to get the applicant's application when you accidentally step on a small shopping bag belonging to the applicant. You hear a distinct crunching. You are certain you have broken whatever is in the small bag.

**Situation 7**: You work in a small department of a large office. Last week the head of the department loaned you a computer program on disk. You can't find the disk, and think you have lost it. You have just finished a meeting with your department when the head of the department passes near you.

**Situation 8**: You are shopping for your friend's birthday and see something in a display case. You want to look at it more closely. A salesclerk comes over to you.

**Situation 9**: You live in a large house. You hold the lease to the house and rent out the other rooms. Each person in the house is responsible for a few hours of chores every week. One of your house-mates asks if you can do extra chores this week because your house-mate is going out of town. You cannot do your house-mate's chores this week because you are very busy at work this week and do not have any extra time.

**Situation 10**: You are the manager in an office that is now hiring new employees. Last week an applicant came into the office and scheduled an interview for tomorrow. Now, that same person is in the office asking to reschedule the interview because of a family funeral. You cannot reschedule because you are about to leave the country for two weeks, your schedule is completely full, and you need to hire before you leave.

**Situation 11**: You work in a small shop. You are working in the back room when you hear the bell that tells you there is a customer in the front room. You are on the phone making an important business call. You finish the call as quickly as you can and go out to help the waiting customer.

**Situation 12**: You want to apply for a job in a small office. You want to get an application form. You go to the office and see the office manager sitting behind a desk.

**Situation 13**: You are the president of the local chapter of a national hiking club. Every month the club goes on a hiking trip and you are responsible for organizing it. You are on this month's trip and have borrowed another member's hiking book. You are hiking by a river and stop to look at the book. The book slips from your hand, falls in the river and washes away. You hike on to the rest stop where you meet up with the owner of the book.

**Situation 14**: You have worked in a small department of a large office for a number of years and are the head of the department. You have just been given an extra heavy work assignment to do. You know that one of your co-workers in the department is especially skilled in the area of this assignment. However, you also know that this person is very busy. You want your co-worker to help with the assignment. You go to the desk of your co-worker.

**Situation 15**: You work in a repair shop. One of your valued customers comes in with an antique that is to be a present for a fiftieth wedding anniversary. The customer asks that it be repaired for the party tomorrow. You look at the antique and realize that you cannot do the job in one day. It will take you at least two weeks to finish.

**Situation 16**: You are the president of the local chapter of a national book club. The club reads and discusses a new book every month. You are at this month's meeting, talking with a member of the book club. You need to get the phone number of Sue Lee, another member of the club. You think this person has Sue's number.

**Situation 17**: You are a teacher at a large school. You see the lead teacher on campus. The lead teacher asks you to call all of the other teachers tonight and tell them that there will be a meeting tomorrow. You cannot do it because you know that it will take hours and you have friends coming over to your house tonight.

**Situation 18**: You are in a small bank buying traveler's checks. You move to take the checks when you accidentally knock over a small ceramic figure on the clerk's desk.  It doesn't break.

**Situation 19**: You work in a bookstore. You are scheduled to start work at noon today. You will take over for your supervisor who is working the morning shift. You go to work and arrive at the bookstore a few minutes after noon. You see your supervisor.

**Situation 20**: You and a few of your co-workers are working on a special project. You have been appointed the project leader. You are walking in the hallway when another co-worker also working on the project asks you to give a message to Mary when you see her at a meeting you and Mary have scheduled this afternoon. You cannot deliver the message because you will not be seeing her. Mary has canceled the meeting.

**Situation 21**: You are walking through a department store. As you walk past a display, a salesclerk asks you to watch a short video demonstration for a new product. You cannot stop because you are on your way to meet someone for lunch.

**Situation 22**: You rent a room in a large house. The person who holds the lease lives in the house as well. You are responsible for mowing the lawn every week, a job that takes you about two hours to do. You want the lease-holder to mow the lawn for you this week because you are going out of town. You are in the living room when the lease-holder walks in.

**Situation 23**: You are an office manager and are hiring to fill a position that has just opened up. Yesterday, many people filled out application forms for the job. The form is very long and takes most people many hours to complete. You are getting ready to interview an applicant, but cannot find the completed application in the files. You want the applicant to resubmit the application. The applicant is now here for the interview.

**Situation 24**: You work as a sales clerk in a department store. A customer is paying for an item and should get three dollars back in change. The customer asks that the three dollars be given in quarters, not dollar bills. You cannot give the change because you do not have enough quarters to spare.

**Situation 1**: You work in a small department of a large office. You have worked here for a number of years and are the head of the department. You are in the office of another member of the department in a meeting. You accidentally knock over a framed picture on the desk. It doesn't break.

**Situation 2**: You are applying for a job in a company. You go into the office to turn in your application form to the manager. You talk to the manager for a few minutes. When you move to give the manager your form, you accidentally knock over a vase on the desk and spill water over a pile of papers.

**Situation 3**: You are applying for a student loan at a small bank. You are now meeting with the loan officer. The loan officer is the only person who reviews the applications at this bank. The loan officer tells you that there are many other applicants and that it should take two weeks to review your application. However, you want the loan to be processed as soon as possible in order to pay your tuition by the deadline.

**Situation 4**: You work for a large company. You and a few of your co-workers are working on a special project. You are just finishing a meeting with the group. The leader of the project asks you to give a message to your secretary. You cannot deliver the message because you are going directly to a meeting scheduled at one of the branch offices.

**Situation 5**: You are a member of the local chapter of a national ski club. Every month the club goes on a ski trip. You are in a meeting with the club president, helping plan this month's. You want to borrow some paper in order to take some notes.

**Situation 6**: You are shopping in a store that sells handmade crafts. You have shopped here a number of times before and usually make a substantial purchase. Today you are looking for a present for your mother's birthday. You are browsing near a clerk. You pick up a small statuette to get a better look at it and drop it on the floor. It breaks.

**Situation 7**: You rent a room in a large house. The person who holds the lease lives in the house as well. Each person in the house is responsible for a few hours of chores every week. Your chore is to vacuum the house. This morning when you were using the lease-holder's vacuum you accidentally dropped it and now it does not work. You are now in the living room and the lease-holder walks in.

**Situation 8**: You are on an airplane. It is dinner time. The flight attendant sets your food on your tray. You need a napkin.

**Situation 9**: You work in a small department of a large office. You have worked here for a number of years and are the head of the department. You have an important meeting scheduled with another member of your department this afternoon. You are in your office when the member stops in and asks to cancel the meeting in order to work on a special project that is due tomorrow. You cannot schedule the meeting for later because you have to report the information to others at a meeting tomorrow.

**Situation 10**: Last week you had trouble with your company car and took it to a company mechanic. The mechanic promised to have it ready tomorrow morning. You are going on a business trip tomorrow afternoon and need the car. You stop by the repair shop to make sure the repairs will be finished in time. Now the mechanic tells you the shop is very busy and asks if you can wait an extra day for your car. You cannot delay your trip.

**Situation 11**: You are in the airport going through customs after a trip to a foreign country. It is your turn, but when the customs officer asks you for your papers, you realize you do not know where they are. You look in your bag for a little while, find them, and give them to the waiting officer.

**Situation 12**: You work in a restaurant. You have just taken a customer's order and are ready to leave the table. The customer is still holding the menu and you need it for another table.

**Situation 13**: You are the president of the local chapter of a national camping club. Every month the club goes on a camping trip and you are responsible for organizing it. Last week you were supposed to meet with another member of the club to plan this month's trip. You had to reschedule because you were too busy. The rescheduled meeting was for 7:30 this morning, but you got caught in heavy traffic and just now arrive at the club headquarters. It is 9:00 a.m.

**Situation 14**: You live in a large house. You hold the lease to the house and rent out the other rooms. The washing machine is broken. It is Saturday and the repair person is scheduled to fix it this morning. However, you will not be home because you have to pick up your parents at the airport. You want one of your house-mates to stay home this morning. You are in the kitchen when a house-mate walks in.

**Situation 15**: You work in a small printing shop. It is late afternoon and a valued customer comes in to ask if you can print 1500 copies of a new advertisement by tomorrow morning. To do this you would have to work into the night. You are tired after a long day and cannot stay late.

**Situation 16**: You work in a small department of a large office. You have worked here for a number of years and are the head of the department.  You are in a meeting with the other members of your department. You need to write some notes, but realize you do not have any paper. You turn to the person sitting next to you.

**Situation 17**: You are a member of the local chapter of a national camping club. Every month the club goes on a camping trip. The president of the club is responsible for organizing the trips, a job that takes a number of hours. You are on this month's trip talking to the president of the club. The president is going to be out of town for a week and asks you to plan the next trip. You cannot plan the trip because you are going to be very busy with work.

**Situation 18**: You are in a small family-owned restaurant. You go up to the counter to pay your bill. When you reach to hand your check to the restaurant worker you accidentally knock a few of the menus on the floor.

**Situation 19**: You teach in a small school. You have a meeting with the lead teacher for your grade at two o'clock today. When you show up at the meeting it is a few minutes after two.

**Situation 20**: You live in a large house. You hold the lease to the house and rent out the other rooms. You are in the living room when one of your house-mates asks to talk to you. Your house-mate explains that it will only take a few minutes and is not important. However, you cannot talk now because you are on your way out.

**Situation 21**: You are on your lunch hour.  You go into a small shop to look for a present for your friend's birthday. You find something you like and buy it. As you are ready to leave the clerk asks to borrow your pen. You cannot lend your pen because you have to hurry back to work.

**Situation 22:** You work for a small department in a large office. The assistant manager of the office gave you a packet of materials to summarize for tomorrow. However, when you start working on the assignment, you realize that you do not have all of the information. You know that the head of the department has the information. You need to get the information, but you know it will take the head of your department about an hour and a half to locate it. You see the head of the department.

**Situation 23**: You are the personnel officer in an office that is now hiring new employees. The application form is quite long and takes most applicants several hours to complete. The form must be typed. An applicant comes in and gives you a completed form. However, it has been typed with a very faint ribbon. The application needs to be retyped.

**Situation 24**: You work in a small store. A customer comes into the store and asks for change for a ten dollar bill. You cannot give the change because you don't have it in the register.

**Situation 1:** You live in a large house. You hold the lease to the house and rent out the other rooms. You and one of your house-mates had planned to meet at 6:00 this evening to talk about house rules. However, you were late leaving work. It is a few minutes after 6:00 and as you enter the house you see your house-mate waiting in the living room.

**Situation 2:** You are a professional photographer. Last month you took many pictures at a company party. You promised that the prints would be ready for the next company newsletter. The editor of the newsletter comes into your office to pick up the prints, but they are not ready now.

**Situation 3:** You have recently moved to a new city and are looking for an apartment to rent. You are looking at a place now. You like it a lot. The landlord explains that you seem like a good person for the apartment, but that there are a few more people who are interested. The landlord says that you will be called next week and told if you have the place. However, you need the landlord to tell you within the next three days.

**Situation 4:** You are a member of the local chapter of a national hiking club. You are on a hike now. You and a few other hikers have just stopped for a rest. The president of the club sits next to you, takes out a bottle of water to share with everyone. The president offers the bottle to you first. You have brought your own water.

**Situation 5:** You are a member of the local chapter of a national ski club. You are on the club bus and have just arrived at the mountain. You are sitting near the club president. You see that the president is applying sun screen lotion. You want to use the president's lotion because you have forgotten to bring your own. You turn to the club president.

**Situation 6:** You are in a computer store sitting at the desk of a salesperson. You have decided to buy several computers for your business and are handing the payment to the salesperson when you accidentally knock over a cup of coffee on the desk. The coffee spills across the desk and onto the salesperson.

**Situation 7:** You are a member of a local charitable organization. Last week you promised the president of the organization that you would borrow your friend's truck to help move furniture from one office to the another today. However, you found out this morning that you cannot borrow the truck. You are now at the office and see the president.

**Situation 8:** You are shopping in the drug store. You need to buy some envelopes, but cannot find them. You see a salesclerk nearby.

**Situation 9:** You live in a large house. You hold the lease to the house and rent out the other rooms. One of your house-mates is talking with you and mentions that it would be a good idea to have a party next weekend. In fact, your house-mate says that the invitations have already been sent out. You cannot allow a party next weekend because you have already scheduled for painters to come and paint the inside of the house that same weekend.

**Situation 10:** You have organized a good-bye party for a co-worker. Everyone in the office has contributed money to have a photograph of all of the office workers framed. The frame store promised that it would be ready today. You go into the store and the clerk tells you that they are very busy now and asks if you can wait another day. You cannot wait because the good-bye party is this evening.

**Situation 11:** You are applying for a loan at a small bank. You have filled out all of the forms and are reaching over the desk to hand them to the loan officer when you accidentally knock over the loan officer's desk calendar.

**Situation 12:** You are a salesperson in a gift shop. You need to get something out of a display case now. However, you are unable to get into the case because a customer is standing in the way and blocking your path.

**Situation 13:** You work in a small department of a large office. You have worked there for a number of years and are the head of the department. Last weekend you borrowed a co-worker's portable computer because you had a lot of extra work to do and were going out of town. However, you accidentally erased some important information that was stored on the computer. It is Monday morning and you see your co-worker.

**Situation 14:** You live in a large house. You hold the lease to the house and rent out the other rooms. This weekend you are going to put new carpeting in all of the bedrooms. Thus, all of the furniture needs to be moved out of your house-mate's bedroom. You are sitting in the kitchen when your house-mate enters the room.

**Situation 15:** You are applying for a job in a large company. You have just finished an interview with the manager and are getting ready to leave the office when the manager explains that it is time for a tour of the company. You cannot go on the tour because you did not know about it and have another meeting scheduled in twenty minutes.

**Situation 16:** You and a few of your co-workers are working on a special project. You have been appointed the project leader. You are working on the project now and are making a few copies on the Xerox machine. One of your co-workers on the project enters the room. You need a paper clip. You notice that your co-worker has a box of paper clips.

**Situation 17**: You rent a room in a large house. The person who holds the lease lives in the house as well. Each person in the house is responsible for a few hours of chores every week. Your chore is to vacuum the house. The lease holder asks if you can vacuum the house tomorrow afternoon because the lease-holder is having visitors tomorrow night. You cannot vacuum tomorrow afternoon because you are going to be very busy all day.

**Situation 18:** You are buying four tickets to a movie. You have a coupon for a free ticket. You tell the ticket clerk about the coupon, but when you look for it you can't find it right away. After a little while you find the coupon. You hand it to the clerk.

**Situation 19:** You and a few of your co-workers are working on a special project. You are at a meeting in the office of the project leader. As you are reaching for your briefcase you accidentally knock over the project leader's umbrella which was leaning against the desk.

**Situation 20:** You are the president of the local chapter of a national camping club. You are on a camping trip now. One of the club members is putting on mosquito repellent and offers some to you. You do not need to use the repellent because you have your own.

**Situation 21**: You are a tourist in a large city. You have taken your film to a photo shop. When you go into the shop to pick up the pictures, the salesperson asks if you would like some coupons for more film developing. You do not need the coupons because you are leaving the city today.

**Situation 22:** You work in a small department of a large office. You had an important meeting with the head of your department last week, but you had to cancel it because you got sick. The rescheduled meeting is for this afternoon. You came into the office this morning and felt okay. However, it is now lunch-hour and you are feeling sick again. You want to postpone today's meeting. You go to the office of the department head.

**Situation 23:** Last week you had trouble with your company car. You took it to a company mechanic. You need the car tomorrow for an out of town meeting. It is Monday morning and the mechanic said your car would be ready this afternoon. However, you have another meeting this afternoon and do not think that you will get out of the meeting until after the shop closes. You go to the shop now. You want someone to stay late this afternoon in order for you to pick up your car.

**Situation 24:** You work as a travel agent in a large department store. You are helping a customer at your desk. The customer gets out a packet of bubble-gum, takes a piece, and offers you a piece. You do not like bubble-gum.

ロールプレイ＃１　自動車整備会社で

> あなた：車の修理を頼んだ客
> いつ　：ある日の昼休み
> どこで：自動車整備会社
> だれと：整備士
> 場面：あなたは、故障の車を先週から整備会社にあずけてあります。
> あなたは整備会社に車を取りにきて、整備士に会います（整備士は弁当
> を食べているところです）。
>
> 1. 車は本当は、あさってできあがる予定ですが、明日の朝までにできない
>    かどうか、あなたは整備士に頼みます。
> 2. 整備士がコーヒーをすすめてくれますが、あなたは断ります。
> 3. 整備士がほかの整備士にききにいっている間に、あなたはあやまって、
>    整備士が飲んでいたコーヒーカップをたおしてしまい、机の上の紙をか
>    なりぬらしてしまいました。

＃１　AT THE CAR GARAGE

> 　　　You go to a mechanic, who is having lunch now, to pick up
> company van, which had some trouble last week.
>
> 1. You want to ask the mechanic to have the van ready by early
>    tomorrow morning, which is one day earlier than it is supposed
>    to be ready.
> 2. The mechanic offers you some coffee but you don't want any.
> 3. After the mechanic leaves to talk with another mechanic about
>    the van, you accidentally knock over his coffee and it spills
>    over some papers on the desk.

あなた：客。有効期限ぎりぎりのギフト券で友達の誕生日のプレゼントを
　　　　買いたいと思っている。（ギフト券は読めないくらいきたない）
いつ　：
どこで：ギフト・ショップで
だれと：店員と
場面　：あなたは来週まで有効のギフト券を持って店に入ります。
　　　　あなたはギフト券で友達に誕生日のプレゼントを買い、土曜日の
　　　　誕生パーティーに持っていこうと思っています。

1.あなたはショーケースの中を見ていて、きれいな花瓶を見つけたので店員
　に見せてくれるようにたのみます。
2.お金をはらう時になって、店員にギフト券を渡そうと思って見ると、その
　ギフト券はたいへん汚れています。
3.あなたは店員に、土曜日にある、店の開店10周年セールに来るように
　勧められますが、断ります。

□WORDS：花瓶＝vase、　ギフト券＝gift certificate、

#2　SHOPPING AT A GIFT SHOP

　　　You walk into a gift shop to use a gift certificate before
it expires next week.  You want to buy a birthday present for your
friend with this certificate which you will give to your friend at
the birthday party this Saturday.  You see a nice vase in a case
and want to get a closer look at it.

1. You ask the salesperson walking by to take it out for you.
2. Now when you take out the gift certificate and hand it to the
   salesperson, you noticed that the gift certificate is very dirty.
3. You are invited to the '10th anniversary sale' on Saturday, but
   you will not go.

ロールプレイ＃3　家で

あなた：大きな家を借りていて、部屋をほかの人に貸している。
いつ　：夕方
どこで：家で
だれと：部屋を貸している人
場面：　部屋を貸している人と、夕方家で会うことになっています。
　　　　あなたは今、外から家に帰って来ました。

1.あなたは約束の時間に少し遅刻してしまいました。
2.その人は、今週の土曜日に部屋でパーティーを開きたいと言いますが、
　あなたは、今週の土曜日はペンキ屋が来ることになったことを伝えます。
3.また、来週の土曜日にはカーペット屋さんが来ることになっているので、
　家具を動かしておくようにたのみます。

□WORDS：ペンキ屋＝a painter、　カーペット屋＝a carpet worker、
　　　　家具＝furniture、　動かす＝to move


#3　AT YOUR HOUSE

　　You hold a lease to a big house and rent out the other rooms.
One of your housemate has asked to see you this evening.

1. You are late for the appointment to talk with him.
2. When you meet him, he will want to hold a party on the coming
   Saturday.  You explain that you have already scheduled painters
   to come this Saturday.
3. You also ask him to move all his furniture out of his bedroom to
   put in new carpeting next Saturday.

あなた：会社のある企画（プロジェクト）のリーダー
いつ　：
どこで：コピー機のところで
だれと：同じ企画のメンバー（あなたはリーダーです）
場面　：あなたがコピーをしていると、同じ企画のメンバーが来ました。

1. あなたは、彼に、メンバーの鈴木さんにメモをわたしてくれるようにたのまれましたが、あなたは、鈴木さんが病気のため、ミーティングがキャンセルになったことを彼に伝えます。
2. あなたはできあがったコピーをとじたいのですが、ホッチキスがありません。彼が、ちょうどホッチキスを持っています。
3. 彼が行ってしまったあと、あなたはそのかりたホッチキスを落としてこわしてしまいました。そこへ彼がもどって来ました。

□WORDS：ミーティング＝meeting、　キャンセルになる＝be canceled
　　　　ホッチキス＝stapler、

#4　AT WORK BY THE PHOTOCOPIER

　　You are the project leader working on a special project with your staff.  When you are at the photocopier, one of your staff members comes in.

1. He asks you to give a memo to Suzuki-san, another staff of yours, this evening.  However,  she is sick and her meeting with you has been canceled.
2. You need to staple some materials you've just copied, but you don't have a stapler.  You notice that the staff member has a stapler.
3. While he is out of the room, you accidentally drop his stapler and it brakes.

ロールプレイ＃５　転職活動

> あなた　：転職のため新しい仕事を探しています。
> いつ　　：朝１１：３０
> どこで　：小さな会社の人事課
> だれと　：人事課長
> 場面　　：あなたは小さな会社の人事課で課長に会います。
>
> 1. あなたは人事課長の部屋に入るとき、人事課長を驚かしてしまいました。
>    人事課長は驚いて、書類を床に落としてしまいました。
> 2. 面接の時間を決めますが、あなたは今の会社の仕事があるので朝がいいと
>    思っています。
> 3. 帰ろうとすると、人事課長が会社の中を案内してくれると言いました。
>    あなたは１：００までに自分の会社にもどらなければなりません。

＃５　APPLYING FOR A NEW JOB

> You go to apply for a new job in a small company at 11:30.
>
> 1. You see and greet the personnel manager but accidentally startle
>    him and he drops some papers on the floor.
> 2. You need to schedule an interview in a morning because you
>    currently work in the afternoons.
> 3. After arranging a morning interview, the personnel manager
>    suggests you come with him on a tour around the company now.
>    But you have to go back to work by 1:00 today.

ロールプレイ＃6　宝石修理店の仕事

あなた：店員。小さな宝石修理店で働いています。
いつ　：
どこで：宝石修理店
だれと：金持ちの客
場面　：店に客が、今日仕上がり予定の骨董品の時計を取りに来ました。

1. 時計は奥の部屋にあります。でも客がそのドアの前に立っています。
   客にどいてもらわなければなりません。
2. 昨夜直すはずだった修理工が、まだ時計を直していないことがわかりました。
3. 客が、電話をかけるために千円札をくずしてくれるようたのみましたが、
   店にはあいにく小銭（１００円玉）がありません。

☐WORDS：くずす＝Change big money to small money (e.g., change one
　　　　thousand yen to ten 100 yen coins)
　　　　小銭＝small coins

#6　WORKING AT A JEWELRY REPAIR SHOP

　　You work in a small jewelry repair shop.  A customer comes into
the shop to pick up his antique watch which is supposed to be ready
today.

1. You want to go into the back room to get the watch, but the
   customer is standing in front of the back room door.
2. You find out that the repairman who comes in at night to do the
   repairs, has not repaired the watch yet.
3. When the customer asks you for some change (from a thousand yen
   to 100 yen coins so that he could use a telephone), you find that
   you have no change.

ロールプレイ＃７　ミーティングのあとで

あなた：社員
いつ　：ミーティングのあとで
どこで：会社の中で
だれと：部長
場面　：ミーティングのあと、部長があなたの前に来ます。

1. 先週、部長から大切な本を借りました。しかし、あなたはその本をなくしてしまいました。
2. 部長が、鈴木商事とのことについて報告するように言いました。しかし、報告書を作るには、情報を受け取った人のリストを部長からもらう必要があります。
3. 部長はさらに、すぐにその報告書を作るように言いました。でもあなたはほかの部で会議があり、今すぐには仕事をはじめることができません。

□WORDS: 報告書＝report、　情報を受け取った人の「リスト」＝a list of who received the information

#7　AT WORK AFTER A DEPARTMENT MEETING

    You work in a small department of a large office. Last week you borrowed an important book from the head of the department and you lost it.

1. Right after the meeting, the head of the department walks over to you and asks you about the book.
2. He asks you to compile a report of the transactions with Suzuki Trading Company. You realize that you need a list of who received the information and you ask the department head to provide you with that list.
3. He asks you to do the report right away but you can't because you have a meeting at one of the branch offices now.

ロールプレイ＃8　写真クラブ

あなた：全国組織の写真クラブの地区会員
いつ　：会社の昼休み
どこで：写真クラブの部屋
だれと：写真クラブ会長
場面　：あなたには安い料金でカメラをなおしてくれる友人がいます。
　　　　写真クラブ会長のカメラをその友人が直すことになりました。
　　　　あなたはカメラを受け取るためクラブの部屋で会長に会います。

1. あなたは少し約束の時間に遅れてしまいました。
2. あなたは前にもらった会長の電話番号をなくしてしまったので、また知りたいと思います。
3. あなたは、次回のミーティングの打ち合わせのため、1時間ほど残るよう頼まれますが、あなたは昼食後にまた会社にもどらなければなりません。

# ＃8　PHOTOGRAPHY CLUB

You are a member of the local chapter of a national photography club. You have arranged to meet the club president to pick up his camera. Your friend, who repairs cameras at home for low prices, will do the repairs.

1. You are a little late for the appointment.
2. You have lost the club president's phone number, so you need to ask him to give it to you again.
3. You are asked to stay for about an hour and help him plan next month's meeting. But you are in a hurry because you have to get back to work after lunch.

三つの SPEECH ACTS［依頼・断り・謝罪］を含むロールプレイ場面

$ ＝被験者

ロールプレイ＃1　自動車整備会社で

あなた：車の修理を頼んだ客
いつ　：ある日の昼休み
どこで：自動車整備会社
だれと：自動車整備会社の整備士
場面　：あなたは、故障の車を先週から整備会社にあずけてあります。
1. あなたは整備会社に車を取りにきて、整備士に会います（整備士は弁当を食べているところです）。
2. 整備士がコーヒーをすすめてくれますが、あなたは断ります。
3. 車は本当は、あさってできあがる予定ですが、明日の朝までにできないかどうか、あなたは整備士に頼みます。
4. 整備士がほかの整備士にききにいっている間に、あなたはあやまって、整備士が飲んでいたコーヒーカップをたおしてしまい、机の上の紙をかなりぬらしてしまいました。

$ Interviewee＝［客］＝挨拶する－（コーヒーを）断る－頼む－謝る

Interviewer＝［整備士］＝挨拶する－客にコーヒーをすすめる

1. 整備工場内の一角で昼食中。客が入ってきたので挨拶をする。
2. コーヒーをすすめる。（客は断る）
3. 修理の仕上げを急ぐよう頼まれるので、できるかどうかほかの整備士に聞きにいく。
4. もどってくると、客が自分の飲み掛けのコーヒーを机の上にこぼし、書類がぬれていた。軽く、書類がぬれていることにたいしてコメントする。

ロールプレイ＃2　ギフト・ショップでの買い物

あなた：客。有効期限ぎりぎりのギフト券で友達の誕生日のプレゼントを買いたいと思っている。（ギフト券は読めないくらいきたない）
いつ　：
どこで：ギフト・ショップで
だれと：店員と
場面　：あなたは来週まで有効のギフト券を持って店に入ります。
　　　　あなたはギフト券で友達に誕生日のプレゼントを買い、土曜日の誕生パーティーに持っていこうと思っています。
1. あなたはショーケースの中を見ていて、きれいな花瓶を見つけたので店員に見せてくれるようにたのみます。
2. お金をはらう時になって、店員にギフト券を渡そうと思って見ると、そのギフト券はたいへん汚れています。
3. あなたは店員に、土曜日にある、店の開店10周年パーティー／セールに来るよう勧められますが、断ります。

$ 客＝頼む－詫びる（商品券が古くてきたない）－（招待を）断る

店員＝商品券がきたなくて判読困難なことを軽くコメントする－店の開店10周年記念パーティー／記念セールに来るよう客に勧める

1. 客が、ショーケースの中の花瓶を見たいというので見せる。
2. 客はギフト券で買い物をする。その券は、期限が有効だが、日付が読めないくらい汚れている（→軽く、そのことについてコメントする）。
3. 客に、今週の土曜日に予定している、店の開店10周年記念パーティー／セールにくるように勧める。

ロールプレイ＃3　家で

> あなた：大きな家を借りていて、部屋をほかの人に貸している。
> いつ　：夕方
> どこで：家で
> だれと：部屋を貸している人
>
> 場面：
> 1. 夕方部屋を貸している人と会うことにしていたが、あなたは約束の時間に遅刻してしまいました。
> 2. その人は、土曜日に部屋でパーティーを開きたいと言いますが、あなたはその土曜日はペンキ屋がくることになったことを伝えます。
> 3. また、来週土曜日には新しいカーペットを敷くことになっているので、家具を動かしておくようにたのみます。

$ 部屋を貸している人＝（遅刻を）詫びる－断る－（家具を動かすよう）依頼

部屋を借りている人＝パーティを開いていいかどうか依頼

> 1. 部屋を貸している人と約束をしていたが、その人は時間に遅れてきた。
> 2. 土曜日に部屋でパーティーをしたいので、その人に了解を求める。
> 3. 来週土曜日に家具を動かしておくように頼まれる。

ロールプレイ＃4　コピー機のところで

> あなた：会社のある企画（プロジェクト）のリーダー
> いつ　：
> どこで：コピー機のところで
> だれと：同じ企画のメンバー（あなたはリーダーです）
> 場面　：あなたがコピーをしていると、同じ企画のメンバーが来ました。
> 1. あなたは、彼に、メンバーの鈴木さんにメモをわたしてくれるようにたのまれましたが、あなたは、鈴木さんが病気のため、ミーティングがキャンセルになったことを彼に伝えます。
> 2. あなたはできあがったコピーをとじたいのですが、ホッチキスがありません。彼が丁度持っていたのでホッチキスをかります。
> 3. 彼が行ってしまったあと、あなたはそのかりたホッチキスを落としてこわしてしまいました。

$ リーダー＝挨拶－（メモをわたすことを）断る－頼む－謝罪

メンバー＝挨拶－頼む

> 1. コピールームへ行くと、同じプロジェクトのリーダーがいた。
> 2. チームメンバーの鈴木さんにメモをわたしてくれるよう、リーダーにたのむ。
> 3. リーダーに、ホッチキスを貸すようたのまれたので貸す。
> 4. リーダーは貸したホッチキスをこわしてしまった。そのことについて、軽くコメントする（リーダーとの応答）。

ロールプレイ＃5　転職活動

> あなた：転職のため新しい仕事を探しています。
> いつ　：朝１１：３０
> どこで：小さな会社の人事課
> だれと：人事課長
> 場面　：あなたは小さな会社の人事課で課長に会います。
> 1.あなたは人事課長の部屋に入るとき、人事課長を驚かしてしまいました。
> 　人事課長は驚いて、書類を床に落としてしまいました。
> 2.面接の時間を決めますが、あなたは今の会社の仕事があるので朝がいいと
> 　思っています。
> 3.帰ろうとすると、人事課長が会社の中を案内してくれると言いました。
> 　あなたは１：００までに自分の会社にもどらなければなりません。

＊転職希望者＝（驚かしたことを）詫びる－（面接時間の調整を）頼む－断る

　人事課長＝驚く－（書類を見せてくれと）頼む－（成績のよいことを）褒める
　　　　　　－会社内見学を勧める

> 1.就職志願の人が急に入ってきたので、驚き、書類を床に落としてしまう。
> 　（志願者謝罪する）
> 2.志願者と面接の日時を決めるにあたって、午後にしようとする。志願者
> 　に午前にしてくれるように頼まれ、そのようにする。
> 3.面談が終わって、志願者が帰ろうとする。あなたは、会社の中を案内しよ
> 　う、と志願者に言う（志願者、断る）。

ロールプレイ＃6　宝石修理店の仕事

> あなた：店員。小さな宝石修理店で働いています。
> いつ　：
> どこで：宝石修理店
> だれと：金持ちの顧客
> 場面　：客が、今日仕上がり予定の骨董品の時計を取りに来ました。
> 1.時計は奥の部屋にあります。でも客がそのドアの前に立っています。
> 　客にどいてもらわなければなりません。
> 2.昨夜直すはずだった修理工が、まだ時計を直していないことがわかりまし
> 　た。あなたは客に説明し、明日もう一度くるようたのみます。
> 3.客がお金をくずしてくれるようたのみましたが、あなたはくずすお金があ
> 　りません。

＄店員＝挨拶する－（客にドアの前をどくように）頼む－（修理が遅れているこ
　　　　とを）詫びる－（金をくずすことを）断る

　　客　＝挨拶する－（時計うけとりを）告げる－（金をくずすことを）頼む

> 1.店に入っていく（あなた＝金持ちの客）。
> 2.修理を依頼している骨董品の時計を受取りにきたことを告げる。
> 3.ドアの前に立っている。店員にどくように頼まれる。（あなたはそのドア
> 　が奥の品物のある部屋の扉だということに気がつかなかった）。どく。
> 4.店員が品物がまだ出来ていないと言う。あなたはまた明日取りに来ること
> 　を了解する（軽く）。
> 5.帰るとき、店員に、電話をかけるため千円札をくずしてくれるよう頼む。
> 　（店員はお金を細かくできない）→了解する。

ロールプレイ＃7　ミーティングのあとで

あなた：社員
いつ　：ミーティングのあとで
どこで：会社の中で
だれと：部長
場面　：ミーティングのあと、部長があなたの前に来ます。
1.先週、部長から大切な本を借りました。しかし、あなたはその本をなくしてしまいました。
2.部長が、鈴木商事とのことについて報告するように言いました。しかし、報告書を作るには、情報を受け取った人のリストを部長からもらう必要があります。
3.部長はさらに、すぐにその報告書を作るように言いました。でもあなたはほかの部で会議があり、今すぐは仕事をはじめることができません。

$ 社員＝挨拶するー（本をなくしたことを）謝罪するー（情報リストを）依頼するー（仕事をすぐ始められないと）断る［？日本人なら詫びる］

部長＝挨拶するー頼む

1.ミーティングのあと、部下のところへいく。先週大事な本をその部下に貸したが、今日返してほしいと告げる。
2.部下は恐縮しながら、なくしたと告げるので、（軽く）了解する。
3.部下に鈴木商事とのことについて報告するように言う。
4.部下から報告書のために情報を受け取った人のリストが必要であると言われる（→あとで渡すと言う）
5.部下に、報告書をすぐにまとめるように言う（→部下は別の会議のため、今すぐには作れないと言うので、了解する）。


ロールプレイ＃8　写真クラブ

あなた：全国組織の写真クラブの地区会員
いつ　：会社の昼休み
どこで：写真クラブ
だれと：写真クラブ会長
場面　：あなたには安い料金でカメラをなおしてくれる友人がいます。
　　　　写真クラブ会長のカメラをその友人が直すことになりました。
　　　　カメラを受け取るため、会長に会います。
1.あなたは少し約束の時間に遅れてしまいました。
2.また、あなたは前にもらった会長の電話番号をなくしてしまったので、再び知りたいと思います。
3.あなたは、次回のミーティングの打ち合わせのため、1時間ほど残るよう頼まれますが、あなたは昼食後にまた会社にもどらなければなりません。

$ 写真クラブメンバー＝挨拶するー（遅刻を）詫びるー（電話番号を）尋ねる／依頼ー（打ち合わせを）断る

写真クラブ会長＝挨拶するー打ち合わせを依頼

1.クラブメンバーと挨拶する。（メンバーは少々遅れてきた）。
2.カメラをメンバーに渡し、紹介された修理人への修理を頼む。
3.電話番号を聞かれたので、教える。
4.次回のミーティングの打ち合わせのため、一時間ほど残ってくれるように頼む（メンバーは都合が悪く残れない）→了解する。

# APPENDIX I: ROLEPLAY RATING SHEET

(HUDSON ET AL. 1995)

Scene One — At the Car Garage

1. Request

|                 |                                   |            |
|-----------------|-----------------------------------|------------|
| very            | 1 - - - 2 - - - 3 - - - 4 - - - 5 | completely |
| unsatisfactory  |                                   | appropriate|

2. Refusal

|                 |                                   |            |
|-----------------|-----------------------------------|------------|
| very            | 1 - - - 2 - - - 3 - - - 4 - - - 5 | completely |
| unsatisfactory  |                                   | appropriate|

3. Apology

|                 |                                   |            |
|-----------------|-----------------------------------|------------|
| very            | 1 - - - 2 - - - 3 - - - 4 - - - 5 | completely |
| unsatisfactory  |                                   | appropriate|

Scene Two — Shopping at a Gift Shop

1. Request

|                 |                                   |            |
|-----------------|-----------------------------------|------------|
| very            | 1 - - - 2 - - - 3 - - - 4 - - - 5 | completely |
| unsatisfactory  |                                   | appropriate|

2. Apology

|                 |                                   |            |
|-----------------|-----------------------------------|------------|
| very            | 1 - - - 2 - - - 3 - - - 4 - - - 5 | completely |
| unsatisfactory  |                                   | appropriate|

3. Refusal

|                 |                                   |            |
|-----------------|-----------------------------------|------------|
| very            | 1 - - - 2 - - - 3 - - - 4 - - - 5 | completely |
| unsatisfactory  |                                   | appropriate|

Scene Three — At Your House

1. Apology

|                 |                                   |            |
|-----------------|-----------------------------------|------------|
| very            | 1 - - - 2 - - - 3 - - - 4 - - - 5 | completely |
| unsatisfactory  |                                   | appropriate|

2. Refusal

|                 |                                   |            |
|-----------------|-----------------------------------|------------|
| very            | 1 - - - 2 - - - 3 - - - 4 - - - 5 | completely |
| unsatisfactory  |                                   | appropriate|

3. Request

|                 |                                   |            |
|-----------------|-----------------------------------|------------|
| very            | 1 - - - 2 - - - 3 - - - 4 - - - 5 | completely |
| unsatisfactory  |                                   | appropriate|

Scene Four — At Work by the Photocopier

1. Refusal

very
unsatisfactory    1 - - - 2 - - - 3 - - - 4 - - - 5    completely
appropriate

2. Request

very
unsatisfactory    1 - - - 2 - - - 3 - - - 4 - - - 5    completely
appropriate

3. Apology

very
unsatisfactory    1 - - - 2 - - - 3 - - - 4 - - - 5    completely
appropriate

Scene Five — Applying for a New Job

1. Apology

very
unsatisfactory    1 - - - 2 - - - 3 - - - 4 - - - 5    completely
appropriate

2. Request

very
unsatisfactory    1 - - - 2 - - - 3 - - - 4 - - - 5    completely
appropriate

3. Refusal

very
unsatisfactory    1 - - - 2 - - - 3 - - - 4 - - - 5    completely
appropriate

Scene Six — Working at a Jewelry Repair Shop

1. Request

very
unsatisfactory    1 - - - 2 - - - 3 - - - 4 - - - 5    completely
appropriate

2. Apology

very
unsatisfactory    1 - - - 2 - - - 3 - - - 4 - - - 5    completely
appropriate

3. Refusal

very
unsatisfactory    1 - - - 2 - - - 3 - - - 4 - - - 5    completely
appropriate

## Scene Seven — At Work after a Department Meeting

### 1. Refusal

very
unsatisfactory   1 - - - 2 - - - 3 - - - 4 - - - 5   completely appropriate

### 2. Apology

very
unsatisfactory   1 - - - 2 - - - 3 - - - 4 - - - 5   completely appropriate

### 3. Request

very
unsatisfactory   1 - - - 2 - - - 3 - - - 4 - - - 5   completely appropriate

## Scene Eight — Photography Club

### 1. Apology

very
unsatisfactory   1 - - - 2 - - - 3 - - - 4 - - - 5   completely appropriate

### 2. Request

very
unsatisfactory   1 - - - 2 - - - 3 - - - 4 - - - 5   completely appropriate

### 3. Refusal

very
unsatisfactory   1 - - - 2 - - - 3 - - - 4 - - - 5   completely appropriate

# APPENDIX J: MCDCT JAPANESE VERSION (FORM A, B, AND C)

Form A

### 場面 1

あなたは大きな家を借りて住んでいます。そして空いている部屋を他の人に貸しています。今、あなたはある部屋に部屋代をもらいに来ました。お金を受け取ろうとしたとき、つくえの上にあった小さい花びんをたおしてしまいました。その花びんには何も入っていませんでした。花びんはこわれませんでした。

a：あ！
b：あ！すみません。われなくて、よかった！
c：あ、すみません。花びんに気がつかなかったもので・・・。

### 場面 2

あなたは宝石の修理をする小さい店で働いています。今大切な客が店に品物を取りに来ました。おくりものにする骨董品の時計です。本当は今日出来上がっているはずでしたが、まだ出来ていません。

a：たいへん申し訳ございませんが、お預かりした時計は修理がまだすんでおりません。申し訳ないのですが、もうしばらくかかりそうです。
b：すみませんが、まだできていません。明日もう一度来てみていただけますか。
c：たいへん申し訳ありませんが、まだお品物は修理がすんでおりません。このところ、仕事がたてこんでおりまして。明日もう一度いらしていただけますでしょうか。

### 場面 3

あなたはある小さい会社に就職したいと思っています。面接の日時を決めたいのですが、人事部長はとても忙しく、午後1時～4時の間しか面接をしてくれません。しかしあなたは今、午後仕事をしているので、午前中に面接をしてほしいと思っています。けさその会社に応募書類を出しに行くと、そこにちょうど人事部長がいました。

a：すみません、就職の応募書類をもってきたものですが、面接の日時について、ご相談させていただきに来ました。通常、こちらでは午後が面接と伺っていますが、私、午後は仕事をしていますので、なんとかご配慮願えませんでしょうか。
b：新しい仕事の面接日時をきめたいのですが。午前中は時間がとれないと伺いましたが、私は午後はちょっと用事があるんですが。
c：すみません。面接の予約を午前中にお願いしたいのですが。

**場面 4**

　あなたは全国組織のスキー・クラブの、地方支部の会員です。そのクラブでは、毎月スキー旅行に行きます。あなたは今、今月のスキー旅行を決めるミーティングに出ています。クラブの会長があなたのとなりにすわっていて、ペンを貸してほしいと言いました。しかし、あなたは1本しか持っていません。そのペンはあなたが自分でノートを取るのに必要です。

a：あ、すみません、これしかないんです。田中さんがもっているかもしれません。きいてみしょう。

b：申し訳ありません。今、これしかないんです。田中さんにきいてみたらいかがでしょう。

c：お貸しできないんです。これしかないものですから。


**場面 5**

　あなたは大きな会社の小さな部で働いています。今その部の会議に出席していますが、ノートを取るのにペンを借りる必要があります。となりにすわっている部長が一本余分に持っているかもしれません。

a：すみませんが、ペンをお借りできますか。

b：あ、メモをとりたいんですが、書くものがないんですよ。

c：すみませんが、お借りできるような、余分なペンをお持ちですか。


**場面 6**

　あなたはある会社の部長です。社員を採用するために面接をしています。今あなたは、ある人と面接中です。その人の書類を取りにたなのところへ行こうとしたとき、うっかりその人の紙袋をふんでしまいました。ガシャっという音がはっきり聞こえました。


a：あ、しつれい。

b：あ、しつれいしました。ふくろが見えなかったもので。何もこわれていないといいのですが。

c：あ、これはしつれい。どうも何かこわれたようです。

場面 7
　あなたは大きな会社の小さな部で働いています。先週あなたは部長からコンピューター・ソフトのフロッピー・ディスクを借りました。そのディスクが見つかりません。どうもなくしてしまったようです。今ちょうど部の会議が終わったところで、部長があなたのそばを通りかかりました。

a：あのう、貸して頂いたディスクが見つからないんです。なくしてしまったかもしれないんです。バックアップコピーはお持ちでしょうか。
b：大変申し訳ありませんが、お借りしたディスクをなくしてしまいました。
c：すみません。先日、私に貸して下さったディスクのことなんですが・・・。ちょっとほかのものとまぎれてしまったようで、見つからなんです。ご入り用とは思いますが、あと一週間お待ちいただけますか。


場面 8
　あなたは友達のために誕生日のプレゼントをさがしています。ショーケースの中のものをよく見たいと思っているところへ店員がやって来ました。

a：すみません、それを見たいんですが、ケースから出していただけますか。
b：すみません！それを見せて下さい。
c：すみません。それを見せていただけますか。


場面 9
　あなたは大きな家を借りて住んでいます。そして空いている部屋をほかの人に貸しています。この家では、みんなが毎週数時間ずつ家事をすることになっています。さてそのうちの一人が、旅行するためあなたに今週かわりに家事をやってもらえるかどうかたずねて来ました。あなたは今週仕事がとても忙しく、空いた時間がぜんぜんないので、かわってあげることができません。

a：ああ、申し訳ない。今週は仕事がとても忙しいんですよ。だれか他の人に聞いたのんでくれますか。
b：できません。今週はとても忙しいんです。
c：かわってあげられるといいんですが、ちょっと忙しくて・・・すみません。

場面 10

　あなたはある会社の部長です。あなたの会社では今社員を募集しています。先週一人応募者が来て、明日面接をすることにしました。ところがその応募者がまた会社に来て、身内の葬式のため、面接の日時を変更してほしいと言いました。

　あなたはまもなく2週間ほど海外に行くことになっており、スケジュールもぎっしりつまっているため、日程を変えることができません。しかし、あなたは出かける前に雇う人を決めなくてはなりません。

a：申し訳ないですが、ほかにあいた時間はありません。ここのところ、ずっとスケジュールがいっぱいで、海外出張もひかえています。新しい社員は、出張の前に決めておかなければならないんですよ。

b：申し訳ありませんが、スケジュールがいっぱいなんですよ。2週間後にはアメリカへの出張がひかえているので、その前に新しい社員を決めなければならないんですよ。

c：申し訳ありませんが、スケジュールがいっぱいで、ほかの時間への変更は無理ですね。


場面 11

　あなたは小さな店の店員です。奥の部屋で大事な仕事の電話をしているとき、表にお客がきてドアのベルを鳴らしました。あなたは急いで電話を終え、待っているお客のところへ出て行きました。

a：すみません。電話に出ていたものですから。何にいたしましょうか。

b：すみません、たいへんお待たせいたしました。

c：いらっしゃいませ。何にいたしますか。ちょっと電話に出ておりまして、すみませんでした。一人で何もかもやらなければならないものですから、大変なんですよ。


場面 12

　あなたはある小さい会社の求人募集に応募しようと思っています。応募用紙を取りに行くと、部長が席に座っています。

a：すみません。貴社の求人募集に応募しようと思っている者ですが、応募用紙をいただけますか。

b：失礼ですが、求人の件でうかがいました。応募用紙を下さいますか。

c：失礼いたします。こちらの求人募集に応募したいと思うんですが。ごめんどうでなければ、応募用紙をいただけないでしょうか。

場面 13
　あなたは全国組織のハイキング・クラブの、地方支部の会長です。クラブでは毎月ハイキングに行きますが、あなたがその企画の責任者です。
　さて、あなたは今、今月のハイキングをしているところです。ある会員からハイキングの本を借りました。ところが、川べりのところで立ち止まってその本を見ようとしたところ、手がすべって本は川に落ちて流れて行ってしまいました。あなたが休憩地点まで来ると、ちょうどそこにあなたに本を貸してくれた会員がいました。

a：ごめんなさい。あなたのハイキングの本が川に落ちてなくなってしまったんです。どうしたらいいでしょう。
b：信じられないことが起こりました。あなたの本が川に落ちて流されてしまったんです。本当にごめんなさい。もどったら、すぐにかわりの本をさがします。
c：本当に申し訳ないんですが、あなたの本をなくしてしまいました。


場面 14
　あなたは大きな会社の小さな部で長年働いていて、今部長です。あなたは今回とても大事な仕事を与えられました。その分野の仕事が特によく出来る同僚が同じ部にいます。この人はとても忙しいのですが、あなたはこの人にぜひ仕事を手伝ってほしいと思っています。あなたはその人の机のところに行きます。

a：大川さん、お忙しいのはよくわかっているんですが、また帳簿に関する仕事が入ってしまったんですよ。あなたは帳簿のベテランだから・・・。
b：大川さん、ちょっと手伝ってくれますか。帳簿に関する仕事なんですよ。
c：大川さん、しつれい、お忙しいところ申し訳ないんですが、ちょっと帳簿に関する仕事が入ってしまったんですよ。手伝っていただけますか。

場面 15
　あなたは修理屋で働いています。お得意さんの一人が結婚50周年のお祝いにするため、骨董品を持って店に来ました。あしたのパーティまでになおしてほしいということです。品物を見てみると、1日でなおすのはとても無理で、少なくとも2週間はかかりそうです。

a：申し訳ありませんが、一日ではちょっと無理ですね。一週間ぐらいかかると思います。あすのパーティーでは品物の目録だけになさって、修理が済んでから品物をさしあげたらいかがですか。
b：たいへん申し訳ありませんが、修理には2週間ほどかかります。もう少し早くお持ち頂ければよろしかったんですが・・・。
c：申し訳ありませんが、少なくとも2週間はかかりますね。

場面 16
　あなたは全国組織の読書クラブの、支部の会長です。このクラブでは、毎月新しい本を読み、話し合います。今、あなたは今月の集まりに出ているところで、クラブの会員と話をしています。あなたは鈴木マリという会員の電話番号が必要ですが、この会員が鈴木さんの電話番号を知っているかもしれません。

a：え〜と、鈴木マリさんに電話しなければならないんですが、電話番号を知らないんですよ。
b：すみません、鈴木マリさんに連絡したいんです。電話番号をご存知ですか。
c：すみません、もしかして鈴木マリさんの電話番号をご存知ないでしょうか。
　　用事があるんですが、ちょっと今電話番号をもっていないんです。


場面 17
　あなたは大きな学校の先生です。学校で主任の先生に会った時、明日会議があるので、今夜他の先生全員に電話をし、そのことを伝えるように頼まれました。しかしそれは非常に時間のかかることです。それに、今夜は家に友達が来るのでできません。

a：あ、今夜はちょっと忙しいんです。だれかべつの人に頼んでくれませんか。
b：本当に申し訳ありませんが、だめなんです。今夜は友人が夕食にくることに
　　なっていますので時間がないんです。だれかほかの先生が手伝ってくれま
　　すよ。ほんとにごめんさい。つぎの時には手伝います。
c：すみませんが、今夜は友人が家へ来ることになっていまして、ちょっと時間
　　がないんです。だれかほかの先生に頼んでいただけないでしょうか。


場面 18
　あなたは小さな銀行でトラベラーズ・チェックを買いました。チェックを受け取ろうとしたとき、机の上にあった陶器の小さい人形を倒してしまいました。人形はこわれませんでした。

a：あ、すみません。こわれていないといいのですが。
b：ああ、すみません。だいじょうぶですか。
c：あ、すみません。こわれなくてよかった。

場面 19
　あなたは本屋の店員です。今日は昼の１２時から仕事に出ることになっていました。あなたの上司が午前のシフトで、あなたはそのあとを引継ぎます。あなたが店に着いたとき、１２時を何分か過ぎていました。入って行くとあなたの上司

がいます。

ａ：おくれて申し訳ありません。もうこれからは遅刻しません。
ｂ：おくれてすみません。すごい渋滞だったんです！
ｃ：おくれてどうもすみません。


場面 20
　あなたは同僚何人かと特別のプロジェクトに係わっています。あなたはそのプロジェクトのリーダーです。今日は同僚の加藤さんと会議をするはずでしたが、加藤さんはその会議を中止しました。
　さて、廊下を歩いていると、同じプロジェクトの同僚に午後の会議で加藤さんに会ったら伝えるよう伝言を頼まれました。しかしあなたは加藤さんに会わないので、伝言はできません。

ａ：すみません、会議が中止になったので、今日の午後は加藤さんに会わないんですよ。
ｂ：すみません、伝えられません。今日の会議は中止になったので。
ｃ：すみませんが、午後の会議が中止になってしまったので、加藤さんには伝言を伝えられないんですよ。大事な伝言じゃないといいんですが。


場面 21
　あなたはデパートでショッピングをしています。ある品物を買うことにし、支払をしようとしました。すると、店員が新製品の特別サービスの説明をし、短いデモンストレーションを見せたいと言いました。あなたは人と昼食の約束があるので、それを見ることはできません。

ａ：あ、だめです。ちょっと急ぎますから。
ｂ：悪いけど、行かなければ。人との約束におくれそうなんですよね。
ｃ：せっかくですが、昼食の約束があるものですから。

場面 22
　あなたは大きな家を借りている人から、空いている部屋を一部屋借りています。その人もやはりその家に住んでいます。あなたは毎週芝かりをすることになっていて、それには大体2時間かかります。あなたは今週旅行に出かけるので、その人に芝かりをかわってほしいと思っています。あなたが居間にいるところへ、その人が入って来ました。

a：すみません。ちょっとお願いがあるんですが。今週旅行に出かけますので、かわりに芝刈りをしていただけませんか。
b：あのね、今週ちょっと旅行にいくんで、芝刈ができないんですけど。いない間芝刈をしてしていただけますか、それとも帰るまでほうっておいていいですか。
c：すみません、来週旅行にでかけるんで、私のかわりに芝刈りをしてくれませんか。


場面 23
　あなたはある会社の部長です。あなたの会社では、ちょうど社員が一人欠員になり、今募集をはじめたところです。昨日はたくさんの応募者が応募書類を書いて行きました。応募書類はとても長いもので、書くのにかなりの時間を要します。さて、あなたは一人の応募者と面接する用意をしていますが、その人の応募書類がファイルの中に見つかりません。そこで書類を再提出してもらおうと思っています。今、その応募者が面接のためにここに来ました。

a：すみませんが、応募書類を完全に書き込んで下さい。
b：大変申し訳ないのですが、あなたの応募書類が見あたりません。面接の後、もう一度書いていただけないでしょうか。
c：すみませんが、応募書類が見あたらないんです。もう一度書いてください。


場面 24
　あなたはデパートの店員です。あるお客が買い物をして、おつりが千円でした。そのお客に千円札ではなく、100円玉でおつりがほしいと言われましたが、100円玉が余分にないのであげることができません。

a：すみませんが、100円玉がちょっと足りないんです。
b：100円玉はあまりないので、さしあげられないんです。
c：すみませんが、100円玉がちょっと足りないんです。500円玉がまざってよろしければありますが。

場面 1

あなたは大きな会社の小さな部で長年働いており、部長をしています。今同じ部の社員の机のところで話をしていて、その人の机の上にあった湯呑み茶碗をうっかりたおしてしまいました。茶碗にはお茶は入っていませんでしたし、こわれませんでした。

a:あ！
b:あ！ごめんなさい。
c:あ、この湯呑み茶碗はがんじょうですね。痛かった！

場面 2

あなたはある会社に就職したいと思っています。あなたはその会社の部長のところに応募書類を提出しに行きました。その時その人と数分話をしました。さて、書類を渡そうとした時、あなたはうっかり机の上の花びんをたおしてしまいました。そしてつんであった書類に水をこぼし、ぬらしてしまいました。

a:ああ、しつれいしました。なんてことでしょう。書類がぬれてしまいました。
b:あ、しつれい。
c:あ、たいへん申し訳ございません。ぞうきんはどこでしょうか。

場面 3

あなたは大学に、学資の貸付申請に来ています。今、あなたは学生部の担当者と会っているところです。貸付申請の書類を調べるのは、ここの大学ではこの人だけです。この人の話では、ほかにも申請した人がたくさんいて、あなたの申請の結果が出るのは2週間後だということです。しかしあなたは今後の予定もあるのでできるだけ早く手続きをすすめて、結果を知らせてほしいと思っています。

a:申請が遅れたのは申し訳ないんですが、学費納入の締切が今月の10日なんです。すみませんが、期限までに学費納入ができるように、手続きを早めていただけませんでしょうか。
b:ずいぶんたくさんの学生が申請しているようで、お忙しいと思います。学費貸付の申請ができるのはたいへんありがたいのですが、早急に学費を払い込まなければならないのです。何とか早くできる方法はありませんか。
c:できるだけ早く私の申請書を検討してくださいませんか。学費納入期限が近いので。

場面 4
　あなたは大きな会社の社員で、同僚何人かと特別なプロジェクトに係わっています。今、ちょうどそのグループのミーティングが終わるところです。プロジェクトのリーダーからあなたの秘書への伝言を頼まれましたが、あなたはこれからすぐに支社での会議に向かうので、伝言を伝えることができません。

a:申し訳ありませんが、このまますぐ支社の会議に出て、4時ごろまでもどらないものですから、伝えられないんですが。
b:すぐ伝言を伝えられるといいんですが、いまから支社の会議なんですよ。会議の後でよろしければ伝えますが。
c:だれかほかの人にたのんでくれませんか。すぐ支社の会議にでなければならないんですよ。

場面 5
　あなたは全国組織のスキークラブの、地方支部の会員です。そのクラブでは、毎月スキー旅行に行きます。あなたは今、クラブの会長と今月の旅行のための相談をしています。あなたはノートをとるために紙を少しもらいたいと思っています。

a:すみませんが、紙を少し下さい。
b:あー、メモをとりたいんですが、紙がないんですよ。
c:紙を少しいただけませんか。

場面 6
　あなたは手作りの工芸品を売る店で買い物をしています。あなたはここに何回も来たことがあり、いつもかなりの値段の買い物をしています。今日はお母さんの誕生日のプレゼントを探していて、店員のそばで品ものをみています。小さい人形を手に取ってよく見ようとしたら、落としてこわしてしまいました。

a:あ、すみません。
b:あ、どうもすみません。代金をお払いします。
c:あ、すみません。でもこういう時のための保険がかけてあってよかった。

## 場面 7

あなたは大きい家を借りている人から空いている部屋を一部屋借りています。その人もやはりその家に住んでいます。この家では、住んでいる人が全員毎週決まった仕事をすることになっていて、あなたの係りは掃除です。

今朝、あなたはこの家を借りている人から電気掃除機を貸してもらったのですが、落としてしまい、そのあと、この掃除機は動かなくなってしまいました。今、あなたは居間にいます。そこへ、掃除機の持ち主が入って来ました。

a:すみません。うっかり掃除機をこわしてしまったんです。今朝使っていたとき、落として、そのあと動かなくなってしまったんです。どこか修理してくれるところをご存知ですか。

b:掃除機をこわしてしまったんですよ。どうしたらいいでしょう。

c:へんなんですよ、掃除機を落としたら、とつぜん動かなくなってしまったんです。そんなにらんぼうに落としたつもりはないんですが。

## 場面 8

あなたは飛行機に乗っています。夕食の時間になり、乗務員がおぼんに食事の用意をしてくれました。あとはナプキンが必要です。

a:すみません、ナプキンがなくなったのですが、もう一枚下さいますか。

b:すみません！ナプキンを下さい。

c:すみません、ナプキンをいただけますか。

## 場面 9

あなたは大きい会社の小さい部で長年働いていて、今部長です。今日の午後、同じ部の社員と大事な会議をする予定になっています。あなたが部屋にいると、その人が会議を取りやめてほしいとたのみにきました。あしたが期限の特別なプロジェクトの仕事をするためです。あなたはあしたの会議で、今日の会議の報告をしなければならないので、延期することはできません。

a:悪いんですが、この会議は延期できないんですよ。明日の会議で今日の会議の報告をしなければならないので、できるだけ早く終わるようにします。

b:だめですね。今日の会議でその報告が必要だから。

c:延期出来るといいんですが。しかし、今日の会議の報告を明日しなければならないですからねえ・・。

場面 10
　先週、会社の車の調子が悪かったので、あなたは車を会社の修理工のところへ持って行きました。修理工は、その時、必ず明日の朝までに直すと約束しました。さて、あなたは急に明日の午後、この車で出張に行くことになりました。それで、確認のために、工場に寄ってみると、修理工は、工場がとても忙しいのでもう1日待てるかどうか聞きました。あなたは出張の予定を遅らせることはできません。

a:しかし、明日の朝までに直すと約束したでしょう。出張にどうしても車がいるんです。急いでやって下さい。
b:すみません。待てないんです。出張で使うのでどうしても明日の朝、車が必要なんです。
c:いや、一日も待てないんです。明日、出張で車がどうしても必要ですから。明日までに直すといったじゃありませんか。

場面 11
　あなたは海外旅行から帰ってきて、今税関を通っているところです。あなたの番になり、係り官に書類を出そうとしましたが、しまった場所がわかりません。かばんの中をしばらくさがすと見つかったので、待っている係官に出しました。

a:あ、ありました。この中にあると思っていたんですよ。お待たせしてすみませんでした。
b:あ、あった。お待たせしてすみませんでした。この次の時はちゃんとすぐわかるようにしておきます。
c:どうも。

場面 12
　あなたはレストランで働いています。注文を取ったので、もどろうと思いますが、お客さんはまだメニューを手に持っています。メニューはほかのテーブルに持って行かなくてはなりません。

a:すみませんが、もうよろしいですか。
b:すみませんが、メニューをいただけますか。こちらで必要なので。
c:すみません。おそれいりますが、メニューを持って行ってよろしいでしょうか。

場面 13

　あなたは全国組織のキャンピング・クラブの、地方支部長です。クラブでは毎月キャンプ旅行に行きますが、あなたがその企画の責任者です。先週あなたはクラブの会員の一人と、今月の旅行の打ち合わせをするはずでしたが、忙しくて都合がつかず、日にちを変えてもらいました。今朝の 7 時半ということになったのですが、渋滞に巻き込まれ、クラブの本部に、今 9 時、やっと着いたところです。

a：ああ、本当に申し訳ありません。渋滞にまきこまれてしまって・・・。まったくひどい渋滞でした。とにかく、わざわざ日にちを変えていただいたのに遅れてしまって・・・すみませんでした。

b：ああ、遅れてしまって大変申し訳ありません。ひどい渋滞にまきこまれてしまって・・・。これから打ち合わせ、いいですか？それとももう遅すぎますか？

c：遅れて大変申し訳ありません。でもしょうがなかったんですよ。渋滞にまきこまれてしまったので・・・。

場面 14

　あなたは大きな家に住んでいて、空いている部屋を他の人に貸しています。今、洗濯機がこわれていて、今日、土曜日の午前中に修理の人が来ることになっています。あなたは空港に両親を迎えに行かなければならないので、家にいられません。そこでほかの人にだれか一人午前中家にいてもらいたいと思います。あなたが台所にいるところへ、だれか入ってきました。

a：あ、こんにちは。両親を迎えに空港へいかなければならないんですが、修理の人が来るんですよ。洗濯機の修理にね。

b：今日の午前中家にいてくれますか。空港へ両親を迎えに行かなければならないんですよ。

c：今日午前中は家にいますか。洗濯機の修理の人が来るんでだれかに家にいてほしいんですよ。私は両親を迎えに空港まで行かなければならないので。

場面 15

　あなたは小さな印刷屋で働いています。夕方おとくいさんが来て、明日の朝までに新しい広告を1500枚印刷できるかどうか聞きました。その仕事をするためには夜遅くまで働かなくてはなりません。あなたは朝からずっと働いて疲れているので、夜遅くまで仕事をすることはできません。

a：すみませんが、もう閉店なんです。明日の朝と言うのはちょっとできないんですが、明日の午後までにでしたら何とかいたしますが。

b：すみませんが、できません。その仕事だと夜遅くまでかかってしまいますでしょ。家へ帰って子供に食事をさせなければならないんですよ。すみません。

c：悪いんですが、明日の朝までに1500枚というのはちょっと無理です。

場面 16
　あなたは大きい会社の小さな部で長年働いていて、今部長です。今、そこの会議をしているところです。ノートを取らなければならないのですが、紙をもっていないのに気がつきました。あなたはとなりにすわっている人の方を向きます。

a: すみません、メモを取りたいのですが、紙を全然持って来なかったんですよ。
b: すみません、紙を貸していただけますか。
c: すみません、紙をお貸しいただけますでしょうか。持ってくるのを忘れてしまったようなのですよ。

場面 17
　あなたは全国組織のキャンピング・クラブの、地方支部の会員です。クラブでは毎月キャンプ旅行に行きますが、クラブの会長がその企画の責任者です。企画をねるのには何時間もかかります。
　さて、あなたは今月の旅行に参加しているところです。会長は一週間家を空けるので、あなたに次の旅行の計画を立ててほしいということです。あなたは仕事がとても忙しくなるのでそれはできません。

a: 今、仕事がとても忙しいので、ちょっと無理です。だれか他の人にたのんでくれませんか。
b: ああ、出来ればお手伝いしたいのですが、実は、仕事が非常に忙しく、時間が取れそうにありません。すみません。
c: お手伝いしたいのですが、今週はちょっと・・・。今週は仕事のスケジュールがいっぱいなんです。

場面 18
　あなたは家族でやっている小さいレストランにいます。カウンターのところへ勘定を払いに行きました。店員にお金を渡そうと手をのばしたら、メニューにぶつかって何枚か床に落としてしまいました。

a: あ、すみません。よごれませんでしたか。
b: あ、よごれなかったでしょうか。私にひろわせて下さい。
c: おっと、すみません。ひろいます。

場面 19
　あなたは小さい学校で教えています。今日の2時から学年主任の先生との会議があります。あなたが会議の場に着くと、2時を何分か過ぎていました。

a:おくれてすみません。でも、たいしたことなかったようですね。
b:おくれてすみません。
c:こんにちは。

場面 20
　あなたは大きな家を借りて住んでいて、空いた部屋を他の人に貸しています。あなたが居間にいたところ、一人が話があるといってやってきました。話は短くてすむし、それほど大事ではないということです。あなたはちょうど外出するところなので、話はできません。

a:すみません、あとでもいいですか。今すぐ出かけなければ、遅れそうなのです。
b:今ちょっと話せません、あとで話しましょう。
c:すみません、今出かけるところなんです。遅れると困るので・・・。帰ってからにして下さい。

場面 21
　今昼休みです。小さい店に友達の誕生日プレゼントを探しに行き、気に入ったものが見つかったのでそれを買いました。帰ろうとすると、店員が、お客についての調査をしたいので、質問表に記入してほしいと言いました。あなたは急いで仕事にもどらなければならないので、記入することはできません。

a:だめです。すぐ仕事にもどらなければなりません。他の人にたのんでくれますか。
b:できればいいんですけど、仕事に遅れそうなので。すみません。
c:すみません、ちょっと急いでいるので・・・。

**場面 22**
　あなたは大きな会社の小さな部で働いています。副部長があなたのところへ資料を1たば持ってきて、明日までにまとめるように言いました。しかしその仕事をはじめてみると、資料が全部そろっていないことに気がつきました。部長が残りの資料を持っているのです。その資料が必要ですが、それを部長に探してもらうのに1時間半くらいはかかってしまいそうです。ちょうどそこへ部長がやって来ました。

a：部長、お願いがあるんですが。申し上げにくいのですが、昨年度の会計報告が必要になっています。お探しいただけないでしょうか。
b：部長、明日までに報告書を書くことになっているのですが、小田さんから受け取った資料が完全ではありません。昨年度の会計報告が必要なんですが、いただけますか。
c：すみません、部長、副部長から明日までにこの資料をまとめるように言われたんですが、部長のところにある昨年度の会計報告が必要です。いただけますか。

**場面 23**
　あなたはある会社の人事担当者です。あなたの会社では今社員を募集しています。応募書類はとても長く、書くのに数時間はかかります。おまけにワープロで打っていなければなりません。応募者の一人が書類を提出しに来ましたが、ワープロの字がうすいのでもう一度打ちなおしてもらわなければなりません。

a：ああ、この書類は結構なんですが、ちょっと読みにくいんですね。もう一度、はっきりとした字に打ち直してきていただけませんでしょうか。
b：悪いんですが、もう少しだれでも読めるようにはっきりと打ち直してきてくれませんか。
c：申し訳ないんですが、この書類は打ち直してもらわなければなりませんね。インクがうすすぎて読めないんですよ。

**場面 24**
　あなたは小さい店の店員です。入ってきたお客に千円札をくずしてほしいと言われましたが、レジに小銭がないのでくずすことができません。

a：申し訳ありませんが、あいにく小銭が1000円分ありません。
b：細かくできないんです。小銭が不足しているので。すみません。
c：申し訳ありませんが、あいにく細かいお金が今ありません。おとなりの店で聞いてみていただけますか。

**場面 1**

　あなたは大きな家を借りて住んでいます。空いている部屋を他の人に貸しています。あなたはそのうちの一人と、今夜6時に会って、家のことで話をすることになっていました。けれども、あなたは仕事から帰るのが遅くなってしまいました。今6時を何分か過ぎたところです。家に着いてみると相手の人は居間で待っていました。

a:　あ、どうも。
b:　あ、どうも。遅れてすみません。なかなか会社を出られなくて。
c:　遅れて申し訳ありません。午後いろいろやることがあったもので。

**場面 2**

　あなたはプロの写真家です。先月あなたはある会社のパーティで、たくさんの写真を撮りました。あなたは会社の次の社内報に間に合うように写真を現像しておくと約束しました。今、その社内報の編集者が写真を取りに来ていますが、まだできていません。

a:　あ、こんにちは。すみませんが、写真、まだできていないんです。午後にはできると思いますから、来る前に電話をしてもう一度来てくれますか。
b:　すみませんが、まだできていません。
c:　ああ、申し訳ありませんが、まだできていないんです。午後にはできると思いますが。

**場面 3**

　あなたは最近引越をしました。アパートを探していて、今一軒見ているところです。あなたはそのアパートがとても気に入りました。大家さんによれば、あなたに貸してもよいのですが、他にも何人か借りたい人がいるとのことでした。大家さんは、そのアパートが借りられるかどうか、来週電話をくれると言っています。しかし、あなたは3日以内にどうしても連絡が欲しいのです。

a:　この部屋がとっても気に入りました。来週までは待てないのですが、何とか3日ぐらいの間にお返事いただけませんか。
b:　う～ん、この部屋がとっても気に入りました。できれば、もう少し早く知りたいのですが。
c:　もう少し早くわかりませんか。今週中に知りたいんですよ。

**場面 4**

　あなたは全国組織のハイキング・クラブの、地方支部の会員です。あなたは今ハイキングをしているところです。他の会員何人かと一緒に休むことにしました。クラブの会長が、あなたのとなりに座って、水筒を出して皆に水をすすめています。会長はあなたに一番先にすすめてくれましたが、あなたは自分の水筒を持ってきています。

a:　ありがとうございます。でも自分のがありますので。
b:　ああ、結構です。私は自分のを持ってきておりますから、それは次の人にまわします。
c:　結構です。

**場面 5**

　あなたは全国組織のスキー・クラブの、地方支部の会員です。あなたは今クラブのバスに乗っていて、山に着いたところです。あなたはクラブの会長のそばに座っています。会長は日焼け止めを塗っています。あなたは自分のを忘れてきたので、会長のを借りたいと思います。

a:　日焼け止め、お借りできますか。
b:　あ〜！日焼け止め、忘れてしまった。どうしましょうか。
c:　あの〜、会長さん、日焼け止めを少々お借りできますか。持って来るのを忘れてしまったので。

**場面 6**

　あなたはコンピューターを売っている店で、店員と話をしています。あなたは会社で使うコンピューターを何台か買うことにしました。店員にお金を渡そうとしたとき、うっかり机の上のコーヒーカップをひっくり返してしまいました。コーヒーは机にこぼれて、店員の服にもかかってしまいました。

a:　あ、すみません。
b:　あ、どうもすみません。あ、わたしがふきますから。
c:　ああ、どうしましょう！だいじょうぶですか。本当に申し訳ありません。

場面 7

あなたは地元のボランティア団体のメンバーです。先週あなたは、事務所の品物を他の事務所に移すために友達のトラックを借りてくる、とその団体の会長に約束しました。今日が移動の日ですが、今朝、トラックが借りられないことがわかりました。あなたが事務所に来てみると、会長がいました。

a:会長、申し訳ありません。友人のトラックを今日借りられないことを今知りまして。だれかトラックを貸してくれる人をご存知ですか。
b:会長、すみません。トラック借りられませんでした。
c:会長、申し訳ありません。トラックを借りられないことが今朝わかりました。どうしましょう。お約束していたのにだめになって本当にすみません。

場面 8

あなたはコンビニエンスストアで買い物をしています。封筒が欲しいのですが、見つかりません。近くに店員がいます。

a:すみません、手紙を出すために封筒を買いたいんですが、どこにあるでしょうか。
b:すみません、封筒を見せて下さい。。
c:すみません、封筒はどこですか。

場面 9

あなたは大きな家を借りて住んでいます。あいている部屋を他の人に貸しています。そのうちのひとりが、今週の土曜日は友達の誕生日で、あなたの家でパーティをする予定になっていると言いました。しかし、その日はもうペンキ屋さんに家の中を塗ってもらうように頼んであるので、パーティをすることはできません。

a:すみません、土曜日はですねえ。ペンキ屋が来るんです。別の日時にしてくれませんか。
b:土曜日はパーティーはできません。ペンキ屋が来るんですよ。
c:ああ、どうしてもっと早く言ってくれなかったんですか。土曜日はペンキ屋が部屋を塗りかえることになっているんですよ。何人くらい来るんですか。来週にのばすことはできますか。その方が部屋もきれいになっていますよ。それともペンキ屋の予定を変更しましょうか。

場面 10
　あなたは同僚の送別会の幹事です。会社のみながお金を出して社員全員の写真を額に入れてもらうようにしました。額縁店は今日でき上がるといっていました。お店に行ってみると、店員が、今とても忙しいので、もう1日待ってほしいと言いました。送別会は今夜なので、待つことはできません。

a:あっ、困りますよ。明日まで待てませんよ。今日受け取るはずだったでしょう。部長に話して2〜3時間待てるかどうか聞いてみますけれど。
b:それは困ります。今夜の送別会のプレゼントの写真なんですよ。だから今1日の5時までにはお願いしたいですね。
c:待てません。今夜必要なんです。今日出来ると約束したじゃありませんか。

場面 11
　あなたは小さな銀行で、融資を申し込んでいるところです。あなたは書類を全部書き終わりました。融資の担当者に渡そうと手をのばしたら、その人の卓上カレンダーをうっかり倒してしまいました。

a:あ、すみません。
b:あら〜。ごめんなさい。こわれなかったでしょうね。
c:あ、すみません。でもなにもこわしませんでしたよね。

場面 12
　あなたはギフトショップの店員です。ショーケースから出すものがあるのですが、お客さんがその前に立っているので出すことができません。
a:すみません、ちょっとそのショーケース出したいものがございますので。
b:すみません、ちょっとそこをとおしていただけますか。ショーケースの中の商品を出しますので。
c:すみません。よろしければちょっとそこをあけて、後ろのショーケースへ行かせていただけますか。

**場面 13**

　あなたは大きい会社の小さな部で長年働いています。今はそこの部長をしています。先週末、たくさん仕事が残っていて、旅行もすることになっていました。そこであなたは同僚からポータブルコンピューターを借りました。ところがあなたはコンピューターに入っていた大事なデータをうっかり消してしまいました。今日は月曜日で、その同僚に会いました。

a.こんにちは、本当にもうしわけないんですがあなたのコンピュータのデータをうっかり消してしまったんです。本当に不注意でごめんなさい。これのバックアップはありますか。

b.ちょっとまずいことになってしまいました。あなたのコンピュータのデータをまちがえて消してしまったんです。本当にすみません。バップアップはとってありましたか。

c.本当に申し訳ないんですが、コンピュータのデータを部分的に消してしまいました。

**場面 14**

　あなたは大きな家を借りて住んでいます。空いている部屋を他の人に貸しています。来週の週末、あなたは全部の部屋に新しいカーペットを入れる予定です。そのため、来週の週末には全員の部屋から家具を出してもらわなければなりません。あなたが台所にいると、だれかが入ってきました。

a.こんにちは、来週の週末は家にいますか。来週部屋に新しいカーペットを敷く予定なんです。

b.来週の週末手伝って頂けませんか。新しいカーペットを入れるので。

c.こんにちは、来週の週末に新しいカーペットをいれるんですが、来週土曜日にあなたの部屋から家具を出しておいてくれますか。

**場面 15**

　あなたはある大きな会社に就職口を求めています。今、人事部長との面接が終わったところです。面接はうまく行きましたが、思ったよりずっと時間がかかりました。帰ろうとすると、人事部長が、これから会社の中を案内すると言いました。あなたは次の約束があるので、ついて行くことができません。

a.すみません。社内見学があることは知りませんでした。実はあと２０分ほどで会議にでなければなりません。また次の機会にさせて頂けますか。

b.えっ、社内見学があるとは知りませんでしたので、２０分後に予定を入れてしまっておりまして。

c.本当に申し訳ありませんが、社内見学には行けません。お聞きしていませんでしたし、午後別の約束も入っておりますので。

場面 16
　あなたは同僚何人かと特別なプロジェクトに関わっています。あなたはそのプロジェクトのリーダーです。ちょうど今あなたはその仕事をしていて、書類のコピーをしています。プロジェクトのメンバーがひとり部屋に入ってきました。あなたはペーパークリップが必要ですが、見るとその人が1箱持っています。

a.あ、クリップがいるんだけど。
b.ペーパークリップをかしてもらえますか。
c.ペーパークリップをおかりできますでしょうか。ちょっと手持ちがなくて。

場面 17
　あなたは大きな家を借りている人から、空いている1部屋を借りています。その人もやはりその家に住んでいます。この家では、みな毎週数時間ずつ家事をすることになっています。あなたの係りは掃除機をかけることです。大家さんが明日の午後掃除をしてくれるかどうかあなたに尋ねてきました。明日の晩、お客さんが来るからです。あなたは明日は1日とても忙しいので、午後掃除をすることはできません。

a.あ〜、あしたの午後はちょっとできないんです。一日中忙しいので。
b.あしたは試験がいくつもあるので、そうじできません。すみませんが、ご自分でできませんか。
c.すみませんが、あしたは一日中忙しいのです。今晩できるだけ掃除機をかけてみますけど。

場面 18
　あなたは映画のチケットを4枚買うところです。1枚分は無料の券を持っています。あなたは窓口でそう言いましたが、なかなかその券が見つかりません。しばらく探すと見つかったので、窓口の人に渡しました。

a.あ、ありました。これが無料の入場券です。
b.ああ、いやだ。もたついてすみません。
c.はい、ありました。すみません、時間がかかって。

場面 19
　あなたは同僚何人かと特別なプロジェクトに関わっています。今、プロジェクトのリーダーの部屋で打ち合わせをしています。ブリーフケースを取ろうと手をのばしたら、机に立てかけてあったリーダーのかさをうっかり倒してしまいました。

a.あ、すみません。そこにあるのに気がつきませんでした。新しいかさでしたか。
b.あら、すみません。
c.あっ！

場面 20
　あなたは全国組織のキャンピングクラブの地方支部の部長です。今、キャンプ旅行に来ています。メンバーのひとりが虫よけの薬をつけていて、あなたにもすすめてくれました。しかし、あなたは自分のを持ってきているので、必要ありません。

a.結構です。自分のがありますので。
b.私は使いませんので。
c.あ、結構です。すごくいい虫よけスプレーを持っているのでそれを使いますから。

場面 21
　あなたは大きな都市に旅行に来ています。写真屋さんにフィルムの現像を頼んでありました。写真を受け取りに来ると、店員が、また今度フィルムを出すときのために、割引券はいりますか、と聞きました。あなたは今日帰ってしまうので、割引券はいりません。

a.結構です。
b.せっかくですけど、もうすぐ町を出ますので使いませんから。
c.結構です。もうこの町を発ちますから。

場面 22
　あなたは大きい会社の小さな部で働いています。先週あなたは部長と重要な打ち合わせの予定がありました。しかし、あなたは具合が悪くなったので、キャンセルしなければなりませんでした。打ち合わせは、今日の午後に予定が変わりました。あなたは、今朝出勤したときは元気でした。しかし、今昼休みで、また具合が悪くなってしまいました。今日の打ち合わせも延期したいと思います。あなたは部長の部屋に行きました。

a.部長、今日の打ち合わせのことなんですが。また延期お願いしてもよろしいでしょうか。朝はなんともなかったんですが、また具合が悪くなってきまして。
b.申し訳ないんですが、まだ体調がよくありません。また打ち合わせの日時を変更しましょう。
c.申し訳ありませんが、まだ具合がよくありません。打ち合わせの日時を変更しましょう。

場面 23
　先週、会社の車の調子が悪くなりました。そこであなたは車を会社の修理工のところへ持って行きました。あなたは明日出張があるので、車が必要です。工場に車を取りに行くと、修理工は、今日の午後にならないとできない、と言いました。しかし、今日の午後は別の会議があって、工場が閉まるまでに来られそうもありません。車が受け取れるように、だれかに今日の夕方遅くまで工場に残っていてほしいと思います。

a.車は午後にはできているといわれたのですが。しかし午後は長い会議があって、店のしまる前には行けそうもないんです。行くまでだれかに待っていてもらいたいんですけど、そういうことができますか。
b.今日中に車が必要なんですが、閉店前に行けそうもないですね。私が取りに来る時間まで、だれか残っていてもらうことはできませんか。
c.う〜ん、今日は午後おそくならないと取りに来られないんです。大事な会議が午後ずっとあって。でも明日一番で車がいるので、だれか私が来るまで残っていてもらいたいんですが。

場面 24
　あなたはある大きなデパートの旅行カウンターで働いています。今お客さんの相手をしているところです。お客さんが、チューインガムを出して、1枚すすめてくれました。しかし、あなたはガムは嫌いです。

a.ありがとうございます。でも勤務中は何もいただけないことになっております。
b.遠慮します。
c.いえ、結構です。

あなたのなまえ（　　　　　　　）　　　　　　　　　　　年　　月　　日

> （　　）にひらがなかかんじを一ついれてください。

　むかしむかし、（　　）るところに、おじ（　　）さんとおばあさん（　　）すんでいました。
おじいさんはまい（　　）山へしばかりに、（　　）ばあさんは川へせ（　　）たくにいきました。
　ある日、おばあ（　　）んが川でせんたく（　　）していると、そこ（　　）大きなももがどん（　　）
らこ、どんぶらこ　、　　とながれてきまし（　　）。おばあさんは、「　おや、まあ、これ（　　）
大きなももだこと　。　　いえへもってかえ（　　）ておじいさんとい（　　）しょにたべましょ（　　）」
といって、いえへ（　　）ってかえりました。
　夕がた、おじい（　　）んは山からかえっ（　　）きました。おじい（　　）んはももを見ると　、
大そうびっくりし（　　）、「おやおや、こ（　　）は大きなももだ。（　　）ばあさん、いっし（　　）
にたべるとしよう　」　　といって、ももを（　　）ろうとしました。（　　）るとそのとき、も（　　）
がまん中からばく（　　）とわれて、中から（　　）わいい男の赤ちゃ（　　）が「おぎゃー」と（　　）
まれました。おじ（　　）さんとおばあさん（　　）とてもおどろきま（　　）た。けれども、子（　　）
もがいないので、（　　）の子を大せつにそ（　　）てることにしまし（　　）。名まえは、もも（　　）
ら生まれたので「（　　）もたろう」にしま（　　）た。
　ももたろうはま（　　）日、まい日大きく（　　）っていきます。そ（　　）ころ、村にわるい（　　）
にがやってきては　、　　村人からたべもの（　　）きるものをとって（　　）き、村人を大へん（　　）
まらせていました　。　　そこで、ももたろ（　　）はおにをたいじし（　　）、おにがしまへい（　　）
ことにしました。（　　）じいさんと、おば（　　）さんは「そんなあ（　　）ないことはやめて（　　）
くれ。おにたべ（　　）れてしまうよ」と（　　）ってしんぱいしま（　　）た。けれども、も（　　）
たろうは、「だい（　　）ょうぶ、きっとぼ（　　）がおにをやっつけ（　　）きます」といいま（　　）
た。おじいさんと（　　）ばあさんは、もも（　　）ろのために、「（　　）本一」とかいたは（　　）
と、日本一のきび（　　）んごをつくって、（　　）たせてやりました。
　「日本一」のは（　　）と、日本一のきび（　　）んごをもったもも（　　）ろうが、げんきよ（　　）
あるいていきました。

　［しつもん］
　あなたはこの話をしっていますか。　□はい－－－＞なんという話ですか。　
　　　　　　　　　　　　　　　　　　　□いいえ、しりません。

昔話「ももたろう」山下・小川他（1994）『インタビュープロジェクト』くろしお出版（pp.63-64）より

覚書

0. ＯＰＤＣＴ（Open ended discourse completion task/ test）は日本語で書かれた２４の場面についてそのとき自分が日本語で何というかを書いて答えたものである。全ての被調査者は日本語で書かれた各場面の説明とその英訳をもとに、回答を書いた。被調査者が英訳を実際にどのくらい参照したかは不明である。辞書の使用も自由とした。

1. 本資料はＯＰＤＣＴ５０名分の手書き原稿をできるだけ忠実にワープロ打ちしたものである。名前のあとのＡＢＣは、質問用紙の各Ｆｏｒｍをあらわすので、それぞれの場面は質問用紙の場面説明を参照のこと。

2. 文法的な誤り及び文字表記の誤りは誤字（漢字、助詞、長音、促音などの誤り）・脱字を含めそのまま打っている。中には単なる表記ミスもあるがそのまま記した。なお、タイプ入力エラーを防ぐため、入力をしたのとは別の人間がダブルチェックをし、入力者側のタイプミスをチェックしたので、認められるエラーは全て被調査者本人のエラーである。

3. 学生が自分で書き込んだ注意書きは（　　）の中に記した。

4. ワープロに打ち直す際の研究者側からの特記事項は[　　]の中に記した。

5. ５０名分の資料は非母語話者４８名と母語話者２名からなり、名前を消去し、ランダムに並べた。非母語話者の日本語レベルは初級から上級まで含む。

6. 分かち書きをしている被調査者がいたが、特に強調する必要があるとき（はっきりさせないと意味がかわる等）以外は分かち書きにはせずに、続けて入力した。


評価に際しての注意

　1. 評価には RATING SHEET-Instrument: DCT Lang Lab とかいてあるシートを使用して下さい。

　2. 1枚のシートには裏表で２４場面のますがあります（Response #1--#24）。各場面ごとに６つのことがらについて1--5（1：全く適切でない--5：非常に適切）で評価して下さい。数字の横の[＋][－]サインについては次の例を参考にして下さい。例えば、回答が長さの点で不適切と判断され、数字の１を付けたとします。その評価が長さが”長すぎる”という理由によるものでれば、長さのところの[＋]に丸をします。また丁寧さが足りないと思われた場合は、数字１あるいは２としたあとに、その点が丁寧さに”欠ける”ためであるので、[－]に丸をします。

３．次に６つの項目について説明します。

Speech act（発語内行為）:

　各場面には、ある speech act（発語内行為--本研究では依頼、断り、謝罪の３つ）が必ず一つ入っています。その場面で現われた speech act が適切かどうか評価して下さい。評価する際の問題点＞speech act は必ずしも１つだけで現われるものではありません。例えば、依頼の時に「すみませんが・・・」という一見謝罪のような表現を使いつつ「・・・して下さいませんか」という表現でまとめた場合でも、はっきり依頼表現が含まれていれば（この場合「・・・下さいませんか」）”適切”として下さい。

　さらに、もしはっきりとした speech act が使われていなかった時でも、その場面の中で適切と思われればそのように評価して下さい（例えば、上司に対して依頼しなければならなかった時に、わざと依頼表現を使わずにすます場合などは、その状況の中では”適切”であると思われればそのように評価して下さい）。

　この項は基本的には speech act が入っているか否かのどちらかなので、あれば　５、なければ１を使って下さい。そのほかに判断が難しいとき（わざと使わないような場合）は中間点を使用して下さって結構です。

Formulaic expressions（慣用的表現）:

　慣用表現や熟語などの使用の適切さを評価して下さい。例えば、「恐れ入りますが・・・」「ご迷惑でなければ・・・」等の表現は慣用表現として考えて下さい。逆に、「ごめんなさいでも・・・」など、母語からの影響が考えられるものは評価が低くなるでしょう。

注意＞ここでは文法が正しく使えているか否かは評価の対象になっていません。例えば動詞の活用形が間違っている、助詞の使い方が正しくない、というような点は評価に含めないで下さい。

評価する際の問題点＞慣用表現からかけ離れた学習者独自の表現（文、表現としておかしいもの）などについては数字で段階的に評価するのは難しいですが、文全体からみてあなた（評価者）が母語話者としてそれをどれだけ許容出来るか、といった観点から評価して下さい。さらに、上記に注意として述べた「非文法的文は評価対象にしない」という点と、表現として”おかしい”文は評価対象にするというのは矛盾するところがあろうと思います。この点も、母語話者の感覚で判断して下さい。

Amount of speech used and information given（発話の長さと情報量）:

　話者がふつう、Speech act（発語内行為）を遂行する時、そのために要する話す長さは、場面によってことなります。例えば、何かこみいったことを依頼する時,あるいは頼みづらいことを頼まなければならないような時、話者はいきなり依頼するのではなく、ある程度そこまでに至る状況説明をしておいてから頼むという形をとることが多いのではないでしょうか。逆に、レストランでメニューを頼むときなどは、簡単にすませます。評価する時は、そのような点を考慮にいれて、その場面でどの程度適切に表現できているかを見て下さい。

　また、学習者は概して母語話者より長い説明をしがちであると言われていますが、その理由は二つ考えられます。（１）簡潔に状況説明をするだけの語学力がないため、余分な言葉を使って遠まわしに説明を試みる、（２）外国語としての知識が豊富なためつい余計な言葉（一見難しい、高度な表現のようだかその場面には則さないような言葉など）を使い過ぎてしまう。いずれの場合も母語話者の一般的な長さ・必要十分な情報量を基準に判断して下さい。

　もちろん、このほかに単純に語学力が不十分なために必要な説明などが言えず、母語話者よ

りも短くぶっきらぼうに聞こえるような言葉になってしまう低いレベルの学習者がいます。また、語学力だけでなく、どのように言うかというのは母語話者の中でも個人差もあるものです。そこで、ここでの評価の基準は、「どの程度その長さと情報量が適切か」ということにおいて下さるとよいでしょう。

評価する際の問題点＞どのくらいの量が適切かというみきわめは母語話者の感覚にも個人差があるので難しいところです。基準としては、あまりに言葉が少なくぶっきらぼうに感じられるもの、あるいは冗長で、不要な情報がだらだらと続いて焦点がぼやける、というようなものは両極端ですが、ともに1や2に近いと考えられます。その際に前者は［－］（長さ、あるいは情報量が足りない）、後者は［＋］（長すぎる）がつくということになります。

## Degrees of Formality, Directness, and Politeness（改まり度、直接さの度合い、丁寧さ）:

### Formality:

　改まり度がどのくらいその場面に対して適切かということを評価します。ポイントは、語彙の選択（例：お宅、家、拙宅）、表現（phrasing）、役職あるいは職業の呼び名（部長さん、お客さんなど）、動詞表現の選択（・・・してもいい？・・・させていただいてもよろしいでしょうかなど）などです。友人間、会社の同僚などがどのくらいの親しさか（informalityの度合い）母語話者としてのあなたの視点、基準で評価して下さい。

### Directness:

　ある speech act を行なう場合に、どの程度直接的にいうのがその場面に対して適切か、ということを評価して下さい。直接的かどうかは場面の中での人物設定（関係）と、それに対する動詞の形や会話の持って行き方で判断して下さい。わかりやすい例を上げましょう。ある部屋にAさんとBさんがいます。かりにAさんを妻、Bさんを夫としておきます。AさんがBさんに「ああ、ここは暑いわねえ」と言って、Bが窓をあけてくれるのを期待しています。ところが、Bは「うん、そうだね」といったきりです。あまりに間接すぎて通じませんでした。そこでAは今度はちょっといらいらして、「ねえ、窓を開けてくれない？」と言いました。この時点でやっとAの要求に気がついたBは、「なんだ、最初からそう言えばいいじゃないか」と言います。母語話者の評価者として、あなたは直接度、間接度がその場面でどのくらい適切か、ということを評価してください。

### Politeness:

　丁寧さは、改まり度や直接度の他に、Politeness markers と呼ばれる指標（例：すみません、よろしければ）も含まれます。丁寧さはその扱う範囲が広いので、ここで評価基準を出すのは難しいのですが、ある発話がその場面に対して全体から見てバランス上どうかという点から評価して下さい。

　　4．この評価では、あなたは一般的母語話者として回答を評価して下さい。語学教師は往々にして、被母語話者の言葉に寛容です。しかし、この評価ではあくまで基準を母語話者ならこう言うであろうという、母語話者を念頭においたあなた自身の判断基準にそって評価して下さい。

　　二人の被調査者からまったく別の表現の回答があった場合でも、どちらの場合も許容できる

範囲であるなら、そのように評価して下さい。

　評価をする上で、「私（評価者本人）ならこういう」という基準では評価せずに、あくまで一般的な母語話者の場合を想定して考えて下さい。

　また、すでに評価した被調査者の回答をもとに新しい回答を判断することはさけて下さい（これは難しいことですが）。一回一回、母語話者を念頭においた基準で評価して下さい。

　５. 一人一人の被調査者のシートの右上に、追加事項として次の２点を加えて下さい。この２点はそれぞれのシートについて２４の場面全部の評価が終わった時点で加えて下さい。
（１）この回答をした被調査者の性別：
　　　　Ｆ＝女性だと思われる場合
　　　　Ｍ＝男性だと思われる場合
　　　　Ｎ＝どちらとも判断できない場合
（２）この回答をした被調査者のレベル：
　　　　１から１０（１・２・３・・・９・１０）のうちのどれかの番号で表して下さい。めやすとしては、
　　　　１＝日本語の学習を始めてからかなり日が浅いと思われる場合
　　　　５＝２・３年学習した中級ぐらいの人と思われる場合
　　　１０＝母語話者（日本人またはそのレベル）

## OVERVIEW

Your responsibilities will be to rate the appropriateness of NS and NNS responses to DCT items on six aspects: correct speech act, formulaic expressions, amount of speech, and the degree of formality, directness and politeness. Explanations of these aspects, including examples and trouble-shooting, are provided below. An explanation of the criteria for rating follows. The manual concludes with some practice examples.

Your packet contains situations followed by the responses of all subjects to that particular situation. NS and NNS responses have been randomly distributed throughout and are not identified. The responses are numbered and you are to indicate your six ratings of a given response on the rating sheet provided.

The scale for rating is a five-point scale with 1 equal to very unsatisfactory and 5 equal to completely appropriate.

```
     very                                       completely
unsatisfactory  1 - - - 2 - - - 3 - - - 4 - - - 5  appropriate
```

When rating the appropriateness of the speech acts and the expressions used in the response, you are to rate using only the five-point scale. When rating the appropriateness of the amount of information given, and the levels of formality, directness, and politeness, you are to rate on the five-point scale and then, in the case of low ratings (1's and 2's), please indicate if you think the response is inappropriate due to a higher or lesser degree of the aspect in question. For example, say you are rating a response and you think it is far too long. Here you would circle 1 (very unsatisfactory) and then the "+" sign to indicate that it is inappropriate because it is too long. Or say you think a response is not quite formal enough. You would circle 2 and then the "−" sign.

## EXPLANATIONS OF THE SIX ASPECTS

### Ability to use the correct speech act

Each situation was designed to elicit a particular speech act. You are to consider and rate the degree to which each response captures what you consider to be the speech act the situation was intended to elicit. The question to answer is: How appropriate is this speech act for this situation?

*Possible problems in* **rating:** As you read the responses, it should become apparent that speech acts are not mutually exclusive. For example, a request might begin with an apology: "I'm sorry, but could you move your car?" This is still a "true" request.

As long as the response includes the speech act within it, it should be considered "appropriate" and rated accordingly. It may also be the case that the response given is very indirect or is intended to introduce a topic without actually getting to the point. In these cases, you should still rate the given response on it's appropriateness in the situation.

It is anticipated that ratings of speech acts will be extreme — either 5 or 1. However, you may use the other numbers on the scale if you think they are appropriate (as might be the case with the very indirect or introduction type responses).

## Formulaic expressions

This category includes use of typical speech, gambits, and so on. Non-typical speech might be due to the non-native speaker not knowing a particular American English phrase or due to some type of transfer. Use of non-typical expressions is not uncommon in these responses and it is anticipated that your native speaker intuitions will serve you well in rating them. The question to ask is: How appropriate is the wording/are the expressions?

Ungrammaticality, however, is not an issue for our purposes. For example, both NNS and NS responses contain errors in verb conjugation and article use. Do *not* let those errors influence your ratings.

Possible problems in **rating:** Although you might find identifying non-typical speech an easy task, assigning a numerical rating might prove difficult. Further complicating the decision is the fact that some responses contain more than one non-typical wording. As with all of the categories, you are judging the acceptability of the response as a whole. You might also be inclined to include ungrammatical responses in your rating of this category. At times, it might be difficult to distinguish between ungrammatical wording and non-typical wording. When in doubt, follow your native speaker intuitions.

## Amount of speech used and information given

Speakers of any language adjust the amount of speech in a given speech act to fit the particular situation. For example, sometimes speakers feel they want to supply a lengthy explanation when making a request. It has been hypothesized that when a non-native speaker uses more speech than the average native speaker, it is due to two possibilities; the non-native speaker might be of a lower proficiency and thus use circumlocution or other less direct strategies, or the non-native speaker might be of a higher proficiency and thus verbose (Wolfson). Of course, non-native speakers of lower proficiency might use very direct and thus shorter-than-the-average-NS utterances, communicating only the most essential information. For example, a refusal might begin with "I can't" without a reason or excuse because the NNS does not have the language to give such an explanation.

It is not implied, however, that all variation in utterance length is due to language proficiency. Of course, there is a degree of individual choice involved in how much one decides to say. The question here is: How appropriate is the amount of speech used/information given?

*Possible problems in* **rating**: Deciding how much speech and/or information is appropriate for a given situation might prove difficult, especially because some individual variation is normal. As a guideline, use your native speaker intuition to judge when a response seems particularly abrupt or seems to "ramble" and provide too much unnecessary information.

## Degrees of Formality, Directness, and Politeness

These three distinct yet often overlapping elements of speech have caused a great deal of discussion and research (in addition to headaches!) in pragmatics. These elements are reviewed below. While rating each response, you should try to keep these three concepts as distinct in your mind as possible. The question is: How appropriate are the levels of formality, directness, and politeness?

*Possible problems in* **rating**: You might find it awkward or annoying to assign a rating to these three speech act elements because they are not 100 percent exclusive. Nonetheless, your ratings will give the researchers an indication of the role each of these elements plays in the data and will therefore help the researchers decide how they want to deal with these aspects in the future.

*Formality*: Formality can be expressed through word choice, phrasing, use of titles, and choice of verb forms. Use of colloquial speech can be appropriate in American English when the situation is informal and between friends, family, and co-workers. Yet here, too, a degree of appropriateness can apply. You are the judge.

*Directness*: Pragmatically defined, most speech is indirect. However, you are to rate the appropriateness of the level of directness found in the responses. Directness can be indicated by verb form or strategy choice. To illustrate, we offer the well-worn example of the couple sitting in the living room having difficulties with direct and indirect request strategies. Person A (stereotypically the wife) says to Person B, "Boy, it's hot in here!" (an indirect form) thinking that Person B will then get up and open the window. However, Person B replies, "Humm, yeah I guess so" and remains seated. The indirect strategy is ineffective, so Person A gets annoyed and now says, "Hey, bozo, open the window!" (direct form). At this point Person B gets annoyed and replies, "Why didn't you just say so in the first place!" Again, use your native speaker intuition to judge the appropriateness of the level of directness used.

*Politeness*: This concept has many dimensions and has been the topic of many discussions in speech act studies. Politeness includes the aspects of formality and directness, among other things such as politeness markers ("thank you", "please", "if you don't mind", etc.). Due to its many elements, it is impossible to prescribe a formula of politeness for a given situation. For example, native speakers of English might use first names in a job situation, but it is not necessarily inappropriate to use Mr./Ms./Mrs. (surname) on the job. Furthermore, if one usually uses politeness markers in addition to first names in work situations, one might be seen by others as appropriately polite.

## CRITERIA FOR RATINGS

In all of your ratings, you are to use your native speaker intuitions and reactions. As someone with a great deal of experience with NNSs, you might be more accepting than other NSs. However, you are not to rate the responses as the all-accepting-and-culturally-sensitive-ESL-teacher. It is assumed that although you might be more accepting of a response than other more linguistically or culturally isolated NSs, you will still *notice* differences in some of the responses. Therefore, focus on what you notice and, using your native speaker intuitions, compare it to what you think the NS norm might be.

When relying on your NS intuitions, it is assumed that you will employ some type of "band of acceptability". For example, you might find that two responses to the same situation have different degrees of formality, but that both seem acceptable. In such a case, you should rate them as you feel is most appropriate.

Do not use what you think you might say as the sole criteria for your ratings. For example, you might be someone who uses humor very often in interacting with strangers. With this in mind you should not rate other responses negatively just because they do not include the humor you would use in the given situation.

While rating, to the best of your ability, judge each response independently of the others. Try not to let the other responses influence your decision of the response in question. This might prove difficult. Try to clear your mind after each response, thus allowing your native speaker intuition a chance to interact with each response without bias from the last one.

## THREE SAMPLES

### Example One

**Situation:** You work in a large company. You and a few of your co-workers are working on a special project. You are talking to the project leader and looking at a copy of the project. You are pointing to something in the paper with your pen and accidentally mark the group leader's copy.

You: _____

_____

_____

**Responses:**

1. Oh, sorry. Want me to use some White-Out on that?

2. Sorry.

3. I'm sorry. This is yours. I have marked on it without notice.

4. Whoops. Sorry about that.

5. I'm sorry. I'm so careless.

## Example Two

**Situation:** You are an officer in a student organization that has grown rapidly. You realize the need for a new financial officer, a job that will involve a lot of work but not much recognition. You know that one member of the organization is studying accounting. You see that member walking by the library.

You: _____

_____

_____

**Responses:**

6. I wanted to ask you if you're interested in a new financial officer position in the organization. It's a lot of work, I know, but I think you're perfect for that position.

7. Personal-name, I was wondering if you'd be interested in becoming club-name's new financial officer. I know you are good at accounting, and thought I'd ask you first.

8. Would you be willing to serve as dub accountant?

9. Could you help our organization's new section?

10. I have a favor to ask you. I heard that you are studying accounting and I was just wondering if you can be the new financial officer for our organization. It would help us quite a lot.

## Example Three

**Situation:** You are president of a student organization. You have a meeting scheduled with another member for this afternoon. You are sitting outside of the library when the member comes over and asks to cancel the meeting in order to work on a term paper that is due tomorrow. You cannot schedule the meeting for later because you have to report the information to several professors at a meeting tomorrow.

You: _____

_____

_____

**Responses:**

11. I know it is very hard, but I need this for tomorrow meeting, so please finish it by tomorrow.

12. I can really sympathize with you, I know the feeling well. However, my meeting with the professors requires the information no later than tomorrow at 10:00 am and I need your data to compile my report. It's very important that I have that information. I need your help on this.

13. I'll have to discuss the project with the boss tomorrow. Could you finish it by tomorrow?

14. Unnn, the problem that I have with that is that I have to report this into several professors tomorrow. Can't we try to squeeze this in?

15. Could you please finish it by tomorrow?

# SLTCC

# TECHNICAL REPORTS

*The Technical Reports of the Second Language Teaching and Curriculum Center
at the University of Hawai'i (SLTCC) report on ongoing curriculum projects,
provide the results of research related to second language learning and teaching,
and also include extensive related bibliographies. SLTCC Technical Reports are available
through University of Hawai'i Press.*

---

**RESEARCH
METHODS
IN
INTERLANGUAGE
PRAGMATICS**

GABRIELE KASPER
MERETE DAHL

This technical report reviews the methods of data collection employed in 39 studies of interlanguage pragmatics, defined narrowly as the investigation of nonnative speakers' comprehension and production of speech acts, and the acquisition of L2-related speech act knowledge. Data collection instruments are distinguished according to the degree to which they constrain informants' responses, and whether they tap speech act perception/comprehension or production. A main focus of discussion is the validity of different types of data, in particular their adequacy to approximate authentic performance of linguistic action. 51 pp.

(SLTCC Technical Report #1)   ISBN 0–8248–1419–3   $10.

---

**A FRAMEWORK
FOR
TESTING
CROSS-
CULTURAL
PRAGMATICS**

THOM HUDSON
EMILY DETMER
J. D. BROWN

This technical report presents a framework for developing methods that assess cross-cultural pragmatic ability. Although the framework has been designed for Japanese and American cross-cultural contrasts, it can serve as a generic approach that can be applied to other language contrasts. The focus is on the variables of social distance, relative power, and the degree of imposition within the speech acts of requests, refusals, and apologies. Evaluation of performance is based on recognition of the speech act, amount of speech, forms or formulæ used, directness, formality, and politeness. 51 pp.

(SLTCC Technical Report #2)   ISBN 0–8248–1463–0   $10.

---

## PRAGMATICS OF JAPANESE AS NATIVE AND TARGET LANGUAGE

GABRIELE KASPER
( Editor )

This technical report includes three contributions to the study of the pragmatics of Japanese:

- A bibliography on speech act performance, discourse management, and other pragmatic and sociolinguistic features of Japanese;
- A study on introspective methods in examining Japanese learners' performance of refusals;
- A longitudinal investigation of the acquisition of the particle *ne* by nonnative speakers of Japanese.

125 pp.

(SLTCC Technical Report #3)  ISBN 0–8248–1462–2  $10.

## A BIBLIOGRAPHY OF PEDAGOGY & RESEARCH IN INTERPRETATION & TRANSLATION

ETILVIA ARJONA

This technical report includes four types of bibliographic information on translation and interpretation studies:

- Research efforts across disciplinary boundaries: cognitive psychology, neurolinguistics, psycholinguistics, sociolinguistics, computational linguistics, measurement, aptitude testing, language policy, decision-making, theses, dissertations;
- Training information covering: program design, curriculum studies, instruction, school administration;
- Instruction information detailing: course syllabi, methodology, models, available textbooks;
- Testing information about aptitude, selection, diagnostic tests.

115 pp.

(SLTCC Technical Report #4)  ISBN 0–8248–1572–6  $10.

## PRAGMATICS OF CHINESE AS NATIVE AND TARGET LANGUAGE

GABRIELE KASPER
( Editor )

This technical report includes six contributions to the study of the pragmatics of Mandarin Chinese:

- A report of an interview study conducted with nonnative speakers of Chinese;
- Five data-based studies on the performance of different speech acts by native speakers of Mandarin: requesting, refusing, complaining, giving bad news, disagreeing, and complimenting.

312 pp.

(SLTCC Technical Report #5)  ISBN 0–8248–1733–8  $15.

## THE ROLE OF PHONOLOGICAL CODING IN READING *KANJI*

SACHIKO MATSUNAGA

In this technical report the author reports the results of a study that she conducted on phonological coding in reading *kanji* using an eye-movement monitor and draws some pedagogical implications. In addition, she reviews current literature on the different schools of thought regarding instruction in reading *kanji* and its role in the teaching of non-alphabetic written languages like Japanese. 64 pp.

(SLTCC Technical Report #6)  ISBN 0–8248–1734–6  $10.

## DEVELOPING PROTOTYPIC MEASURES OF CROSS-CULTURAL PRAGMATICS

THOM HUDSON
EMILY DETMER
J. D. BROWN

Although the study of cross-cultural pragmatics has gained importance in applied linguistics, there are no standard forms of assessment that might make research comparable across studies and languages. The present volume describes the process through which six forms of cross-cultural assessment were developed for second language learners of English. The models may be used for second language learners of other languages. The six forms of assessment involve two forms each of indirect discourse completion tests, oral language production, and self assessment. The procedures involve the assessment of requests, apologies, and refusals. 198 pp.

(SLTCC Technical Report #7) ISBN 0–8248–1763–X $15.

## VIRTUAL CONNECTIONS: ONLINE ACTIVITIES & PROJECTS FOR NETWORKING LANGUAGE LEARNERS

MARK WARSCHAUER
(Editor)

Computer networking has created dramatic new possibilities for connecting language learners in a single classroom or across the globe. This collection of activities and projects makes use of e-mail, the World Wide Web, computer conferencing, and other forms of computer-mediated communication for the foreign and second language classroom at any level of instruction. Teachers from around the world submitted the activities compiled in this volume — activities that they have used successfully in their own classrooms. 417 pp.

(SLTCC Technical Report #8) ISBN 0–8248–1793–1 $30.

## ATTENTION & AWARENESS IN FOREIGN LANGUAGE LEARNING

RICHARD SCHMIDT
(Editor)

Issues related to the role of attention and awareness in learning lie at the heart of many theoretical and practical controversies in the foreign language field. This collection of papers presents research into the learning of Spanish, Japanese, Finnish, Hawaiian, and English as a second language (with additional comments and examples from French, German, and miniature artificial languages) that bear on these crucial questions for foreign language pedagogy. 394 pp.

(SLTCC Technical Report #9) ISBN 0–8248–1794–X $20.

**LINGUISTICS AND LANGUAGE TEACHING: PROCEEDINGS OF THE SIXTH JOINT LSH-HATESL CONFERENCE**

C. REVES,
C. STEELE,
C. S. P. WONG
(*Editors*)

Technical Report #10 contains 18 articles revolving around the following three topics:

- Linguistic issues: These six papers discuss various linguistics issues: ideophones, syllabic nasals, linguistic areas, computation, tonal melody classification, and *wh*-words.
- Sociolinguistics: Sociolinguistic phenomena in Swahili, signing, Hawaiian, and Japanese are discussed in four of the papers.
- Language teaching and learning: These eight papers cover prosodic modification, note taking, planning in oral production, oral testing, language policy, L2 essay organization, access to dative alternation rules, and child noun phrase structure development.

364 pp.

(SLTCC Technical Report #10) ISBN 0–8248–1851–2 $20.

---

**LANGUAGE LEARNING MOTIVATION: PATHWAYS TO THE NEW CENTURY**

REBECCA L. OXFORD
(*Editor*)

This volume chronicles a revolution in our thinking about what makes students want to learn languages and what causes them to persist in that difficult and rewarding adventure. Topics in this book include the internal structures of and external connections with foreign language motivation; exploring adult language learning motivation, self-efficacy, and anxiety; comparing the motivations and learning strategies of students of Japanese and Spanish; and enhancing the theory of language learning motivation from many psychological and social perspectives. 218 pp.

(SLTCC Technical Report #11) ISBN 0–8248–1849–0 $20.

---

**TELECOLLABORATION IN FOREIGN LANGUAGE LEARNING: PROCEEDINGS OF THE HAWAI'I SYMPOSIUM**

MARK WARSCHAUER
(*Editor*)

The Symposium on Local & Global Electronic Networking in Foreign Language Learning & Research, part of the National Foreign Language Resource Center's 1995 Summer Institute on Technology & the Human Factor in Foreign Language Education included presentations of papers and hands-on workshops conducted by Symposium participants to facilitate the sharing of resources, ideas, and information about all aspects of electronic networking for foreign language teaching and research, including electronic discussion and conferencing, international cultural exchanges, real-time communication and simulations, research and resource retrieval via the Internet, and research using networks. This collection presents a sampling of those presentations. 252 p.

(SLTCC Technical Report #12) ISBN 0–8248–1867–9 $20.

## LANGUAGE LEARNING STRATEGIES AROUND THE WORLD: CROSS-CULTURAL PERSPECTIVES

REBECCA L. OXFORD
(*Editor*)

Language learning strategies are the specific steps students take to improve their progress in learning a second or foreign language. Optimizing learning strategies improves language performance. This ground-breaking book presents new information about cultural influences on the use of language learning strategies. It also shows innovative ways to assess students' strategy use and remarkable techniques for helping students improve their choice of strategies, with the goal of peak language learning. 166 pp.

(SLTCC Technical Report #13) ISBN 0–8248–1910–1 $20.

---

## SIX MEASURES OF JSL PRAGMATICS

SAYOKO OKADA YAMASHITA

This book investigates differences among tests that can be used to measure the cross-cultural pragmatic ability of English speaking learners of Japanese. Building on the work of Hudson, Detmer, and Brown (Technical Reports #2 and #7 in this series), the author modified six test types which she used to gather data from North American learners of Japanese. She found numerous problems with the multiple-choice discourse completion test but reported that the other five tests all proved highly reliable and reasonably valid. Practical issues involved in creating and using such language tests are discussed from a variety of perspectives. 213 pp.

(SLTCC Technical Report #14) ISBN 0–8248–1914–4 $15.